TRAVELLERS' ARCHITECTURE

TRAVELLERS' ARCHITECTURE

by

Harry Holland F.R.I.B.A.

GEORGE G. HARRAP & CO. LTD
LONDON   TORONTO   WELLINGTON   SYDNEY

First published in Great Britain 1971
by GEORGE G. HARRAP & CO. LTD
182-184 High Holborn, London W.C.1

© *Text and illustrations George G. Harrap & Co. Ltd 1971*
Copyright   All rights reserved

ISBN 0 245 59068 4

Designed by W. Bainbridge and K. Anderson
Composed in Centaur type and printed by
Jarrold & Sons Ltd, Norwich

Made in Great Britain

PREFACE

This book represents an attempt to put into narrative form a subject which basically is technical in character.

The subject matter relating to railway architecture is mainly derived from personal experience assimilated over a period of about thirty-six years, while based at Euston Headquarters – and enlivened by many journeys on the country's railway systems in connection with the design, construction and supervision of stations and ancillary buildings.

The railways and public transport generally are the centre of public attention, particularly since nationalization. And, in the rapid development of other forms of travel by sea, by air, and by public highways, a new and exciting vista is open in which the results of research and the fundamental processes of design and planning are being translated into construction of buildings and vehicles, for the service of travellers and the trade of the nation.

With the wide publicity distributed by travel agencies and the expanding routes of air and sea lines the world today has few inaccessible places; thus, the popularity of holiday travel and the ease of foreign business conferences in this Machine-Age. This is an important part of our existence, and we may rightly assume that people today are better informed and more interested in matters which are 'in the News' (the Press, TV and Sound-Radio) than others of an earlier era. They tend also to be more critical and conscious of the services and buildings which are associated with their means of travel; perhaps what follows may expand and stimulate that interest.

H. H.
Chester

ACKNOWLEDGMENTS

The author gratefully acknowledges the supply of material, with permission to reproduce – from the following sources:
The Royal Institute of British Architects; with special reference to photographs from original drawings in the Bannister Fletcher Library of architects' work. Also for the co-operation of the former Librarian, James Palmes, in securing the loan of current photographs and material.

Roads

Berni Inns Ltd. City of Birmingham Information Department. Nelson Foley, A.R.I.B.A., A.I.L.A., Chief architect, Trust Hotels, London.

Railways

Ian Allan Group, Shepperton, Middx. Central Argentine Railway F.C.C.A. (John Taylor, former Chief Engineer). British Railways Board. Canadian Pacific Railway Co. B. W. C. Cooke, Assoc.Inst.T., Editor-in-chief, Railway Publications. Dr F. C. Curtis, F.R.I.B.A., former Chief architect, British Railways Board. Information Service of India. Italian Ministry of Transport and Civil Aviation, Rome. Italian State Railways, Rome. Japan Information Centre, London. R. L. Moorcroft, F.R.I.B.A., Regional architect, British Rail (LMR). New South Wales Office, London. H. H. Powel, M.B.E., B.Arch., F.R.I.B.A., Regional architect, British Rail (NE). J. M. Richards, Editor-in-chief, Architectural Press. South African Railways, Johannesburg. E. A. Taber, A.R.I.B.A., Regional architect, British Rail (WR). N. D. T. Wikeley, Dip.Arch., A.R.I.B.A., Regional architect, British Rail (SR).

Seaports

British Rail Hovercraft Ltd. British Transport Docks Board, Southampton. Dover Harbour Board (W. Taylor-Allen, Chief Engineer). Massachusetts Port Authority, Boston (Frank Kyper, Editorial coordinator). New York Port Authority (Public Relations Manager). Port of San Francisco (Charles Siefert, P.R.O.).

Airports

Alitalia Airlines, Rome, Dr Giuseppe Richichi, Director. British Airport Authority, Heathrow. British Overseas Airways Corporation, London. Canada Airlines, Ottawa and London. Canadian Department of Transport, Ottawa. Daily Telegraph, London. Deutsche Lufthansa A.G., Frankfurt/Main. Federal Aviation Administration, Washington. Hawker Siddeley Group Ltd, London. Italian Embassy, London, Air Attaché. KLM Royal Dutch Airlines. Lufthansa German Airlines. Pan American World Airways, New York. Trans World Airways, New York & London. Dr C. Susskind.

Photographic credits

A. F. Kersting, A.I.I.P., F.R.P.S. (Euston: The former Classical Portico). Alex Nicoll and Partners Ltd, Architectural Photographers, Southampton. K. M. Anderson.

CONTENTS

INTRODUCTION

'Travel, in the younger sort, is a part of education; in the elder, a part of experience. The things to be seen and observed are churches and monasteries, with the monuments which are therein extant; the walls and fortifications of cities and towns; and to conclude, whatsoever is memorable in the places where they go.'

Francis Bacon, Lord Verulam – introduces 'Essay XVIII: OF TRAVEL' in the above words, continuing with advice and exhortation on the pleasures and educational value to be gained.

In the 'Golden Age of Travel' during the eighteenth century and in the nineteenth when Baedeker was a trusty companion, travel was a somewhat leisurely affair conducted in the grand manner; that is, with as much dignity as the means of transport then permitted. In the present era, the speed and variety of transport opens up an expanding vista for travellers, and the manner in which we make our journey will depend upon the facilities provided to enable us to travel.

Throughout our journey, by whatever form of transport we select, we cannot be unaffected by the measures, either successful or not, provided for our safety and comfort on our way between home and destination. The planning and design of the buildings, equipment, and décor associated with our journey and with which we come into contact intimately, constitute what we may describe as 'Travellers' Architecture'; for we, the travellers, find that these matters loom large in our experience on journey, by land, sea, and air.

Clearly, any exploration of the means of transport in modern Britain would be inadequate without a brief reference to the earlier modes of conveyance and communications. From many points of view the most important event in the early history of travel in Britain was the Roman Conquest, for it introduced the far-reaching effects of the Roman military highway. If one compares the maps of Roman and present-day Britain, one is at once aware how the road system of the former persists in spite of the manner in which modern motor highways have carved up the countryside.

London was created by the invaders as a gateway of advance, and from thence roads were projected towards those districts in which the seats of tribal government existed; the exploitation of those centres seemed to present a rewarding accomplishment. It was on this framework of communication that all subsequent roads, up to the 1920s, were firmly based.

Great Britain became a world power through transport; in the eighteenth century, coal, iron, timber, wool, and manufactured articles were carried by inland waterways and horse-drawn wagons to coastal ports and so, across the seas, linking the continents of the world.

So it came about that Britain, pioneer of steam power for ships and trains, and having faith in the great potential of her inventions, embarked her commerce upon a course hitherto undreamt of by her unsuspecting rivals.

Unquestionably, we may say, transport is the life blood of modern civilization, and the traveller's first impression of a country's progress is influenced by the standard of its airport, railway terminal, or maritime station. These are, indeed, the gateways to the land or city.

The natural sequence of modes of travel in Britain started with the roads. Today they continue to be an all-absorbing problem; this problem was high-lighted in the Buchanan report on 'Traffic in Towns'. The operative symbol in the report is, of course, the road-vehicle; for, by the end of 1964 there were over 8 million private car owners in Britain – out of a total $12\frac{1}{2}$ million vehicles on the roads. The significance of planning for their accommodation and control will be very apparent.

The emergence of the railways, early in the nineteenth century, at once introduced and stimulated the Industrial era which was then developing for overseas markets. The railways, as they also expanded, provided a country-wide means of travel for the individual.

This development has been described in many books, which are full of interest for the railway enthusiast; a selection of these books will be found in the bibliography – preceding the Index. As a footnote, in the present era, we should refer to the most astounding achievements connected with the entire reconstruction of the old London to Birmingham railway – to provide for the electrified system to supersede steam traction; it became fully operative on March 6th, 1967.

As this book is primarily concerned with the architectural aspect of travel, we shall examine in detail this particular type of building, both in this country and abroad, and we will follow the various changes brought about by evolution, geographical location, change of ownership, and change of emphasis, not only in the realms of railway travel, but in those of road, sea, and air transport.

In the case of railways, it will be interesting to note what an influence the English architectural style has had on countries abroad. It could also be said that buildings connected with sea transport all over the world show a strong British stimulation; this might, on the other hand, be refuted by an early English example, the Customs House at King's Lynn, built in 1683, and showing a strong Dutch influence. Later structures in this country, however, undoubtedly suggest a very definite native aspect, and it is this style which spread so widely overseas.

Finally, we will turn our attention towards the newest form of travel and examine buildings associated with the aeroplane. The establishment in 1940 of the 'Atlantic Bridge' by night-flying Hudsons of the Royal Air Force, set the pattern for world air travel, and from this pioneer beginning stemmed the modern traffic lines of communication.

The development of airports has been rapid and spectacular, and we shall find many exciting and stimulating examples of this new form of architecture and planning on both sides of the Atlantic; here, in Britain, with its forty or more air terminals, several rebuilt, famous European examples, and the astounding complex of New York's air termini on Kennedy airfield.

In the pages which follow we hope the reader may find some examples of the more commonplace, yet familiar, type of building, some that are unfamiliar yet rewarding, and some which are conspicuously commendable. If he is stimulated to further study and exploration the author will deem his labours to have been well worth while.

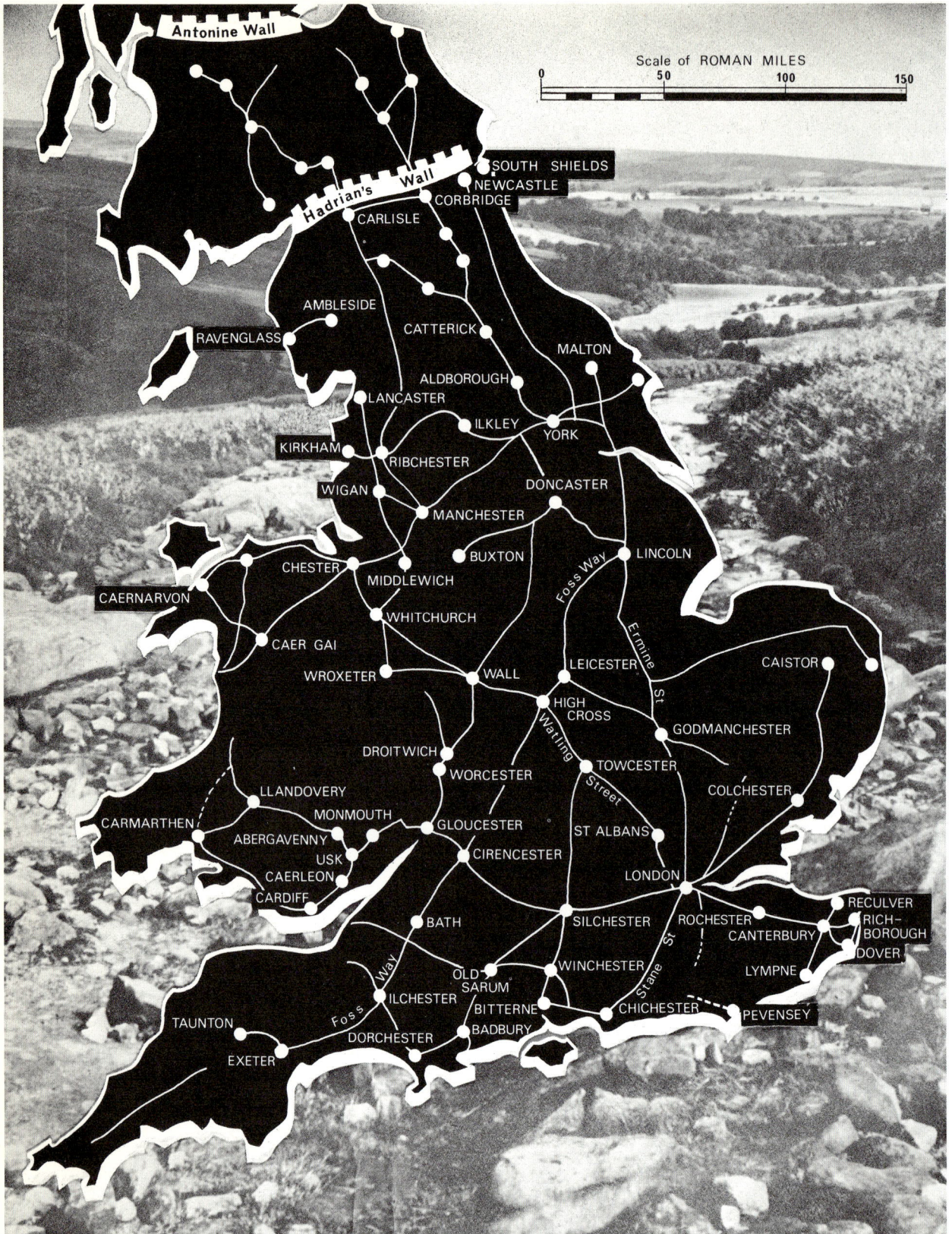

Scale of ROMAN MILES

0   50   100   150

Antonine Wall

SOUTH SHIELDS
NEWCASTLE
CORBRIDGE
Hadrian's Wall
CARLISLE

AMBLESIDE
CATTERICK
RAVENGLASS
MALTON
ALDBOROUGH
LANCASTER
ILKLEY
YORK
KIRKHAM
RIBCHESTER
WIGAN
DONCASTER
MANCHESTER
BUXTON
LINCOLN
CHESTER
MIDDLEWICH
CAERNARVON
WHITCHURCH
CAER GAI
WROXETER
WALL
LEICESTER
CAISTOR
Foss Way
Ermine St
HIGH CROSS
GODMANCHESTER
DROITWICH
Watling Street
TOWCESTER
COLCHESTER
WORCESTER
LLANDOVERY
MONMOUTH
ST ALBANS
CARMARTHEN
GLOUCESTER
ABERGAVENNY
CIRENCESTER
USK
LONDON
CAERLEON
CARDIFF
RECULVER
RICH-
BOROUGH
BATH
SILCHESTER
ROCHESTER
CANTERBURY
DOVER
WINCHESTER
LYMPNE
Foss Way
OLD SARUM
Stane St
TAUNTON
ILCHESTER
BITTERNE
CHICHESTER
PEVENSEY
DORCHESTER
BADBURY
EXETER

Map showing Roman road system in Britain, based upon the Antonine Itinerary.

Foss Way, Ermine and Watling Streets had their origin in pre-Roman times.
The Romans found rough tracks which they adapted and fitted them into a system of
magnificently engineered roads which lasted for centuries in spite of subsequent neglect.

CHAPTER 1 ROADS AND INNS

Travel and adventure were among the earliest instincts of Man . . . that is, in relation to the land he occupied from the birth of civilization, and there are several ways of looking at the past. The most common approach, the romantic, is that of the sentimental majority, to whom a sense of high adventure is paramount. There is also the point of view of the level-headed 'realist', who is by no means prevented from sharing the pleasures of the romantic, but, he regards the past primarily as an approach to the future.

Glancing back into history, we readily discover that the earliest of the routes for travel were the tracks and primitive roads which eventually formed our system of land communications. Regarding these, Geoffrey Boumphrey, has, with a wealth of detail and trenchant reality, traced the development from prehistoric times up to the basic types of high-speed motorways, with which we are familiar in this mechanized age.

ROMAN ROADS

The *Antonine Itinerary* describes fifteen British roads, of which no less than eight connected with London. The first to be formed was most probably the great road to the West, which crossed the Thames at Staines, and so on to Silchester, a few miles south-west of Reading. From Silchester the road sent out branches to Winchester, Towcester, Cirencester, and to Old Sarum from which the Mendips of Exeter were reached. A map will usefully indicate the link-up with important centres from as far south as Dover and Chichester, northward to Hadrian's Wall.

TRAVEL IN THE MIDDLE AGES

Medieval travel in the early part of the fourteenth century was, according to some records, a mixture of occasional discomfort with a general air of jollity; there was undoubtedly a spirit of good comradeship among travellers. A prominent feature of travel along the medieval roads comprised groups of pilgrims – including those of Chaucer's Canterbury followers.

Refreshment and rest would be found at the taverns, or ale-houses, usually at the cross-roads. Many of the taverns had 'alestakes' projecting over the doorway; in taverns where wine was sold within, the projecting pole was surmounted at the end with a bush of leaves. This fact, no doubt, fathered the expression 'Good wine, needs no bush'.

The city of London, in 1375, at the 'prayer of the commonalty', decreed that the length of the poles of alestakes, or bushes, should be within seven feet; this was because the greater length impeded the King's Highway. The penalty for excessive length was forty pounds paid to the Chamber of Guildhall.[1]

[1] *Chaucer's World* by Edith Rickert

An impression of Chaucer's pilgrims arriving at a 14th-century roadside Inn, with the projecting 'alestake' or 'bush' above the door.

THE INNS

Many of the medieval inns were rough places – providing little, except shelter, a verminous bed or pallet and a fire, on which the traveller could cook what food he had, or could buy locally. On the other hand, there existed hostels for poor travellers in other areas. The Gild Merchants of Coventry, in 1340, provided a hostel with thirteen beds for poor men, passing on pilgrimage; a governor presided over it and there was a woman to keep it clean. The upkeep was £10 a year.

Inns were generally used by the middle or merchant classes; monastic guest houses by the very poor by necessity – or, by the very rich and powerful by privilege. Examples of the latter may be found at Glastonbury and at Dunster in Somerset.

Very early the horse was an obvious means of travel, providing a longer journey, with less exertion to the traveller; following the two-horse litter, used by the noble medieval lady, the horse-drawn carriage became the next step to the coach. The seventeenth century saw the coach days fully developed, although the richer and more independent preferred to travel by horse. Samuel Pepys certainly preferred this mode of travel upon his various journeyings to visit his brother John in Cambridge and more sportive trips to Epsom. So, also – but with more serious intent, at a later date –

William Cobbett, who travelled through the shires, on his Rural Rides, to fulfil his self-imposed missions. Cobbett was far from being unmindful of the villages, towns and countryside through which he passed, as the following from his writings, will illustrate:

> From the hill, you keep on descending all the way to Dover, a distance of about six miles and it is absolutely six miles of down hill. On your right you have the lofty land which forms a series of chalk cliffs, from the top of which you look into the sea. . . . The town of Dover is like other sea-port towns, but really more clean and with less blackguard people in it that I have ever observed in any sea-port before. . . .

So, from individual travel on roads, we ultimately arrive at the bustling and exciting days of the stagecoach at its zenith, about which so much has been written. Of the many books on that interesting era, the most recent (1961), is Leslie Gardiner's *Stage Coach to John O'Groats*. Unlike some earlier, but repetitive chroniclers, it breaks new ground with lively anecdotes, and provides many historical facts, unrecorded by earlier writers.

We realize the immense fortitude required in those days to undertake long journeys in all conditions of weather. Their descendants, in this present century, are able to travel in luxury motor-coaches, upon wide and speedy highways and, while remaining in those coaches, bridge the sea gap to the European continent, and continue their holiday tours. But, on our roads today, we have – inevitably, at public holiday times – a sad and fluctuating casualty rate among private motorists; the sixteenth- and seventeenth-century road travellers were, proportionally, less 'accident-prone', except, perhaps for the surprise Highwayman.

To some extent the toils of the journey by stagecoach were a little mollified on arrival at the roadside inns, which marked each stage of the journey; there, rest and refreshment awaited the tired traveller. Many and famous were those inns; a notable example in London was *The Bull and Mouth*, established in Sherman's Yard, St Martins-le-Grand, facing the General Post Office. This romantic and historical hostelry is here recalled. In our illustration we see an indication of the activities at the time when the travellers arrive; their luggage is being collected adjoining the Coffee Rooms, into which they will go, and there we will leave them to sort themselves out, and repair the ravages of their journey.

The accommodation was generally arranged in tiered buildings, which surrounded the central courtyard – and here

The George Inn, Glastonbury, built about 1470 as a pilgrims' hostelry.

The Old Bull and Mouth Coaching Inn, St Martin's-le-Grand, London.

The New Inn, Gloucester.

extensive stabling accommodation provided below ground. The accommodation included areas for grooming the horses, cleaning and repairing coaches and harness, and all the other odd jobs carried out by ostlers.

The yard foreman, who supervised this work, was a person of very considerable importance in his own field; he occupied a post to which great prestige accrued. Inevitably, responsibility for ensuring that the Royal Mail coaches arrived and departed on schedule was a very exacting business. Perhaps the best example of a galleried inn remaining in England is the *New Inn* at Gloucester.

On reflection, we see that these terminal coaching inns, and their yards, played a considerable part in the life of London, and the provincial cities; a few of them still stand, mostly modified in form. They are like the sheltered drifts of winter's snow left behind, in the advance of the spring of a new generation of civilization.

Even in this present decade, it is interesting to recall that a similar old inn survives; *The George*, 71, Borough High Street, Southwark, is reputed to have been built shortly after the fire of 1666; what now remains comprises one side of the typical galleries in the courtyard. The early design conditions the germ of the English theatre, and figures prominently in many eighteenth and nineteenth-century novels.

the coaches entered by way of an archway, over which the first floor bedrooms spanned. Most of the upper rooms had covered balconies facing the courtyard; this feature is prominent in the illustration. In a much modified form we shall find this feature recurring in the present era – in the holiday 'Motel' on the sunlit bays on the coast of Florida, U.S.A., to be described in a later chapter.

In the larger sort of stagecoach inn, serving several routes, there was sometimes

Its relevance to early English theatres may be amplified by the fact that occasionally on Shakespeare's birthday some of his plays are enacted in the courtyard, either a loading bay or a flat-topped lorry being used as a stage. In the old days spectators would crowd the galleries to watch the

The Angel Inn, Islington, London.

performance, as can be seen in the accompanying reconstruction of the scene.

The partial eclipse of the *George Inn* took place in 1889, when the Great Northern Railway, who owned the premises, decided to demolish the north wing and centre. To the east of the remaining galleried part there is a larger plain brick section, with a few vertical and segment-headed windows. At least, here we do have part of the characteristic inn design surviving, in spite of modern encroachment.

Less happy is the case of *The Old Malthouse* at Kingston-upon-Thames, which was a 400-year-old coaching inn; it is a bleak example of the sacrifice of the Old, deliberately demolished in 1966, in the name of progress, to make way for the New. So, we are left with, mainly, a memory of the romantic and artistic inns of the coaching days; long may the memory survive! For those who are blessed with a sense of romance, and still care a little for the enlivening records of travel in the days of the stagecoach, that sense may be indulged in the collection of facets, by a kindred soul, Rowland Watson, in his *Scrapbook of Inns*.

FAREWELL TO COACHING DAYS

The first three decades of the nineteenth century had been a glorious age for coaching – both for the private owner and for the traveller at large. Inevitably, the first signs of the industrial revolution in transport began with increased 'horse-power', without the use of horses; in fact, with mechanically propelled vehicles.

Although some people tended to deride the triumphs of the engineer, George Stephenson – whose early steam-engines hauled wagons, loaded with coal, iron, and stone, along the first short railways – by the year 1830 mails and passengers were being

The White Hart Inn, Bishopsgate, London, showing the yard beyond the arch.

carried between Liverpool and Manchester by means of the steam-engine.

So, at last, the stagecoach was superseded by another type of vehicle for public transport; the future development of transport by rail will provide the opportunity for enlargement in later chapters of this book.

London's only surviving coaching inn – the George, Southwark. The drawing shows how Shakespeare's birthday is celebrated by scenes from his plays acted in the open courtyard in the medieval manner, with spectators lining the balustraded galleries.

THREE OLD CHESTER INNS

left

The Old King's Head is mainly 17th-century but incorporates older work. The first floor contains a fine contemporary dining-room.

bottom left

The Bear and Billet Inn. Its half-timbered front dates from 1664 and although restored much original material is retained. A small hoist was housed in the great gable behind folding doors. The continuous ranges of windows are a great feature.

below

Nearby stands the Falcon Inn which has a 15th-century stone base and upper storeys of timber dating from 1626. The great ranges of windows are again a feature of the carefully restored frontage.

Sir Goldsworth Gurney's (1829) and Walter Hancock's (1831) steam road coaches ran for such a short period that they hardly retarded the flight of travellers from road coaches to railways, nor did they have time to influence the layout or architecture of inns.

THE MOTOR VEHICLE

By the year 1860, the French engineer, Lenoir, produced a gas-engine, the fore-runner of the internal combustion principle of vehicle propulsion. So, the first motor car's seething progeny of thousands, which we are today trying to tame, is today threatening our towns and cities with traffic chaos and our highways with rising human casualties.

BUILDINGS FOR THE MOTOR VEHICLE

In the sphere of public transport, the motor vehicle very soon commenced extending its influence after the end of the First World War. One result of demobilization of the Forces was the dispersal of large numbers of men, who had first-hand experience of the management and maintenance of motor transport fleets (R.E.M.E.). Some of the men took up repair work and petrol sales, starting the wide distribution of garages up and down the country; others established themselves as carriers of passengers and goods.

ROAD TRANSPORT ARCHITECTURE

Parallel with the development of the motor vehicle, the need for garages – public and private – bus and coach stations opened up a new field of design for architects. The countryside and townscape supply evidence of buildings and installations connected in its many aspects; even domestic buildings have some element, in the form of the humble garage. The 'Petrol Age' has been responsible for some good – and many bad things; on the one hand it has created a wider freedom of travel for a greater number of people. That is a good thing. How we use this freedom to go where we like, when we like, will influence our personal lives and, to a large extent, our fellow-creatures. So, if the use of the motor vehicle becomes a dominant factor in our existence it is then a bad thing, and our priorities must be adjusted to control its use more effectively.

Whilst the traffic experts endeavour to propound a panacea for the urban and metropolitan street scramble, perhaps we may scan the townscape perimeter (as from a helicopter) and observe the inward and outward surge of motor vehicles. From this vantage hover-point, we may consider the theory, inspired by Dr F. F. C. Curtis, F.R.I.B.A. in his 'Alfred Bossom' lecture on Architecture in Transport, delivered before the Royal Society of Arts in January 1961, that one might apply the medieval principle of a ring of fortresses, but, for 'fortress', substitute satellite multi-storey parking buildings. Access to these 'parking-towers' would be achieved by ramps, flowing from ring roads on the outer fringes of the town or city. Perhaps, an interesting theory, which we may consider in detail later, after we have briefly traced the evolution of those buildings designed specifically for the accommodation of motor vehicles.

Multi-storey garages in town and city provide accommodation and services for private cars and commercial vehicles, and it

Catford Garage and Filling Station.

will be useful to consider the rapidly expanding growth of the motor-coach business, which succeeded the stagecoach. The problem of the motor-coach in cities became alive about forty years ago, when the Pickford Company, with other London coach-owners, formed London Coastal Coaches Ltd, operating from Belgrave Square. After three years they moved to Lupus Street, S.W.1, and, during an Easter weekend, about 1,200 loaded coaches travelled from the terminal to various parts of the country. In 1932, owing to the severely restricted site conditions for operating the expanding services with coaches from twenty companies, a new and more appropriate site was obtained nearer Victoria (Southern Railway) Station.

In this new field we may refer to two simple early examples, in areas far apart; one in London and the other New York.

The London example is represented by a garage and filling station at Catford, illustrated by the accompanying sketch which indicates its happy grouping with the neighbouring buildings.

The New York motor-coach station, designed by Thomas Lamb, is a forthright example of a problem well resolved. The ground floor plan here illustrated, indicates saw-tooth embayments for the road coaches, enabling passengers to arrive and depart under the cover of a canopy adjoining the main waiting hall, which latter extends upwards and provides extensive side-lighting.

On the ground floor the accommodation includes a restaurant, an information bureau and a booking office. The first floor provides accommodation for offices and public toilets; these are separated in the end blocks, whilst the space between forms the upper part of the main hall.

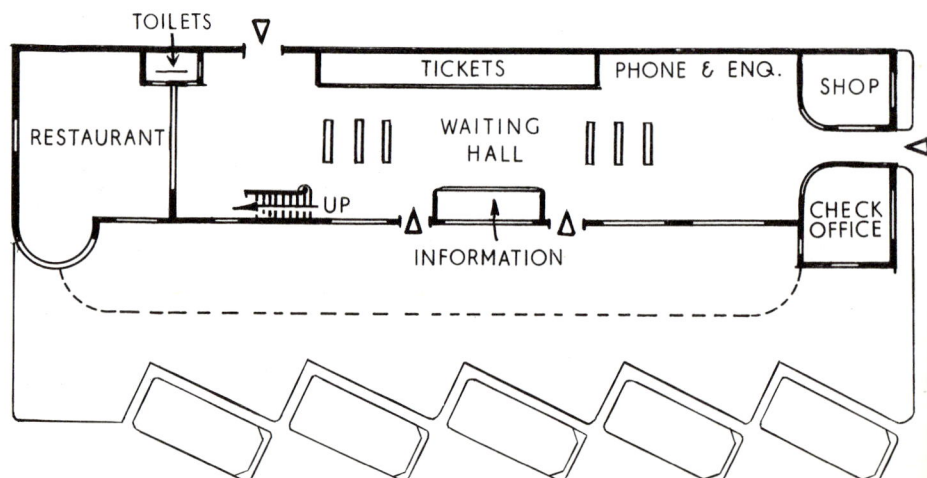

Coach Station, New York.

Victoria Coach Station, Buckingham Palace Road, London S.W.1. Architects Wallis, Gilbert & Partners, 1931-2.

VICTORIA COACH STATION

To many travellers by road coach, this Terminal, situated on the corner of Buckingham Palace Road and Elizabeth Street, will be familiar; a year or so prior to 1932 the writer was closely associated with preliminary designs for a similar project upon the same site, and it is therefore of particular interest to him. The illustration displays the characteristic prominence of the dominant corner block – uniting the façades of the adjacent streets.

The magnitude of the problems of handling large numbers of coaches and passengers may not at first be very apparent to the prospective traveller when he books his coach seat at an agency. From the operating point of view, the complexities of traffic facing the booking office staff – dealing with the variety of requirements of the affiliated companies – indicates that a highly specialized type of planning precision is fundamental.

A pivotal feature initiated at this station relates to the Chart Room, under the control of the Traffic Manager. The control is divided into geographical zones, corresponding with the operating companies. Here, the bookings for numerous agencies throughout the country are dealt with; a separate department undertakes bookings for inclusive extended tours in Britain and European countries.

What has happened in the way of travel by road coach, originating at Victoria Terminal, is now multiplying in most provincial cities in Britain; the author's own experience bears this out, also, as far north as the city of Chester, whose Roman and Medieval character is in the throes of rebuilding and the application of new highways planning.

The examination of any parking area at an airport, factory, office block, etc. demonstrates forcibly enough that this is an

The 'openwork' garage ramp at Hemel Hempstead, Herts. is an example of design which respects its surroundings while fulfilling its practical functions.

Summer Row, Birmingham: Here in 1964 'a proving project' of demountable units was erected to deal with urgent parking problems in an expanding situation.

intolerable waste of ground space, and that vertical or 'layer' parking is the logical solution.

The development of modern techniques in prefabricated building-units simplifies construction and cuts down time and also the inconveniences of paving vast areas of ground.

The New Town of Hemel Hempstead provides a modest essay in a ramped 'openwork' flat spiral building – as illustrated.

A more ambitious project is the example at Summer Row, Birmingham, comprising a multi-arch, three-tier parking ramp. This is unique in the fact that the whole structure is demountable. The main elements are a structural steel framework, with pre-formed reinforced concrete floor slabs, laid as ramps. It was built in 1964 and accommodates 400 cars; the combined floor areas amount to 28,600 square feet, whilst parking on open ground would use up 72,000 square feet. The simplicity of the construction, at an early stage, is indicated in the adjoining photo; it may be regarded as a 'proving project'. Birmingham had a

much greater project in the making at New Street Station, which we shall be examining in a later chapter.

ROAD AND RAIL

Before adventuring into the wider field of 'Architecture on the Highway', we are bound to look at the case of the 'commuter' who is also a car-owner. Hitherto he regularly travelled to work into London, or his nearest provincial city – by car, until by the slow silting-up of traffic lanes he became a semi-commuter, which means that he proceeded by car to the outer perimeter of the city, parked his car, and completed the journey by public transport.

The architect and town planner, in conjunction with the engineer, have an opportunity and a duty to devise and promote the most satisfactory means for ending the conflict that bedevils our road transport system in towns. During the years following the Second World War, the impetus of the New Towns and the major expansion of the highways throughout Britain have provided a breadth and variety of scope comparable with the railways.

In the planning of the new Motorways the road cannot be considered in isolation – nor merely as a track for motorists; it is an all-embracing, all-penetrating network, which, together with the vehicles upon it, the bridges and the roadside ancillaries, is an integral part of our life and landscape.

Some other forms of transportation have, in their time, evolved an acceptable aesthetic, which has developed from their own particular functions; consequently, they frequently manage to be compatible with their surroundings.

The railways, particularly (built during the emergence of high engineering innovation), provided some large-scale structures in the landscape which may have appeared, at the time, unnatural components for the native scene. Yet, hard, functional, and linear engineering became embedded in small-scale landscape as readily as pretty wayside stations.

Inevitably, it was the motor-car habit which wrought most havoc with its environment. The early attraction was 'The Open Road' and the urge to go where you like, stop where you like, and when you like – no more fixed points of embarkation – no terminus!

We are, by controls, accepting the position that was obvious in the eighteenth century and adopted by common consent then, of grouping 'staging' facilities at sensible intervals. As we have seen, in the eighteenth century, taste in building was such that the essential services were offered in modern buildings, and they have stood the test of time. Many of them were so architecturally meritorious as to be worthy of preservation, and are listed under the Town and Country Planning Act – 1947. Garages and filling stations are unlikely to be protected by industrial archaeologists as they are being constantly altered and brought up-to-date, and would therefore never reflect the taste of a given period. Their architecture is ephemeral.

What should concern us now is whether the service areas on motorways will be as appropriate in design for this age as buildings

The 'road style' for filling stations in Britain on a 'solus' site (selling only one brand of petrol).

The Allertal service area on Hamburg–Hanover Autobahn, Germany.

were in the stage-coach era, a time when buildings and vehicles, as well as being embraced by their characteristic style, were enlightened by a satisfactory relationship. Will, for instance, the service area at the Watford Gap, on the M1, be as appropriate and as fine as Colnbrook village was on the Bath Road (where a staging post for coaches still survives), as an inn serving the traveller of the twentieth century?

SERVICE AREAS

A car journey towards London along the M1 will reveal the Gargantuan proportions of fly-overs and bypass highways under construction, and this example is indicative of the development ahead in Britain's trunk road systems.

In order to establish a 'touchstone' for what we may anticipate architecturally in the service-areas, it may be relevant to look at some examples from Continental and American systems. At Allertal, on the Hamburg–Hanover Autobahn, there is a simple and direct car-service area, comprising two halves, almost identical, which are staggered, each being planned in relation to the other (as on the railway principle of UP and DOWN), serving the traffic lanes. The petrol pump units have a simple cantilever reinforced concrete roof, each wing overlapping on the main supporting piers. The rear wings of each pump unit provide shelter for the entrances to the large blocks of restaurant and 'comfort' accommodation, which adjoin the roadside. By an interesting coincidence, the roof section over the service pumps resembles a prototype 'cranked' roof, developed by the L.M.S. Railway during the Second World War as an experimental unit of modular construction at Queens Park Station. The latter will be referred to in Section 2: Review and Analysis.

Lakeside service areas on the Munich–Austria Autobahn at Bad Reichenau, on the Chiem See, Germany.

In Italy, at Firenzuola, on the famous Autostrada del Sol, on an otherwise well-laid-out service site, a strikingly elaborate overbridge restaurant spans the motor highway; while resting travellers may enjoy an extensive vista from their lofty restaurant, the flag-bedecked 'Pavesi' may tend to distract the approaching motorist.

An appropriate example, with similar characteristics, may be quoted from the western continent. In the State of Oklahoma, at Vinita on the Rogers Turnpike motorway, an overbridge restaurant spans the dual highways. Linking them is an arched structure, superimposed and integrated with the rectangular restaurant buildings. Although somewhat distracting, it is less so than at Firenzuola, nor is it so flamboyant.

Firenzuola on the Autostrada del Sol, Italy.

Vinita on the Will Rogers Turnpike, Oklahoma, U.S.A.

An overbridge restaurant spanning the Tri-State and North-West Tollway,
Illinois, U.S.A.

From the United States, also, comes another example of an overbridge restaurant, spanning the Tri-State and North-West Tollway system in the state of Illinois. It is one of a series of similar structures, rational and simple in character, well related to the car-parks and filling stations.

The highway, which runs along an embankment, has spur-roadways ramped up to the level of the overbridge to provide access to the adjoining car-parks on each side. The design of the building is rational and restrained; particularly satisfactory is the emphasis of the abutments, linking it with the car-parks. The superimposed topography, due to the establishment of the car-parks and connecting road spurs, indicates the immense engineering require-

ments of this and similar undertakings. Like the vast engineering problems in the development of the trunk railways, the new motor highways of the world demonstrate the ingenuity of their designers and con-structors. By comparison, they have the advantages of new skills and new types of engineering equipment.

Contrasting with the overbridge type of service-area buildings, America's West Palm Beach – Sunshine Parkway, Florida, provides an example of a centre island service area. A rectangular building with a main restaurant at first-floor level, and a second floor over one-half of the main block. The first floor is cantilevered from a central 'spine' beam, providing a paved circulating area at ground level under the building. Also, at Pompano on the Sunshine State Parkway, Florida, the centrally sited service area becomes a major feature, in a well-wooded parkland. The main motorways form an elongated island; one road sweeps round in a slow curve, the other runs die-straight, forming a segment within which the service area is planned in a broad and expansive manner reminiscent of the countryside around St Cloud.

The placing of service areas along motorways on the Continental scale predicates a limitless landscape. In Britain the long 'Freeways' soon run into the countryside; the thatched garage of the nineteen-thirties, which presumably was an attempt to belong to the countryside, was unconscious of the impending development of a national road system. A motorway designed with circumspection, could be both functional, and be also embedded in the landscape. A service area could be part of both; it should *appear* correct, from the road, from the landscape, and from its internal planning. Unfortunately, in many cases this has not been achieved; service areas properly conceived could help to bring about, if not a marriage, at least, a measure of harmony between scenery and services.

Newport Pagnell, on the M1, provides a

The Pompano service area on the Sunshine State Parkway, Florida, U.S.A.

somewhat unhappy example of the lack of unity of parts – completely out of harmony with the countryside. The illustration of the service area indicates the disruptive nature in siting and the awkward inter-penetration of bridges and roads, with an entire absence of flow characteristics of motorway traffic. Perhaps a reason for the disharmony stems from the use of radial planning on the basis of official diagramma-tic projects for service-area layouts.

Here and there, one may find roadside buildings of acceptable character – such as *The Ox in Flames* restaurant on the Farn-borough bypass; the influence of petrol companies may have a bearing upon some service buildings. An overhaul in the design and character of filling-stations following upon the changeover to 'Solus Sites', indicates how a 'New Look' may be happily placed for commercial ends, whilst retaining a traditional vogue. As illustrated, this trend may provide useful ideas for a developed road-style for motoring. (page 21)

THE GROWTH OF MOTELS

In the Continents, where road distances are measured in thousands of miles (instead of hundreds), particularly in the case of U.S.A., the problems of catering for travellers are many and various. [1]Records have indicated that in 1952, 85 per cent of all travellers in the United States went by car; and, the predicted number for 1953 was 40,000,000 people, two-thirds of these would stop at 'Motels' – that portmanteau word with which we are now familiar. The influences of air-travel, also, had its effects in some locales; tourists, 'resort vacationists' [*sic*], and businessmen arrive by air, rent a car, and drive to a motel, where they have reserved rooms.

The name 'Gold Coast' has been applied

[1] See *Architectural Record*, July, 1953

An aerial view of the service area at Newport Pagnell, Bucks.

A view from the road and parking area of The Caribe Motel, *Miami Beach, Florida. The narrow and deep site is designed on an 'H' plan and provides a secluded bathing pool behind the administrative block facing the sea.*

CARIBE MOTEL
MIAMI BEACH, FLORIDA

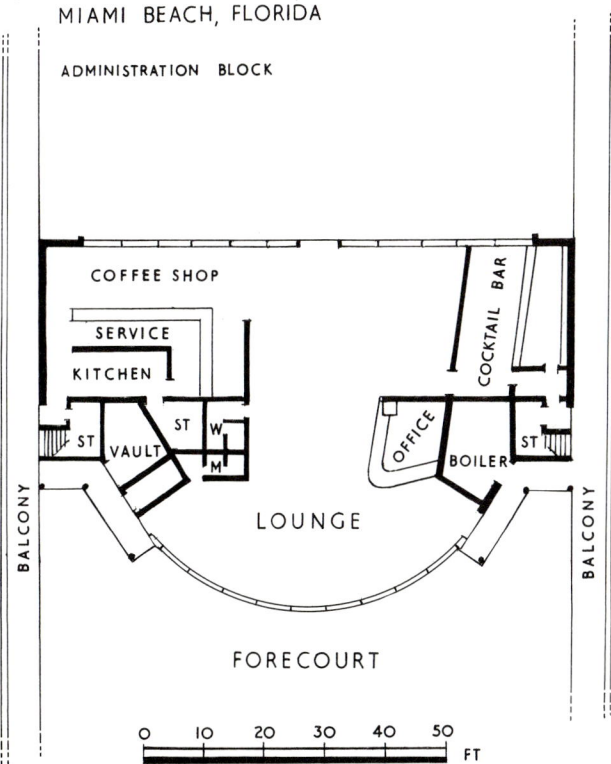

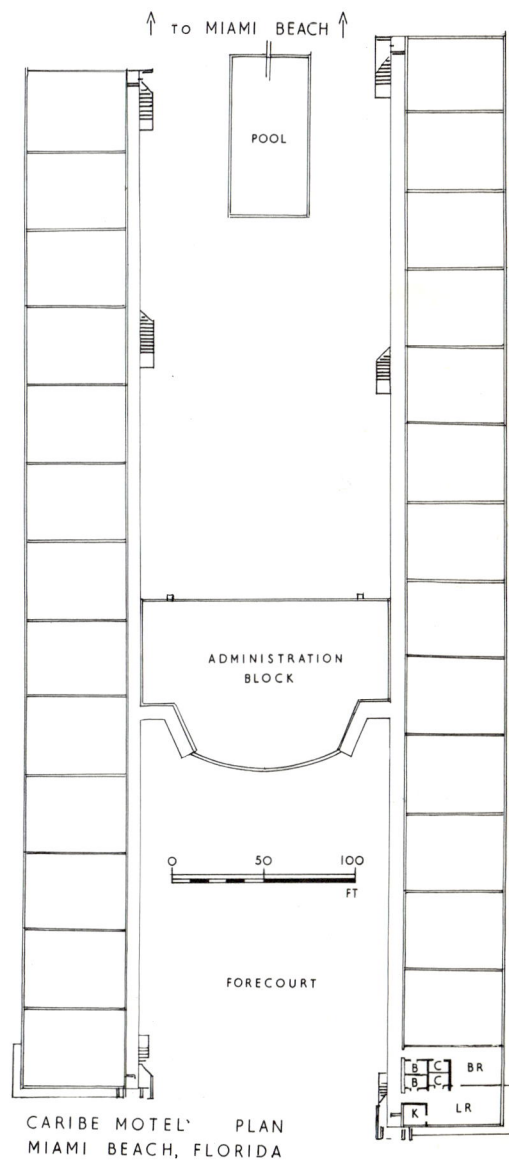

ADMINISTRATION BLOCK

COFFEE SHOP

SERVICE

KITCHEN

COCKTAIL BAR

ST

ST   VAULT   W   M

OFFICE   BOILER   ST

BALCONY

LOUNGE

BALCONY

FORECOURT

0 10 20 30 40 50
FT

TO MIAMI BEACH

POOL

ADMINISTRATION
BLOCK

0   50   100
FT

FORECOURT

B C
B C   BR

K   LR

CARIBE MOTEL PLAN
MIAMI BEACH, FLORIDA

27

to several coastal holiday regions; the current version in Miami Beach is a fashionable strip of land, developed with motels, which rank with Big-Business; the Florida coast indicated a motel-building boom. It will be interesting to glance at a few types representing the planning requirements, in respect of accommodation and site location.

HOLIDAY PLANNING

Between the years 1951 to 1953 that golden strip of Miami Beach on the coast of Florida experienced phenomenal development; motels and the like were planned for the holiday atmosphere in romantic surroundings.

A typical example was *The Caribe*, designed by Norman M. Giller as a holiday hotel for guests who intend staying over a period of three months. The narrow, deep site was developed as an 'H' plan, in which the parking areas face the front.

The guest's accommodation comprises a living-room with dining recess; bathroom and bedroom: this accommodation is located in the long wings which have galleries along the inner faces for access to the first floor. This principle brings back memories of the galleried arrangement of the coaching inn of the far-off days.

The short connecting single-storey block contains the administration offices and includes entrance lobby, office, coffee shop and cocktail lounge. The units of accommodation are typical although the arrangements vary in planning positions to suit particular sites. A swimming pool is provided in the court formed by the two wings, and sited behind the admininstrative block; the sketch gives a general impression of the layout.

Flexibility in the layout of the rooms and sites become more important with the growing variety of patronage. Commercial and resort visitors tend to prefer rooms with convertible sofa-beds, used as living-rooms by day, while 'transient' tourists prefer the standard bedroom arrangement. The newer type of motels tends increasingly to approach hotel standards in interior furnishings and amenities. More attention has been given to the provision of noise-control and adequate protection from glare of flashing headlights. This has been achieved in some cases by the arrangement of entrance, cloaks, and bathroom on the

Casa Mañana Motel, *San Antonio, Texas, U.S.A., showing how the units are angled to secure privacy. Architect: Thomas B. Thompson.*

28

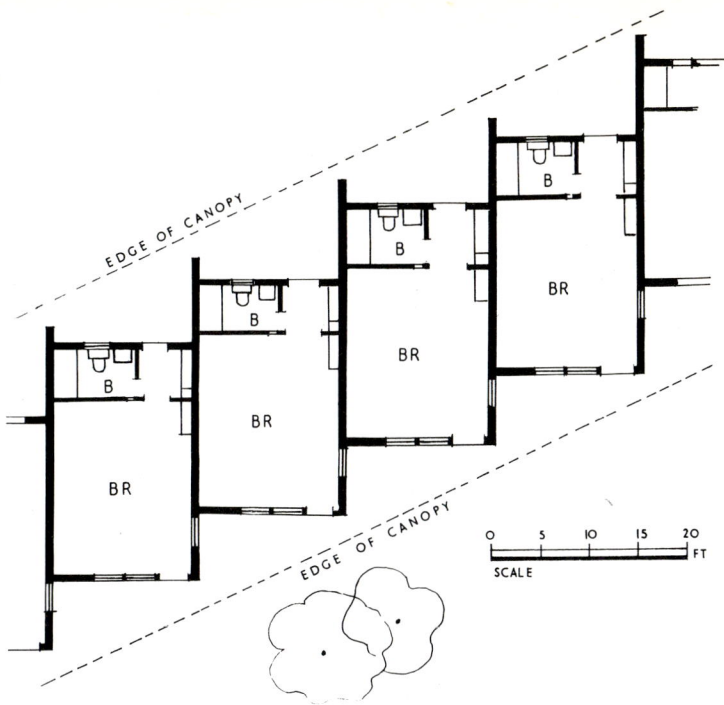

Casa Mañana Motel: *part of a typical plan of units which are arranged in blocks of eight.*

side adjoining the parking area, to form a baffle between it and the living accommodation, as at the *Red Horse Motor Inn*, at Dayton, Ohio.

Another interesting type is the *Casa Mañana Motel* at San Antonio in Texas, where we find the buildings arranged in groups of eight units, the blocks being angled to secure privacy and to provide an interesting elevation.

Several national motel companies in U.S.A. strive to keep patrons within their own affiliated orbits by providing more or less standard accommodation. The influence of air travel is also a factor which may tend to have its effect in some locales. Perhaps we in Britain may some day investigate the possibility of well designed and suitably sited motels of moderate size, as a substitute for seaside caravan sprawl. Contemplation of such a possibility might lead us to the creation of a holiday environment, somewhat more secluded than the holiday camp or the caravan town. We may not have our Golden Coast of Florida or

Daytona Beach, but we have examples such as Port Merion, which, thanks to its originator, preserves its protected seclusion.

MOTELS IN EUROPE

The pioneer of motels in Britain was the late Graham Lyon (*d.* 1930) who had travelled extensively in U.S.A. where, for a time, he stayed. After the early introduction of the idea into Britain, some thirty-five years ago, one now finds a chain of this type of 'rest-houses' for motorists, extending from the *Oakwood Motel* at Elgin in Morayshire, down to the *Dover Stage*, well known to travellers using the Channel Ferry.

It is reasonable to assume that, in some instances, their development took the form of extensions to existing garages or refreshment rooms, adjoining parking areas near main motorways. Where space permitted at country inns, travelling motorists were encouraged by providing a group of small bedrooms with car-ports near by.

An example of this type of development

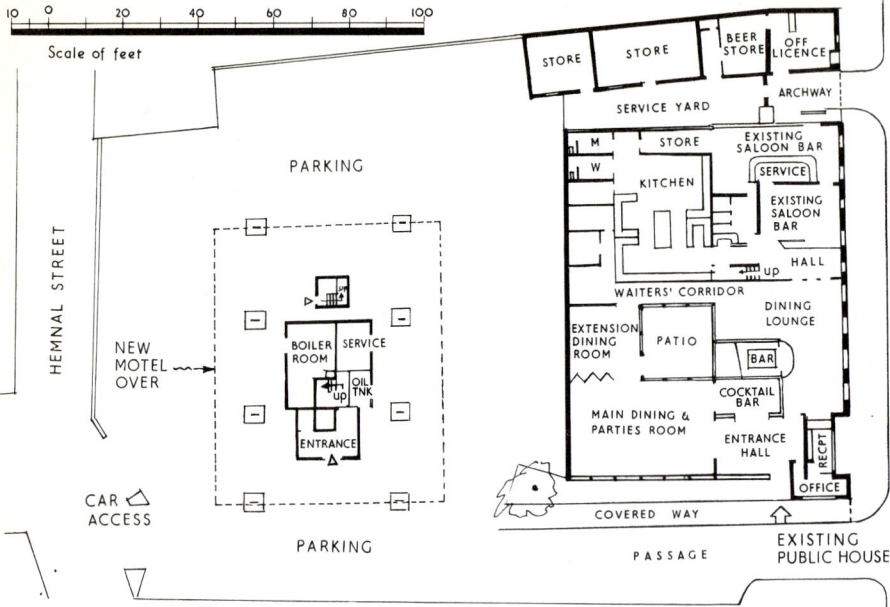

The layout plan of the Epping motel, adjacent to an existing replanned Georgian 'pub', indicates a fortuitous site arrangement governed by access roads and parking areas. Architects: Erdi & Rabson.

is the motel at Epping, which was designed by Erdi & Rabson in 1963. They successfully achieved the integration of a new block, three storeys high, with an existing High-Street inn which has a Georgian façade.

The block plan indicates an ideal site condition where, by reason of a secondary street, parallel with the High Street with a connecting side-street, passes at right-angles to the existing inn; this provides very satisfactory traffic circulation and access to the private parking area.

The plan gives a clear picture of the layout, with its interesting patio, opening from the dining-room extension.

This view of the new block indicates how it is raised on 'V' stilts to provide under-cover parking for visitors' cars. The unique system of supports is reminiscent of buildings in Italy and elsewhere, which typifies Professor P. L. Nervi's structural system.

Examples of completely modern motels, planned exclusively as such, are to be found in three of the new towns; at Harlow, Stevenage, and Hemel Hempstead. The latter is selected as an appropriate example to discuss and illustrate.

The new motel block at Epping. Owing to the restricted site the bedroom block is raised off the ground to allow parking space beneath.

The main façade of the Breakspear Motor Hotel, *Hemel Hempstead, Herts., dominates the composition by expressing its height by vertical ribs.*

The *Breakspear Motor Hotel* at Hemel Hempstead was designed by Mr Nelson Foley, A.R.I.B.A., and was completed in the autumn of 1964. The site is conveniently near to the M1 motorway, yet adjacent to an area where the rural landscape provides a background of trees. The general composition of the buildings forms an interesting group, as will be apparent from the illustrations. Approaching from Breakspear Way one is faced by the tall narrow end, perfectly plain except for the characteristic motif of modern Trust House buildings.

The main façade dominates the composition by expressing its height, achieved in the form of vertical ribs spaced in relation to the width of the end elevation. The front entrance is asymmetrically placed and is emphasized by a deep and widely projecting canopy. An interesting feature of this elevation is the long sculptured panel forming a screen to the terrace; the artist who designed the panel was Henry Haig.

The end view of the Breakspear Motor Hotel. *The hotel was designed by Mr Nelson Foley and completed in 1964.*

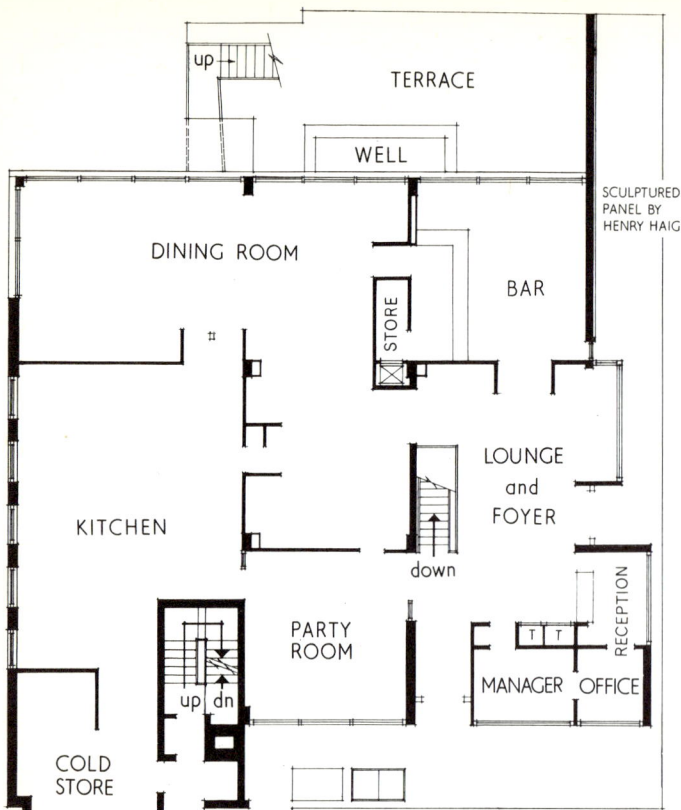

Ground Floor Plan

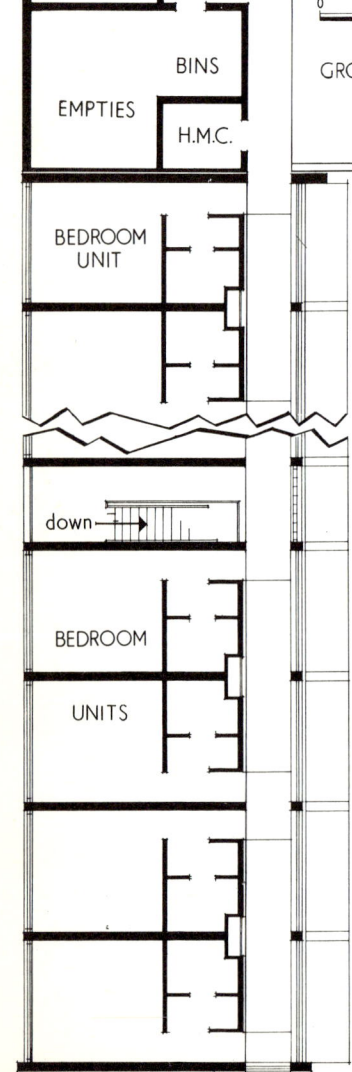

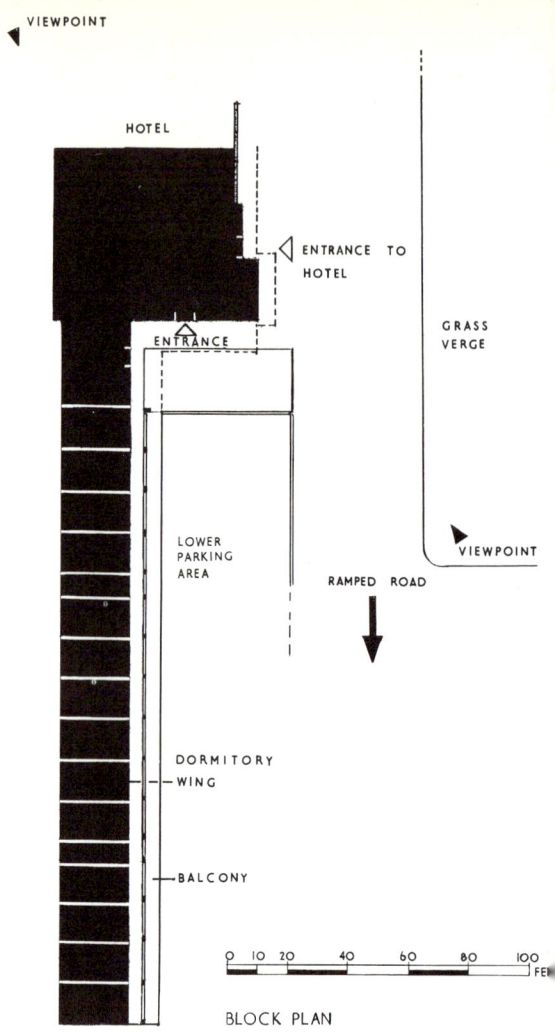

- up
- TERRACE
- WELL
- DINING ROOM
- BAR
- STORE
- SCULPTURED PANEL BY HENRY HAIG
- LOUNGE and FOYER
- KITCHEN
- down
- PARTY ROOM
- RECEPTION
- up dn
- MANAGER OFFICE
- COLD STORE
- T T
- BINS
- EMPTIES
- H.M.C.
- BEDROOM UNIT
- down
- BEDROOM UNITS

```
0    5   10        20        30  FEET
```

GROUND FLOOR PLAN

Block Plan

- VIEWPOINT
- HOTEL
- ENTRANCE TO HOTEL
- ENTRANCE
- GRASS VERGE
- VIEWPOINT
- LOWER PARKING AREA
- RAMPED ROAD
- DORMITORY WING
- BALCONY

```
0  10 20     40      60      80     100 FEET
```

BLOCK PLAN

The Breakspear Motor Hotel. *Ground floor and block plans.*

The adjoining plans of the ground floor, illustrate the sub-division of accommodation, which has been planned in a rational way. As the ground formation inclines steeply down from the main block, the bedroom units have been so arranged that the roof line of the upper range of bedrooms coincides with the underside of the canopy of the main block. There are twenty-eight bedroom units (designated 'studio' units) compactly planned with a bathroom entered from the lobby of each unit.

In the main tall block, the ground floor comprises the public hotel with foyer lounge, giving access to the bar and dining-room; there is also a room for private parties. On the first floor, a staff dining-room with living-room and kitchen are provided; recreation rooms and bedrooms take up the two floors above for the resident staff.

In contrast with the solidly built Break-spear Motor Hotel at Hemel Hempstead, it may be interesting to refer to the recently built (1965) *Coylum Bridge Motor Hotel* at Aviemore, Inverness-shire, designed by Russell, Hodgson & Leigh for a motoring organization; it is one of many other projects which extend also upon the European continent.

The illustration depicts the special purpose of the Aviemore project, which is a combined motor inn/ski hotel serving a mountain resort catering for winter sports; it provides two blocks of buildings arranged around an open forecourt with separate garage blocks.

The residential buildings express an interesting application of rough stone walls on the lower part, combined with vertical boarding above first floor level.

We have examined a limited but representative series of buildings from medieval to modern times, designed to serve the traveller, whether he drives his own vehicle – or is conveyed by public transport. No doubt the present road system will proliferate in the future and, in Section 5 of this book we will refer to the trends to be expected.

The transition of horse-power to steam leads naturally to the industrial era and the railways, which rapidly competed with the roads. The development from the early nineteenth century onwards provides us with many new and interesting types of railway architecture, which will be the subject of Section 2, a subject which is daily a part of the traveller's experience.

The Coylum Bridge Motor Hotel, *Aviemore, Inverness-shire, designed by Russell, Hodgson & Leigh. Situated at the foot of mountain slopes among pine trees, these buildings reflect in their construction the stone and timber of their surroundings and blend perfectly into the landscape.*

The Great Hall, Euston station, 1840. Reproduced from a water-colour drawing by the architect, P. C. Hardwick. A survival of this splendid hall is the sculptural group at the head of the stairs which is now in the Waiting Room of the New Euston.

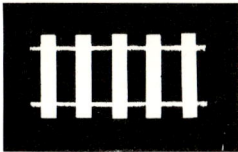

CHAPTER 4 HISTORICAL BACKGROUND

In the General Introduction to the four systems of transport we have briefly referred to the genesis of land communications in Britain from the time of the Roman invasion. Similarly, in Section I, the development of the road systems of the coaching era brought us to the point where a new type of transport vehicle appeared in the form of the rail-wagon and steam-engine.

It is not the author's intention, in this place, to go into details in tracing the pre-history of track forms used for carrying stone from quarries, and iron and coal from mining areas to seaports and centres of industry. Many interesting facts of this sort relating to early locomotive types, details of permanent-way tracks, to signalling – all are to be found in books written by those railway enthusiasts who make these matters their particular concern. A list of study books is supplied, as an appendix to this book, for those readers who have graduated from the 'spotter' stage to being fully fledged model-railway builders with an urge to find out how it all began.

BRITAIN'S EARLY RAILWAYS

It is now the author's intention to evaluate those buildings the travellers will observe during railway journeys. Today's examples may be usefully compared with and related to early specimens, so few of which now survive.

The first railway trains to carry passengers exclusively in Britain, travelled along the Liverpool and Manchester Railway on September 15th, 1830 – a memorable day in railway history. The promoters of the project had experienced an arduous struggle which was equalled only by the vigorous and competent efforts of George Stephenson, its designer and engineer; their united efforts ultimately secured a victory over their opponents.

Objectors to this project were many, and cunning in their cross-examinations; each applied his own interests in the framing of his question. Although some of the answers were quite unexpected, as for instance, to the question, "What will become of the harness-maker and coachman; the horse-breeders and dealers, the roadside innkeepers?" Stephenson's friends replied,

Chesterfield Station (c. 1870), a mature example of straightforward building in the classical idiom, in harmony with its surroundings.

"They will probably become shareholders in the New Railway." An interesting speculation, indeed!

The scope of that project will perhaps be gauged by this brief outline of a few of the facts relating to its construction. The route for the railway required sixty-three bridges, with a viaduct of nine giant arches – and a cutting through the Pennines.

As a further hazard, the almost intractable Chat Moss, a peat-bog, about 12 miles square, upon whose bosom the rail-track and its loaded trains had to be sustained. . . . For weeks on end, during the hours of daylight – and, by the light of torches at night – hundreds of navvies ceaselessly tipped loads of turf, hurdles laced with brushwood and heather – finally barrels of clay to take ballast and sleepers for the tracks. And, so it was that in 1830 George Stephenson's *Rocket* hauled the first passenger train from Liverpool to Manchester, with the august Duke of Wellington at the 'saluting base'.

The success of this first passenger-carrying railway provided a great impetus to railway development; many large groups, with commercial interests, sought parliamentary powers to build more railways throughout Britain to link up with industrial towns and seaports. The various companies vied with each other to provide imposing

termini, stately viaducts, and Doric or Gothic frontispieces to their tunnels. Typical examples of two great trunk lines show an interesting comparison in their respective forms of development: one, the line joining London and the provincial city of Birmingham, a large and direct project, complete; the other, the somewhat piecemeal construction of branch lines between provincial centres of industry, finally forming the nucleus of the Midland Railway.

It is, however, with the former London to Birmingham line we are primarily concerned, as it formed the basis of the London and North Western Railway, known as 'The Premier Line' in those days.

Thus, we glance back over 125 years to its completion, which leads us to the firm establishment of a new form of architectural expression, arising in the era of transport.

As an introduction to the consideration of particular examples of the more important railway stations of long standing, it will perhaps be appropriate to recall the impressions of a nineteenth-century writer and critic, Frank Williams, writing in 1852, who gives an interesting survey of the railway architecture at that time, ranging over a fairly wide field.

In his view, the treatment varied consider-

Different architectural treatment of tunnel entrances; a typical Classical frontispiece at Box in Wiltshire (ABOVE) *and a castellated example at Shugborough Park, Staffordshire.*

Battle station, Sussex, 1852. Designed by William Tress; a Gothic-style building, reminiscent of a rural vicarage, with its walls of native stone, with Caen stone dressings and alternating bands of plain and ornamented roofing tiles.

ably in both "style" and quality of style. Occasionally, buildings were "heavy and massive", or "large and handsome;" at other places they were 'neat and picturesque', whilst *modo et forma* "they had no quality to apologize for their existence." He stressed the fact that the characteristics of the neighbourhood in which they were erected, frequently determined their style. As an example Battle station, on the Tunbridge Wells and Hastings Railway, was in the Gothic style, built with native stone walls and having Caen dressings. Another example, this on the line joining Bedford with the London to Birmingham Railway, is at Woburn. Of this latter Frank Williams exclaimed: "The tasteful arrangements of the building and the contrast of the clean white walls with the framings, have, by the skill of the architect, combined to make it an ornament to a very beautiful neighbourhood."

The above quotations may appear to our modern sophisticated colleagues as a trifle effusive; nevertheless the general idea to be conveyed was an enthusiasm – generated in an exciting period of development – sparked off by the railway pioneers.

NORTH PERIMETER

In referring to the London and Birmingham Railway, we find naturally, from an architectural point of view, our interest is primarily focused on Euston, where now a new station has arisen. This will be the first entirely new terminal station in Britain's capital city in this twentieth century. In a later chapter we shall see the new vogue in planning and design for an electrified system of rail travel, and the co-ordinating of 'Traffic in Towns', vehicular and pedestrian, where these converge.

Let us now, however, dwell, nostalgically perhaps, upon the Euston of an earlier era – Philip Hardwick's classical masterpiece which survived well over 100 years.

The London to Birmingham Railway, rather more than three times longer than the Liverpool to Manchester line, was an

The style of the former rural station at Woburn, Bedfordshire, was perhaps influenced by the works on village architecture by John C. Louden (1783–1843).

The Euston Portico, built in the Greek Doric style, by Philip Hardwick 1836. The magnificent fluted columns were 44 feet high and formed an impressive entrance to the station yard. Unfortunately this feature was demolished in 1965.

*Entrance portico of Euston station. A lithograph by T. Allom showing the original
aspect of the entrance complex. One can see the secondary blocks flanking the main portico.*

accomplishment of supreme significance in that it established a powerful and firmly based means of transport, from Britain's capital city, linking it with the industrial Midlands and feeder communications with seaports. The promoters, who appointed the engineers, George Stephenson and his son Robert, to construct the new railway, wisely recognized also the national importance of suitable architecture for buildings associated with the terminal stations of that great adventure. In commissioning Philip Hardwick with the task of designing the Euston terminal, they symbolized the gateway through which one entered the railway system to travel north, and, appropriately that same gateway was used for entering London, coming from the provinces of the North Midlands.

In Hardwick's view the symbolism of Euston deserved and achieved a Classical significance; he therefore produced, appropriately, a Greek Doric propylaeum, a noble and dignified piece of architecture.

That its impact, as a masterpiece of Victorian architecture, expressed a literary idea became quite evident and vocal as the time for its demolition approached; this distressing event will be recorded in a later chapter.

To remind ourselves of Euston's pristine appearance, set in the open space which then (1838) existed in Seymour Place and Euston Grove, the illustration will convey an impression of Hardwick's intention. The portico was composed of a central mass of the Classical order, flanked on either side by pedestrian entrance blocks which formed the secondary features.

In order to appreciate the scale of the 44-foot-high fluted columns of the portico, and the magnificent cast-iron gates, the illustration provides a wonderfully evocative sensation of the play of light and shade upon the finely sculptured surfaces of the Craigleith stonework, and the vigorous details of the ornamental gates and wing-panels.

With regard to the cast-iron gates, it is

Euston station, a detailed sketch of the superb cast-iron gates in the portico, designed by Philip Hardwick in 1838, and cast by Bramah.

interesting to observe that symbolism was carried into the design in the form of the lock plates, these are an heraldic representation of the coat of arms of the London and Birmingham Railway; this was in scale with the general pattern of the gates which were of the order of 10 ft high. The lock-plate was about 12 in. high and 8 in. wide; the coat of arms superimposed in low relief and, as the writer remembers, when the gates were repainted for a special occasion, the lock-plate emblems were picked out in their true heraldic colours.

In considering the relationship between Hardwick's portico, and the station beyond, it is vitally important to have our facts aligned. The earliest simple layout of the rail-head at Euston, in 1838, comprised two platforms, a ticket office, and an administrative block of simple form – as illustrated in the plan below.

It is a sad fact that some writers, whilst

Plan of Euston station, 1838, showing the initial simplicity of an early rail-head station. Later it was elaborated by the addition of P. C. Hardwick's Great Hall.

acknowledging the noble portico, have, in effect denigrated it as a piece of Victorian stage scenery. . . . An example of this view is represented by the following extract: ". . . At Euston, Hardwicke [sic] adorned his vast Greek Doric gateway, with superb cast-iron gates and railings, but, behind this impressive portal the station itself was just a series of sheds. . . ." This would seem to be a premature comparison, for Euston, in 1847–8, was much more than that. The group of buildings approached from the portico, was begun in 1846, by the twenty-four-year-old P. C. Hardwick, son of Philip Hardwick, designer of the immaculate stone Greek Doric propylaeum, earlier illustrated.

The central feature of station buildings was the Great Hall projected as a waiting concourse where passengers would move in and out of the adjacent booking halls and refreshment rooms, before joining the trains. Leading up from the Great Hall, the wide stone stairway ascended to the gallery level and so to the noble meeting room for the shareholders, also the suites of committee rooms and offices.

The magnificence of the interior of the Great Hall, as conceived by the younger Hardwick, is recaptured in the splendid water-colour drawing, which the writer was privileged to examine in the library of the Royal Institute of British Architects. The illustration on page 34 is a reproduction of it and may convey some idea of the hall's former grandeur.

It is interesting to record that Hardwick's intention for the treatment of the walls above the gallery level was to have a series of large panels enriched by painted murals, and representing Classical landscape subjects. A fortuitous relationship was the impression created by the mingling of this mural treatment, the exuberant deeply coffered ceiling, and the vigorous scrolls of the huge consoles, which support the framed ceiling beams spanning the 61 ft wide hall.

With the exception of the murals, the Great Hall was built very much as the illustration indicates. As completed it formed part of a group of Classic buildings of great dignity and purpose justifying the noble portico. Here, indeed, was a terminal where 'The Gateway to the North' achieved an integral composition. Between 1848 and the early 1960s, while the main structure remained, the hall suffered many expensive transgressions from its original purpose as a great waiting concourse. It also miraculously survived two wars.

STATIONS OF THE LONDON REGIONS

In order to relate the London termini to the pattern of the metropolis, the accompanying diagram – in the form of a roughly elliptical *ceinture* – provides a location reference.

Most of these termini incorporate interchange stations for London's Underground Railways, which developed in the twentieth century to link up with the whole transport system, and to which we will refer in later chapters. From the diagram (page 42) it will be seen that upon the northern perimeter we have Paddington, Marylebone, Euston, St Pancras, King's Cross, and Liverpool Street. The southern perimeter aptly links up the Southern Group of railways, with their termini at Victoria, Waterloo, and London Bridge – all serving the southern counties and Channel ports. Each terminal has interesting historical associations as well as significant characteristics of planning and design.

While pride of place has been accorded to the London and North Western Railway,

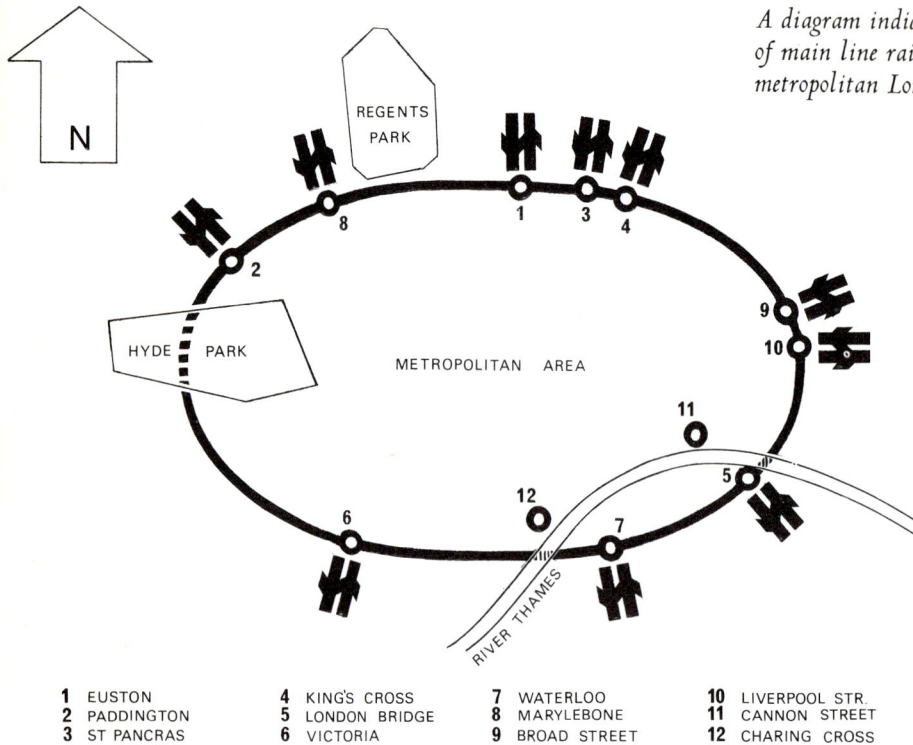

A diagram indicating the approximate position of main line railway termini in relation to metropolitan London in the nineteenth century.

1 EUSTON	**4** KING'S CROSS	**7** WATERLOO	**10** LIVERPOOL STR.
2 PADDINGTON	**5** LONDON BRIDGE	**8** MARYLEBONE	**11** CANNON STREET
3 ST PANCRAS	**6** VICTORIA	**9** BROAD STREET	**12** CHARING CROSS

for the principal reason that it was the pioneer of all great railways, we should respect the Great Western as the only one of the Big Four that, despite ultimate amalgamation, preserved its original title and individuality. In fact, that individuality was early expressed in the choice of the gauge of 7 ft for its track, continuing with that dimension until 1892, when it changed over to the standard of 4 ft 8½ in.

Influenced by the progress in railway transport so successfully achieved by the promoters of the London to Birmingham Railway, the Bristol Chamber of Commerce with the Merchant Adventurers and others, initiated in 1833 the scheme for their projected railway to London. The promoters appointed Isambard K. Brunel (1806–59), then twenty-seven years old, to be their engineer and to construct their ambitious undertaking. The selection of Brunel was

interesting, from the fact that his father, M. I. Brunel (1769–1849, who formerly served in the French navy), worked as an architect in New York. Isambard, who was educated in Paris, was trained as an engineer in his father's office there.

The projected route of the Great Western Railway, linking London with Bristol was boldly conceived, running north of the Marlborough Downs, via Reading and Bath. It necessitated the building of a great viaduct near the Thames at Maidenhead. The first section from Paddington to Taplow was completed in 1838, and the final stage to Bristol two years later, enabled the system to become operative. To bring about such achievements Stephenson and Brunel, and their peers of that era, predicated courage and knowledge on a par with those facing the highway engineers of today – in the complexity of great motor transport requirements. This may be an understatement; for example, the building of the London to Birmingham Railway was a much greater undertaking than the construction of the M1, that is in relation to the technical resources available at that time.

PADDINGTON STATION

In the building of Paddington station, it seemed inevitable that the principle which initiated the 'broad gauge' should apply to the associated structures as well as with the conception of the system as a whole. Thus, the great semicircular train-shed principle which we also find at some other London terminals, as at King's Cross and St Pancras for example; the notable exception on the northern perimeter was Euston, with its orthodox series of pitched roofs.

At Paddington we find the inevitable fusion between wrought- and cast-iron structures as seen at termini with similar characteristics. Engineers and architects often worked together in the design of the stations – sometimes with agreeable results. This was so at Paddington, where the combined efforts of Brunel and Sir Matthew Digby Wyatt (1820–77), produced in 1854 the remarkable structure of five spans, embodied in a unified single design.

A general impression of its character will be evident from the adjoining illustration.

Although during its lifetime, the booking offices and public rooms have been re-designed, the aura of the great train shed lives on. Here is no ordinary station; by comparison St Pancras and King's Cross are grand and straightforward train sheds; there is an unexpected and suave allusiveness about Paddington. The plan, with its double 'transepts', suggests faintly the configuration of a cathedral layout. Digby Wyatt's Gothic ornamentation heightens the effect.

Passing from the platforms through the barriers to the wide area of concourse known as 'The Lawns', one arrives, inevitably, at

Paddington station, 1852–4. View along the 700-foot length of platform in the new cast- and wrought-iron and glass architecture of the day, designed by Isambard K. Brunel and Sir Matthew Digby Wyatt. Note the 'transept' inter-penetration of the roofing system.

Paddington Hotel. The original water-colour drawing of this fine French château-type building, designed by Philip C. Hardwick (1792–1870), is preserved in the Bannister Fletcher Library of the Royal Institute of British Architects.

Paddington station. Detail of the transept end on the main departure platform, showing the semi-Classical arcaded entrance to the office block, carried out in enriched cast-iron and plasterwork.

44

the Station Hotel, as formerly was the case at most head-of-line termini.

The original hotel was designed by Philip C. Hardwick (1792–1870) and, a fine water-colour drawing of its French château-type exterior, keeps company with his splendid drawing of Euston Great Hall; they repose in the R.I.B.A. Bannister Fletcher Library of drawings. Submerged by twentieth-century extensions, Paddington Hotel, largely remodelled internally, no longer preserves the entity which Hardwick's drawing conveys.

Before leaving Paddington, it is interesting to reflect that the Great Western was the first railway to call itself 'great'; this may derive from the fact that while it terminated at Bristol, its traffic was carried on by other companies westward and on to Wales; steamers such as Brunel's *Great Western* conveyed the traffic across the Atlantic.

ST PANCRAS STATION

Still on the northern periphery of London's main-line termini, we pass to St Pancras, of the former Midland Railway Company. Historically the development of the Midland line, already referred to as somewhat piecemeal from its inception in 1830, with the section between Leicester and the important area of Swannington built by George and Robert Stephenson. Subsequent progress was slow, the final section in 1870 provided a through route between London and Birmingham, via Sheffield, and so westwards and to the north.

The difficulties of selecting a suitable site for the passenger terminal station were numerous and formidable. The old Midland Railway Company had its own goods station at St Pancras linked up with the Great Northern system, but the rapidly increasing traffic rendered the very restricted site unsuitable for the handling of numerous passengers; consequently a fresh site became imperative. The determining factor for the layout of the new station was the Regent's Canal, which barred the approach of the tracks to the station site, about half a mile away.

The problem of the canal posed two alternatives: under or over. To proceed in tunnel would predicate a low-level terminal station, with all the disadvantages of transfer between road and rail for both vehicular and passenger circulation. A bridge approach, the method adopted, provided for the rail level at the station, running through at between 12 and 17 ft above Euston Road, and being connected to it by the fine upward sweep of the approach drive-in.

St Pancras station, 1865. W. H. Barlow designed this vast cast-iron and glass roof which springs from below track-level, from girders resting on piers both supporting the tracks and forming ties across the basement ceiling.

45

The decision upon the high-level approach, provided the designer and engineer of the station, W. H. Barlow (1812–1902), with a fortuitious opportunity to design his vast arched roof, with a 240 ft span clear of intermediate supports at platform level. It has been described by Ian Nairn (*Nairn's London*) as "... this is one huge all-embracing sweep.... A vast throbbing hangar...."

Constructionally, the St Pancras train terminal has some quite interesting aspects, arising from its unique traffic considerations; for, apart from the service in the carrying of passengers, its goods traffic was equally important from a revenue point of view. The latter was enhanced by the carriage and storage requirements of the brewers of Burton-on-Trent. Thus, William Barlow combined a station and storehouse in one of the most remarkable engineering feats of the last century.

In the basement beer-cellar, below platform level, vaults were formed with brick piers supporting tracks and platforms. From the top of these vaults the great cast-iron ribs, soaring aloft to their apex, were placed parallel like a series of tightly strung bows and strengthened by tie-beams which, in turn, supported the rail-tracks. This glass and iron roof had flexible links along the apex to allow for expansion and contraction, under varying weather conditions.

Externally the roof-end of the station is masked by Sir Gilbert Scott's incredibly clever Victorian Gothic hotel building, with its multiplicity of dormers, pinnacles,

St Pancras Hotel. This photograph shows the original detail for the turret feature, designed by George Gilbert Scott, and completed in 1872.

46

St Pancras Hotel. Typical details of windows and balcony; an original drawing by George Gilbert Scott.

and chimneys; the whole bound horizontally by strong stone cornices. It was completed in 1872.

Sir Gilbert Scott, during that era, was at the peak of his architectural profession, and won the competition for the hotel in 1865.

As an experienced architect, of a family which carried on the tradition, he had been, for several years previously, building huge houses in that style, notably at Kelham in Nottinghamshire, he also was architect for the Broad Sanctuary building adjacent to Westminster Abbey and for many cathedral restorations.

The vogue for placing hotels across the fronts of railway termini in London, had been established at Paddington, Cannon Street, and Charing Cross. We have referred to the case of Paddington, where the public rooms were at station level in

Hardwick's French château-type building. Scott's designs for St Pancras Hotel are also at the R.I.B.A., and we are fortunate in having permission to reproduce one of them here.

The exterior of the building has been criticized as "heartless and fussy" but with an admission that the building had not been inspected internally. Fortunately, admirers of Scott's work, quoted by Professor Pevsner, describe it as "Standing without rival . . . for palatial beauty, comfort, and convenience" (Walford 1897).

To assess reasonably the merits of Scott's design of the hotel building, one should examine the interior planning and details. In the heyday of its public functions as a railway hotel, it was reckoned as the most sumptuous in London, with accommodation for 600 guests.

47

St Pancras Hotel. The Dining Room interior, as designed by George Gilbert Scott. Photograph of original drawing.

The great Gothic porch on Euston Road, leads up by stone steps of easy 'going' to the main staircase, ascending to most of the upper floors. This staircase, with its ornamental cast-iron balustrade and weaving handrails, carries the eye upwards to the lofty vaulted, cathedral-like ceilings, which in their pristine colours of blue, star-spangled panels between the ribs, must have added lustre to the general grandeur of Scott's inspired design. Many of the large rooms had magnificent stone fireplaces, and the tiled wall surfaces, robust and well-fitting doors, survived into the present century, as John Betjeman has confirmed.

The building eventually (1935) ceased to be an hotel, and so was converted into offices under the reorganization of a central engineering and architectural staff; the building now bears the name of 'Midland Chambers'. Hanging over this building and its adjoining neighbour, King's Cross, is the uncertainty of their survival beyond the present decade, due to unspecified reorientation of traffic and transport requirements. That, however, will be another chapter – in several senses!

KING'S CROSS STATION

We follow, naturally, to King's Cross, terminal of the London and North Eastern Railway. It is interesting to recall that this terminal accommodates the product of seven separate companies, serving northern, eastern, and central England and Scotland. They represent one of the most powerful

King's Cross station, 1852. The Euston Road façade plainly showing the two bold arches of the twin sheds, each of a span of 71 ft.

legal battles, contended in Parliament between 1845 and 1846, over a single railway project. By 1850 the towns of Doncaster, Lincoln, Grantham, Peterborough, and Hitchin were linked up with the London terminus at King's Cross, and it is interesting to compare its buildings with Scott's fantastic Victorian Gothic façade.

King's Cross, designed and built in 1851–2 by Lewis Cubitt, member of a celebrated family of builders, is a simple and dignified structure, with no romanticism or associational motive. The twin arches of the roofs of the arrival and departure sheds, each with a span of 71 ft, are quite frankly displayed upon the end wall, facing Euston Road.

Lewis Cubitt faced the ends of his train sheds, with two great glazed arches set in yellow brickwork, with the rings of the arches emphasized by recesses. An attempt to convert a duality of purpose into unity of appearance, forms the central accent of the square turret with a clock face; the turret is 120 ft high, the factual height is not so apparent by reason of the straight line of the coping, just above the high crowns of the arches, and by the strong vertical dominance of the two end brick pylons. During the first two or three decades of the present century there was uncontrolled encroachment around the forward areas, one also remembers the 'rash' of the early Underground Tube stations faced with cherry-red faience of that era.

King's Cross, as a passenger station, was well contrived; we should also refer to the fact that its operations included a well developed goods station for the handling

Plan of King's Cross station 1851–2, designed by Lewis Cubitt.

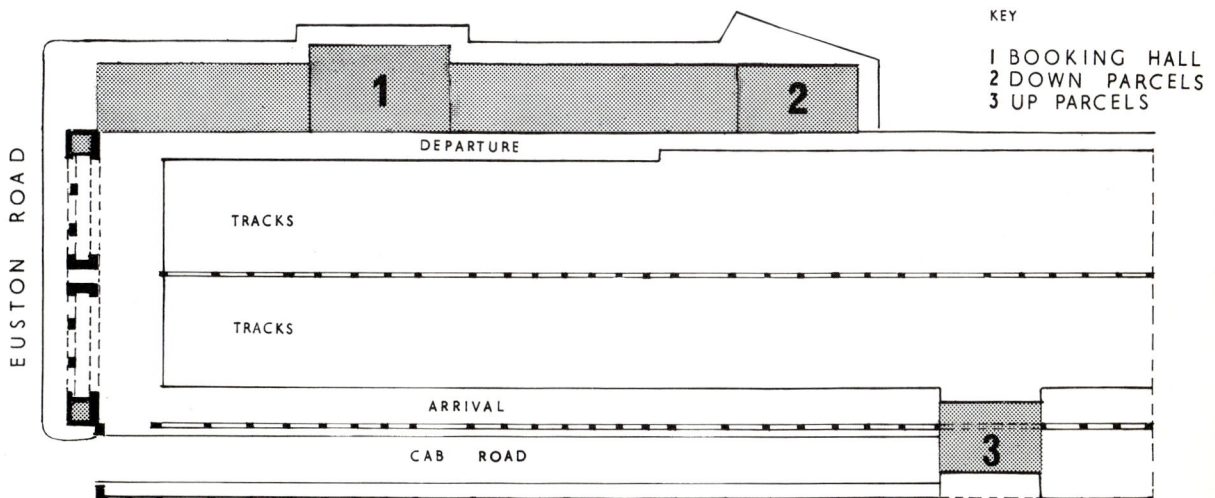

KEY
1 BOOKING HALL
2 DOWN PARCELS
3 UP PARCELS

King's Cross station. Interior view of the twin-arched roof.

of freight. The latter was built alongside the Regent's Canal, and it included a loading dock for barges inside. The building was well lighted, both through the glass roof and by lamps, equipped with cranes and planned to provide easy interchange between road, canal, and railway. It was an outstanding example of transport co-ordination in the 1850s, and an earnest for future traffic integration in succeeding years.

SOUTH PERIMETER

Travelling from the northern perimeter and across to the group of termini serving the south-eastern counties and the Channel ports, we are introduced to the first of the British railway companies to install electric power for traction, with exciting results.

In contrast to this example of progressive achievement, the Southern Railway holds some interesting records of antiquity; at Mitcham is a railway station which has been claimed to be the oldest in the world! It was built for the Surrey Iron Railway, which obtained an Act of Parliament in 1801 to enable it to construct a railway between Wandsworth (Rainfield) and Croydon (Pitlake Meadow), and a branch between Mitcham and Hackbridge.

In those early days when the trucks were hauled by horses or donkeys, the railway

was constructed for goods only, as were several other primitive lines in Britain. This small Mitcham line ceased its operation in 1846. Yet, the old station still survives, protected by Section 30 of the Town and Country Planning Act of 1947, as a building of special architectural or historic interest. The illustration indicates its semi-domestic character.

Of the earliest stations for passenger-carrying railways we have a number of remarkable examples which will be illustrated in succeeding pages. Of particular

London Bridge station. Cast-iron column base of 1836 showing the attention paid to detail by early railway architects.

Mitcham station, reputed to be the oldest in Britain and listed as an historical building.

interest is the station upon the first line to enter London, at Greenwich in 1836, designed by George Smith. By way of contrast, Waterloo was the latest Southern terminal, begun in 1907 and, eventually opened in 1922. Briefly the railway is the smallest of the Big Four group, which comprised London and South Western; London, Brighton, and South Coast; and, South Eastern and Chatham Railways.

Before concluding the historical background to the Southern Railway it will be interesting to refer to several examples from early days, when some of the finest architects of that era designed station buildings of grace, charm, and functional satisfaction.

We have referred, in an earlier chapter, to Frank Williams's survey in 1852 upon the architectural characteristics of railway stations in those far-off days; and, it will be appropriate here, to translate his word-picture into visual reproduction in the form of selected examples of former railway buildings, some of which still survive.

It must be obvious that in our own

Rye station, Sussex. View from the forecourt.

Horley station.

Reigate station.

Brighton station, 1841.

Greenwich Station, 1836. George Smith, architect.
The outward terminus of London's first railway.

country's railway network there are thousands of stations, representing every size and category; and, their prototypes in many instances are still on record. By fortunate circumstances, the author has obtained interesting examples in the form of original photographs of many types. They indicate an idea of sociability as well as sensitive application of architectural form – by architects of undoubted ability. Already we have examined some examples of London's great termini, each displaying a phenomenal diversity in design; now, we may travel further afield.

By way of contrast, let us travel south-wards; the Southern Railway, which has been briefly described in an earlier chapter, provides many buildings of historical significance. The first line to enter London from the south came in from Greenwich on its fringes, and a station designed by George Smith was built in 1836. Later in 1878 the line was extended, and George Smith's building was taken down and re-erected upon a slightly different site.

The accompanying photograph is an interesting example of the nineteenth-century Classical Renaissance building functioning in the present (1970s) highly mechanized era.

53

The original terminus of the London and Southampton Railway was at Nine Elms. The station was designed by Sir William Tite in 1849. Nine Elms is now a goods depot, and the terminus is at Waterloo.

Detail of cast-iron column and decorative capital at Nine Elms supporting the timber roof.

The former London and Southampton Railway, entered London near Vauxhall, at Nine Elms Road, where a fine Italianate station was built in 1849. It was designed by Sir William Tite (1798–1873), who was also the architect for Southampton terminal (1839).

The building was later used as a goods depot; it had a very fine trussed timber roof, supported by beautifully designed cast-iron columns and brackets. A drawing of one of the latter is here shown. The building now exists as the Transport Museum.

SOME PROVINCIAL STATIONS

As mentioned above, Sir William Tite designed Southampton (S.R.) terminus; in fact he designed a number of fine stations, including Carlisle. Windsor station (1849) is also attributed to him. The Windsor line originally terminated at Datchet, and at that point was opened in August, 1848; powers were then given to take the railway across the Home Park to Windsor, where it was opened a year later. The station includes a special royal entrance

Windsor station, 1849, Sir William Tite, architect. The now disused Royal Waiting Room entrance.

and waiting room, as was originally the case at Paddington. The crown and arms still remain over the doors.

In commenting upon a variety of railway stations which have historical backgrounds, we have briefly referred to the architects responsible for their design. And, in the light of present-day tendencies in the design of buildings, we must pay our respects to the men who contributed to the design of stations for the pioneer railways.

These men existed amid the stimulating excitement of an expanding, industrial era in which many new prospects in railway building were opening up. They realized that these buildings were not merely to accommodate railway trains, but they also existed for people; consequently, they applied their arts and educated intelligence to the purpose of humanizing the buildings with which they were associated.

In comparing some of those buildings – representing the nineteenth-century vintage – it is possible to trace resemblances in style, which seem to suggest an established 'railway tradition', consequent upon the

In contrast with the somewhat severe Italianate style of Thompson, James Pritchett, senior, designed the Classical station at Huddersfield in 1847, with a noble portico which still survives.

The small station at Holywell in North Wales, by Francis Thompson (1848), is now closed. It is a successful example of simple planning on the line between Chester and Holyhead.

close association between leading architects of that period.

For example: David Mocatta (1806–82), the architect who designed Brighton station, was formerly a pupil of Sir John Soane (1753–1837); and Sir Robert Smirke (1780–1867) taught Sancton Wood, who designed the delightful little station at Tunbridge Wells. John Dobson (1787–1865) designer of Croydon station and, far northwards, the fine station at Newcastle-upon-Tyne; he, too, was a pupil of Smirke.

We referred earlier to Sir William Tite, whose name is well remembered by architectural prizemen, who have benefited by the competition which bears his name. Tite and Charles Fowler were trained in the office of David Laing (1774–1856), who was also one of Sir John Soane's pupils. Other names are remembered by those buildings which they designed and which still survive. Francis Thompson was the architect for the station serving the ancient city of Chester. The Italianate elevation facing the City Road has a length of about 1000 ft. Thompson also built the neat little station at Holywell, on the Chester–Holyhead line; both these stations are illustrated.

Across the border from Chester, into the heart of Yorkshire, we find at Huddersfield a railway station which has been regarded as a notable example of Classical architecture; James Pritchett (senior), 1786–1868, designed the fine portico in 1847; he was a member of the gifted family, known in those days for their notable contributions to architecture in the North. From the illustration we are enabled to appreciate the dignified proportions of the Corinthian order as applied to the 'portico-in-antis', its relation to the main mass of the station buildings, and its setting in the wide forecourt.

Also by Thompson is the more important station at Chester, 1837.

56

RAILWAYS IN SCOTLAND

To complete our outline survey of the historical background of railways in Britain we travel northwards to Scotland, which provides some spectacular examples of engineering and architecture in its early development of railways.

Many of the earliest railways in Scotland were local concerns and bore purely local names; two of the earliest examples appear to be primitive tracks serving coal-mines. They are: Tranent – to the small harbour of Cockenzie on the Firth of Forth, in 1722: Alloa, on the Firth of Forth, to the mines, completed in 1760. These examples would probably bear comparison with the wagon-way constructed at Tanfield, near Newcastle, during 1712–25. Also comparable with the Stockton and Darlington Railway (September 1825), the Scottish Railway between Garkirk and Glasgow (1826) indicates that the idea of the 'iron road' was becoming established north of the Border. In those early days it became evident that, south of the Border, the conception of this new form of transport was on a much wider scale.

It was realized that the railways projected in Scotland were to become links in the communication between London and the Scottish cities. And, anticipating the importance of the line from Edinburgh to Berwick, they selected the bold name of North British Railway.

Whilst Edinburgh was the immediate goal of the English Railway, but to the companies who had invested in the North British Glasgow was the main objective of the Grand Junction – the greatest line of that day. The first railway bridge across the Clyde, in Glasgow itself, was built in 1870; the Caledonian extension northward over the Clyde was completed in 1879, when Glasgow Central terminus opened. The Midland Company built Glasgow's other terminal station – St Enoch's – between 1874 and 1878. The Midland did not attempt to rival their triumphal station at St Pancras in London – the Scottish station in fact was 45 ft less in span, and the roof arches are not pointed. The actual roof span of St Enoch's was 198 ft, with a maximum height of 80 ft and a length of 518 ft.

GLASGOW CENTRAL STATION

Two decades after the completion of this important railway station, the attraction of passengers and freight from the surrounding country and towns had built up a volume of business which was sufficiently compelling as to warrant a comprehensive extension of accommodation and improvements in efficiency. Thus, from 1899 onwards, a series of reconstruction works enlarged both the permanent way and public accommodation. At that time the station comprised nine platforms, and was approached by a quadruple-track bridge over the River Clyde. The project envisaged thirteen reconstructed platforms and a new bridge across the Clyde carrying nine tracks abreast, not the least intricate part of the works was the crossing of Argyll Street, where the foundations had to be carried to a depth of 40 ft below street-level in order to avoid difficulties from the drainage system of the Glasgow Underground Railway.

The new bridge over the Clyde was an imposing piece of work, five spans wide, supported by steel caissons, sunk to a depth of about 68 ft below high-water mark. The magnitude of the engineering work involved in these great bridges is self-evident, but on the railways of Scotland there are some great works which, with familiarity and in less romantic situations,

Part of façade of Glasgow Central Terminal (1908) showing the Argyll Street Bridge.

become almost commonplaces, and voluntary appreciation is not always apparent. The reconstruction of the station itself represented a pleasing and satisfactory piece of work in which both architect and engineer combined to produce a new concourse of a character vast and impressive; adjoining the concourse, and readily accessible, the station offices, bureaux, waiting rooms, and other public amenities are positioned; train arrival and departure indicators are of exceptional size and clarity.

COHERENCE OR CHAOS

In late Victorian days, when early station layouts were cramped and inconvenient in many places, the Caledonian, the North British, the Glasgow and South Western, in turn, carried out very thorough reconstruction. St Enoch's station in Glasgow was greatly enlarged in 1901 and, in Edinburgh, the North British completely rebuilt Waverley station in 1899;

this latter is considered by Scots to be the model of what a large 'through' station should be, being built on an island-platform principle with all the offices readily available. During the latter part of the nineteenth century many of the pioneering railways on both sides of the Border showed a manifestation of expanding traffic against a background of limited accommodation. Coherence in planning this accommodation could only be achieved if design was rationalized and subordinated to structural needs and fitness of purpose. If the extensions were primarily 'architectural' they could lead to chaos for both passengers and for station management; the use of space could not be sacrificed to grandiloquence. As the implications of the foregoing *obiter dictum* can only be satisfactorily measured in the light of modern requirements, we should defer until a later stage a more comprehensive examination of the problem.

58

Having discussed the development of the trunk railways of Britain against their historical background, we should, to avoid insularity, now study the railways of Europe, America, and the Commonwealth, and those of other countries which show comparable development and local characteristics. Whilst the range for selection is very wide it is not desirable, in this place, to expand beyond the limits of the examples selected for their representative and intrinsic interest.

Chronologically the first European country to embark on railway construction was Belgium, an early starter. It may therefore be appropriate to record one fairly general principle applied to the design of prototype continental railway stations during their primary stages of development. In permanent buildings of simple structural elements, it would seem to be a matter of 'trial and error' if they could at any time be extended, reduced, or even rebuilt without disrupting traffic. The ultimate dimensions and appliances could not, in many instances, be determined until the lines had been in operation for a reasonable period of time. Here then we shall pass on to a brief description of the historical background existing when the countries nearest to Britain received and began to develop the idea of the 'iron road'.

The earliest evidence of embryo railway tracks in Europe is to be found in certain historic exhibits in the Verkehrs-und Baumuseum in Berlin; they comprised wooden wagons and sections of rounded wooden bars laid on wooden sleepers and reputed to date from the sixteenth century. The examples were stated to have been originally in use adjacent to medieval gold-mines in Transylvania, once a province of Hungary and now part of Romania.

As in Britain, horses and donkeys were presumably used to haul the trucks from mines and quarries to the nearest ports.

BELGIUM

In the continent of Europe, one of the first countries to avail herself of the benefits of railway locomotion was Belgium; and so, although railway systems had achieved practical and successful distinction by the construction of the earliest line in Britain, no similar system of transport for passengers existed in any other European country. The undoubted success of the railway systems in Britain attracted the attention of continental engineers and groups of business supporters. In Belgium social, political, and general considerations all urged the expediency of the establishment of a railway system throughout the country.

The system was conceived upon the basis of an intelligent relevance to the adjoining countries of Germany, Holland, and France; the project visualized routes running west to east and north to south, intersecting at Malines. From the coastal town and port of Ostend on the west it proceeded via Aachen to Cologne.

The line from north to south commenced at Antwerp, proceeding to French territory near Valenciennes, by way of Brussels and Mons; the programme provided for 347 miles of line. In contrast to the difficulties which the promoters of Britain's early projects encountered, Belgium's legislative assembly adopted the project immediately after it was promoted; the enactment was passed in May, 1834 and, ten years later, the work was completed in 1844.

FRANCE

The railway system in France was developed on principles differing considerably from those adopted in Britain and Belgium; here again the primitive tracks originated in colliery and quarry areas, before the introduction of steam locomotives. The earliest of these 'mineral lines' was in the Loire area, in 1829. In the same year France saw her first locomotives; the first that is, since the tragi-comic performance of Nicholas Joseph Cugot's 'steam carriage' in 1760!

It was not until 1837, three years later than Belgium, that France turned her attention to providing a railway system; by way of preparation, two locomotives of the Stephenson type were purchased for the engineer M. Seguin, to serve as models for the French railway system.

Development of a railway system was initially sporadic, owing to the fact that the power of private energy and resources proved inadequate; several private companies promoted schemes which, through lack of official co-operation, failed to materialize. As a matter of national urgency the Government, in 1842, took over the various systems; seven main routes were projected from Paris to the seaboard. One of the first to be completed, and opened to the public, was that from Paris to Rouen in 1848.

Political disturbances in that year somewhat retarded progress of other lines, but the schemes were eventually brought to a successful conclusion, and the Government then permitted the companies to regard themselves as tenants or lessees of the lines.

EARLY DEVELOPMENT IN PARIS

The first railway constructed in Paris was that of the Compagnie des Chemins de Fer, Paris à St Germain, whose station in the Place de l' Europe, was the predecessor of the Gare St Lazare, opened in 1844. It was proposed in the first place to build the station near the Place de la Madeleine, but finally the Place de l'Europe was selected.

The present Gare St Lazare was designed by J.-J.-G. Lisch (b. 1828) and completed in 1889; it replaced a very plain structure of three storeys, which was laid out in the form of a centre block and two side wings, forming an open square. During the Franco-Prussian war of 1870, the waiting rooms of the old station were converted into a temporary hospital for wounded soldiers.

The present Gare St Lazare occupies the most central and convenient situation of any railway terminus in Paris. It has the largest suburban traffic serving the populous district on the western side of Paris, such as Asnières, Colombes, Argenteuil, and Versailles – its design will be compared with that of the Gare du Nord below.

This large terminal station of the Compagnie des Chemins de Fer du Nord, faces the Place de Roubaix, and was erected in 1846. The original façade designed by the architect Rénaud, was removed piece by piece to Lille, where it was reconstructed about 1864. In 1863, owing to the great expansion of traffic, the company decided to reconstruct the terminus. The present station, designed by J.-I. Hittorff (1792–1867) is in the form of a quadrilateral, 540 ft by 620 ft; it comprises five principal sections: including a grand hall, salle de départ, a salle d'arrivé, booking offices, and covered accommodation for vehicles.

As in the case of St Lazare station – reconstructed in 1889 and which will be compared with the Gare du Nord in a later chapter, we will briefly refer to the

Gare St Lazare, in 1912.

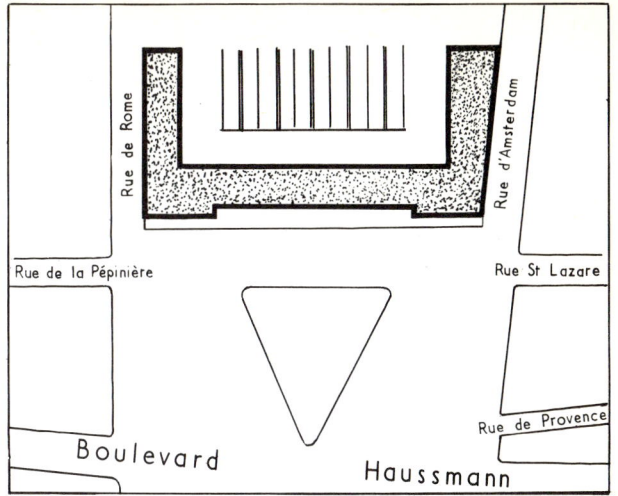
(map: Rue de Rome, Rue d'Amsterdam, Rue de la Pépinière, Rue St Lazare, Rue de Provence, Boulevard Haussmann)

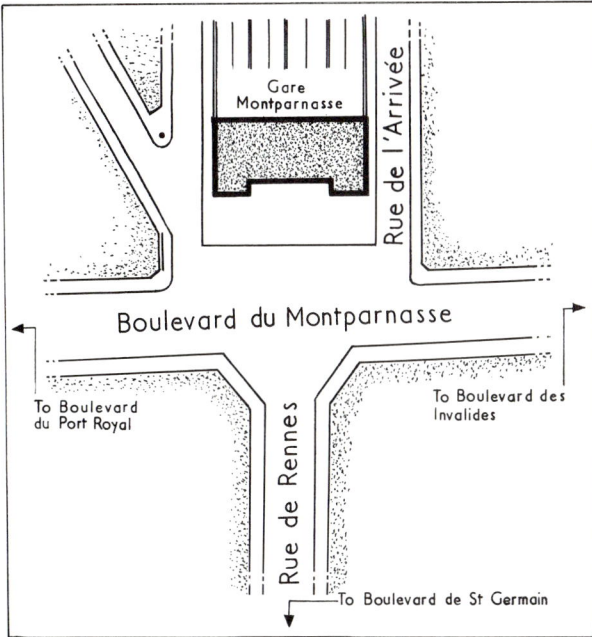
(map: Gare Montparnasse, Rue de l'Arrivée, Boulevard du Montparnasse, To Boulevard du Port Royal, To Boulevard des Invalides, Rue de Rennes, To Boulevard de St Germain)

Gare Montparnasse.

Three Paris termini and plans of their approaches

Gare du Nord, in 1912.

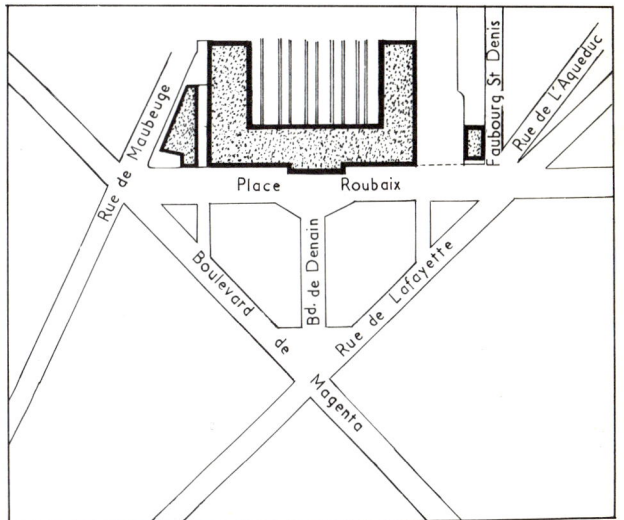
(map: Rue de Maubeuge, Faubourg St Denis, Rue de L'Aqueduc, Place Roubaix, Boulevard de Denain, Rue de Lafayette, Magenta)

general character of the latter, as to its position in the first part of the twentieth century; thus, deferring to later chapters a more detailed appraisal of the main characteristics of those elderly buildings still striving to function and 'hold their own' architecturally in an era of rapidly changing conditions.

There appeared to be two main characteristics relevant to the above stations, which were evident to the author during a stay in Paris, a few years prior to World War I. In the case of Gare St Lazare, its open situation in the space between Rue de Rome on the left and Rue d'Amsterdam on the right, provided a viewpoint from which one is able to appreciate its typical château-like façade as a whole.

On the other hand, the Gare du Nord has a complex of surrounding side streets, and less depth of foreground in the Place Roubaix; so that one has mainly angular views of a building which contains an intricacy of Classical features. By standing far back at the intersection of Boulevard de Magenta and Rue de la Fayette, one may secure a vista towards the centre feature, which comprises a 20 ft high semicircular window, set within the pedimented Ionic order with pairs of tall fluted pilasters.

Situated at the northern end of the Boulevard de Strasbourg, and built in 1856, Gare de l'Est was designed by the architects Duquesnay and de Sernet. When first opened it had only two platforms; these were increased to eight in 1878, and fourteen in 1889. A further extension was carried out in 1928; the original façade in Rue de Strasbourg was preserved and a similar structure built in Rue du Faubourg St Martin. The new and existing were linked by a central gallery, providing a total length of about 550 ft.

In view of the great new development around Gare Montparnasse, on the south side of the Seine, we should refer briefly to the situation and historical background relating to the old terminal. The railway which started from the terminal station (1840), belonged to the Chemin de Fer de l'Etat; it was constructed by the Compagnie des Chemins de Fer de l'Ouest and completed in 1855.

The diagram on page 61 indicates the complex of streets about the terminal; the classical façade on the south side of the Boulevard du Montparnasse, is also reproduced.

On page 123 of this book we shall see the total removal of the station, between Boulevard du Montparnasse, is also repro-Pasteur, involving the disappearance of the 78-year-old building.

GERMANY

It is a remarkable fact that in a supposedly advanced country, that is advanced in science and engineering, railways did not at first materialize in Germany until a decade after their appearance in Britain. And, it is still more remarkable when one considers that both the neighbouring countries of Belgium and France had early taken up the innovation from the British pioneers. However, when Germany did commence, it was a State undertaking from the start; the railways were well and economically constructed and were planned with strict conformity to military and strategic requirements; public and private considerations were a secondary factor.

In order to maintain constant efficiency several of the principal stations were rebuilt just prior to World War I; and, whilst many of them were either wholly or in part demolished by bombing in World

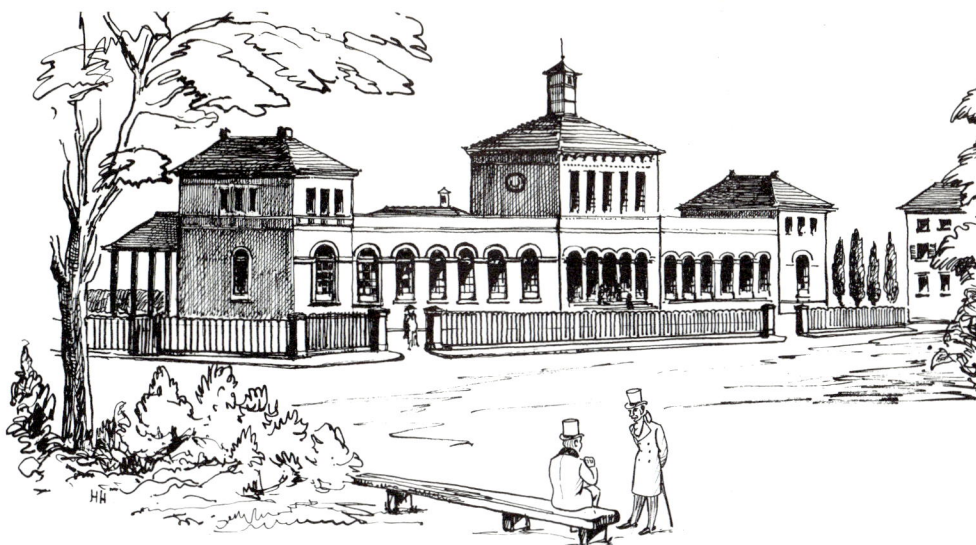

Frankfurt-on-Main station was built in the Classic Renaissance style.

War II, a brief description of some may help to establish their motive and character in respect of layout and general design.

Emanuele Calma, an Italian engineer, carried out in 1921 an examination of several of the more important German stations, and his observations were recorded in the journal *Revista Tecnica delle Ferrovie Italiane*, the Italian equivalent to our *Railway Gazette*. He divided the stations quite simply into two groups: *statione di testa* (terminal) and *statione di transite* (route). Illustrations of selected types from the 1921 era may provide a comparison with contemporary stations in other countries.

Before proceeding to examine the principal features of the more sophisticated stations in that era, it may be interesting to glance at the illustrations of their prototypes of a more romantic age.

EARLY GERMAN STATIONS

Both those of Frankfurt-on-Main and Weisbaden have much in common in their simple, symmetrical, and Classic Renaissance design, but once again they illustrate an incongruity in relation to purpose as may be seen in the 'serpent' lamp standard, shown in the sketch of Weisbaden station. The illustration of the station at Hochst

Weisbaden station was very similar but without flanking pavilions.

A small level-crossing station at Hochst (c. 1845) on the Taunas line formerly linking Frankfurt-on-Main and Weisbaden.

depicts a building which might be a chapel or house and shows the casual manner which, in this case, the railway track meanders across the village green.

SWITZERLAND

Following close upon the heels of France, this small but efficient nation achieved wonders in the way of railway construction. The first railway in Switzerland was that joining Baden and Zurich, constructed in 1846. This was followed by the sublime achievement, eleven years later, by the line passing through the St Gothard tunnel. Since that time large-scale electrification developments have taken place, happily unhampered by wars or other disturbances. It will be interesting to recall that Britain, the pioneer for railways, has gained valuable experience from the early start of Swiss electric traction.

ITALY

In Italy, the early ancestry of railway track has been traced back to the wagon tracks in the green lava paving of the streets of Pompeii and Herculaneum, which were covered for 1800 years. They were in the form of ruts, and carefully checked data indicated an average gauge of 4 ft 9 in. to the centre of the ruts.

Apart from these interesting facts, the railways as commercial undertakings developed in Italy contemporaneously with those of the neighbouring countries of Austria, Switzerland, and France. After functioning for something over seventy years they arrived at a period of drastic reorientation, part of the national upsurge promoted by the dynamic Duce in his most ambitious moments.

Obviously, during the final stages of World War II, many of the country's railways were disrupted or destroyed, as were those in other European countries. Their rehabilitation during the post-war period of twenty years should provide us with some interesting types of new station buildings, and, in Italy particularly, we may find some exceptionally fine examples for comparison which we will examine in a later chapter.

Having briefly looked at the early beginnings of railways in the main countries of Europe, we should expand somewhat the survey to include those in countries of the Western Hemisphere and Commonwealth, where the development of examples pioneered in Britain took on many interesting interpretations.

6 RAILWAYS IN THE UNITED STATES HISTORICAL BACKGROUND

News of the successful début of the railway system in Britain was received with acclamation in the United States of America. Although the Americans had no railway locomotives of their own, they were carefully watching the various experiments that were in progress in Britain, with such engines as the *Pen-y-daren* at Merthyr Tydfil and the Rainhill trials which included Stephenson's *Rocket*.

EARLY RAILWAY STATIONS

American business groups believing in the future success of railways had several districts laid out with tracks in order to be ready for the advent of workable locomotives. Thus, in the year 1830, the State of South Carolina embarked upon a scheme for the construction of a railway, from Charleston to Augusta in Georgia, a distance of 135 miles. It was completed in three years at the low cost of $1,336,615, which sum also included the cost of rolling-stock and all the necessary equipment.

This was the first railway of importance to be constructed in the United States, and it was the cheapest and most successful among its contemporaries. Following almost immediately upon the example set by South Carolina, a company in the State of New York organized a scheme for a line from the Hudson River to Lake Erie, a distance of about 469 miles, at a cost of $23,500,000. The construction was completed in May 1851 and the line was put into operation in the same month.

It is interesting to note that the State advanced $6,000,000 towards the cost of the work and then released the company from the obligation to repay the loan! The

comparatively low cost of railways in America was due, *inter alia*, to the following causes:

(*a*) Promoters were spared all expenses attending congressional inquiries.

(*b*) There were no adverse interests to be 'bought off', nor any exorbitant compensatory claims for land.

The advantage of the railway system to adjoining owners and occupiers was realized by them to the extent of their promoting the undertaking by a cession of land where it was required, either as a gift or on terms compatable with the market price. The next step in railway development was the Gargantuan stride, of traversing the American continent from New York to San Francisco. This formidable undertaking was commenced in 1863 and it was completed on May 10th, 1869.

As a preliminary to the description of particular buildings, a brief general survey of the physical facts will provide a background and explain features of the general plans and design, which might not, at first sight, be apparent. A little over sixty years ago the chief characteristics of American railway stations, of the larger size, consisted of a vast train shed covering the tracks. These in themselves were almost purely engineering works and were very impressive on account of their great spans and lofty height. Spans from 250 ft to 300 ft and from 75 ft to 100 ft high being typical.

The south station at Boston, the old Pennsylvania terminal at Jersey City, and the stations of Chicago, Pittsburgh, and St Louis, all have train sheds of similar dimensions. However, in New York, where trains enter over electrified lines from places remote from the city, they approach the station through subways.

In cities where lines are not electrified there are separate, smaller sheds, each parallel to and covering two tracks. This method was first used in the Delaware and Lackawanna station at Hoboken, and subsequently at Washington and Kansas City, the latter being a 'route' station through which pass transcontinental lines.

In Boston, New York, and other eastern cities, there is a heavy suburban commuter traffic which requires an intricate, extensive track layout, which tends to cause a large amount of congestion at the peak periods – morning and evening.

In Chicago the stations are mainly terminals for lines which converge there; to a lesser degree this applies to St Louis

station. On the western coast the stations are principally a 'combination' type – *i.e.*, terminations for some transcontinental lines and 'route' stations for coast lines.

In Washington there is a particular and unique problem. The terminal, which would have been adequate for the ordinary traffic to and from the capital, would have been quite inadequate for dealing with the enormous crowds visiting the Capitol every four years to attend the Presidential Inauguration, so the station was designed to accommodate these quadrennial crowds.

Having described the general types and characteristics of the stations it will be interesting to glance at some of the outstanding features in some of the more important examples and note their success or failure. The south station at Boston was built over seventy-five years ago by Shepley,

Pennsylvania Station, New York, 1906–10, McKim, Mead & White, architects.

1 *Entrance vestibule*	4 *(M) Men's waiting room*	7 *Grand concourse*
2 *Entrance arcade*	5 *Ramped cab roads*	8 *Dining room*
3 *General waiting room*	6 *Shops*	9 *Lunch room*
4 *(W) Women's waiting room*	6 *(a) Bank*	10 *Foyer*

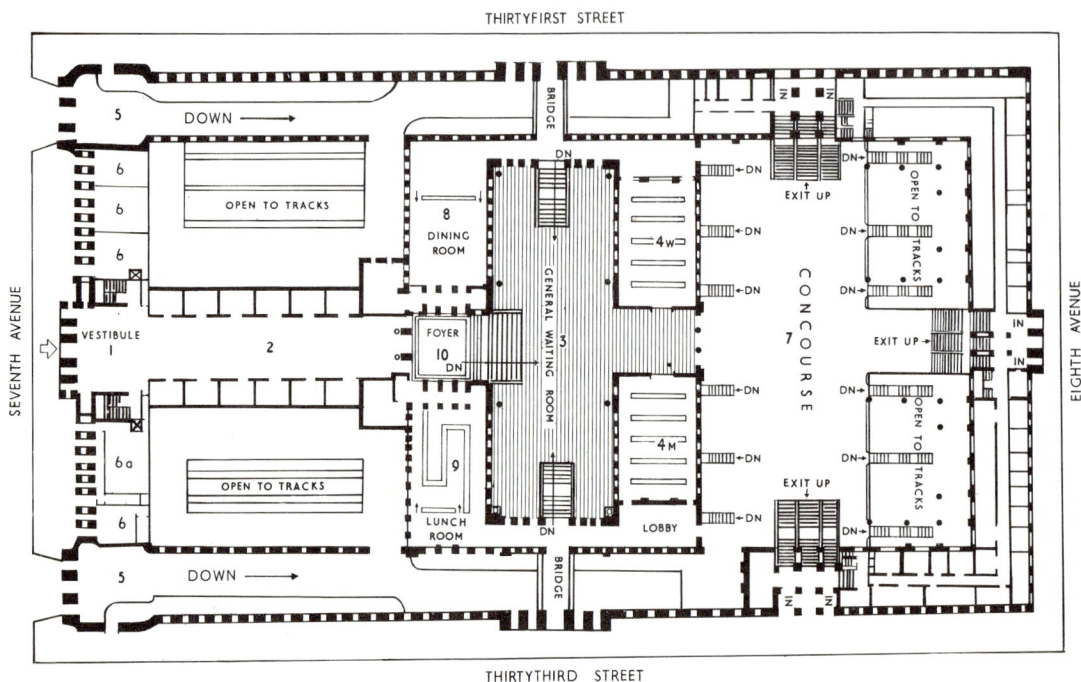

66

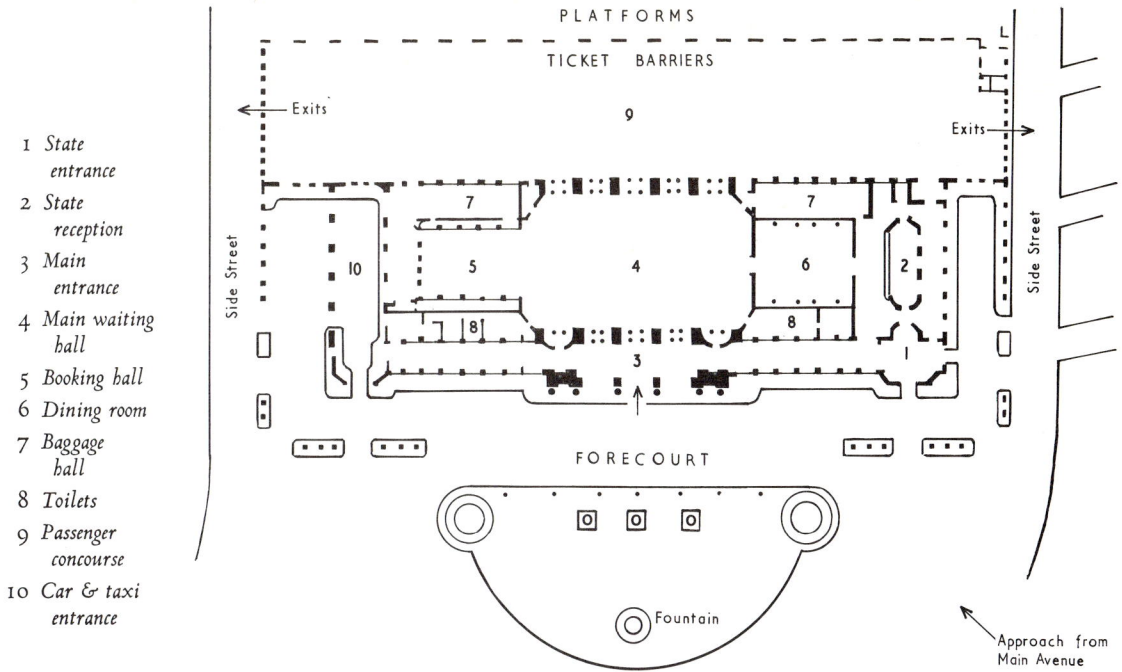

1 State entrance
2 State reception
3 Main entrance
4 Main waiting hall
5 Booking hall
6 Dining room
7 Baggage hall
8 Toilets
9 Passenger concourse
10 Car & taxi entrance

PLATFORMS

TICKET BARRIERS

Exits

9

Exits

Side Street

Side Street

7

10

5

4

6

2

8

8

3

FORECOURT

Fountain

Approach from Main Avenue

Union station, Washington, 1903–07. D. Burnham & Co., architects. Designed for ceremonial and ordinary passenger traffic, and replacing the original building of 1873, designed by Joseph Wilson. The concourse is sufficiently large to allow the uninterrupted flow of inward and outward terminal passengers.

Rutan, and Coolidge, architects. It is one of the largest and busiest stations in the country, more than 700 trains arriving and departing every day. It has a large train shed; the plan is not noteworthy, in fact it developed serious faults with use. The design is very simple, going very little beyond the utilitarian requirement of its purpose.

NEW YORK

The Grand Central terminal in New York City is one of the later and most complete stations in the country. Messrs Reed and Stem, with Warren and Wetmore, were the architects. This terminal will be described in a later section of the book. The first Grand Central station was built and opened in 1871, this was enlarged in 1886 and again in 1900. The growth of the suburban traffic soon indicated that the

then existing station could not be expanded to meet future needs without rebuilding on a very much larger scale. Electrification was also being considered at that time. Matters were finally brought to a critical stage as the result of an accident in the Park Avenue tunnel. The New York Legislature passed an Act requiring trains to be electrically operated after a certain date. Plans were therefore commenced for the present station, which was opened in 1913. It can be assumed that many of the original stations of the larger sort, such as Pennsylvania (New York), Philadelphia, Detroit, etc., and probably some of the small suburban stations, became outmoded and were rebuilt. Examples of buildings of a variety of types will illustrate their authors' versatility of interpretation in this highly specialized subject.

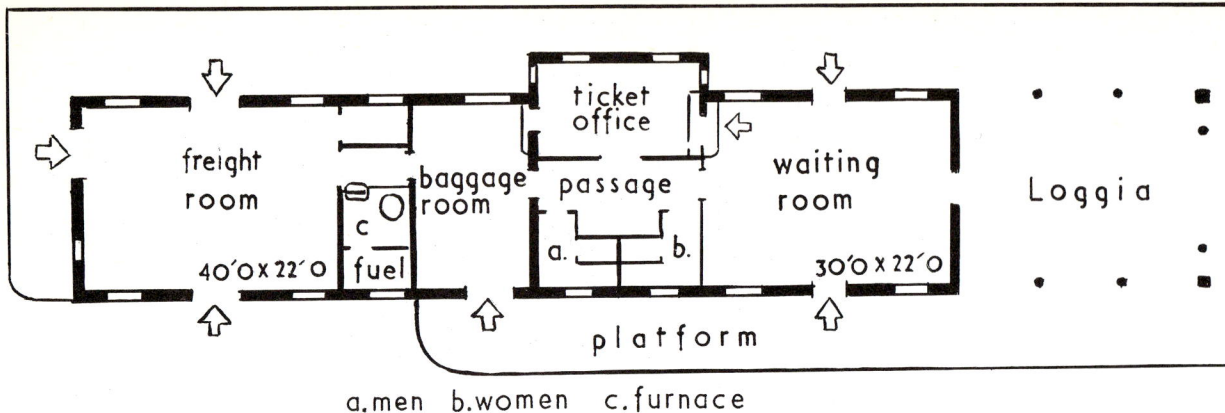

Examples of two small American stations showing the disposition of passenger and freight accommodation.
Above: *Delaware, Lackawanna & Western railway type.* Below: *the Lehigh Valley type.*

WAYSIDE OR 'ROUTE' STATIONS

Having traced the historical development and touched upon the physical facts providing a background to discussion upon particular examples, it will be interesting here to refer briefly to some of the smaller stations built prior to 1914. From the 85,000 or more in the U.S.A. a few will suffice to illustrate the variety of types of small stations spread over this vast country of varied communities and differing geographical surroundings. They may be divided into two main categories, in respect of their architectural character. Examples are:

(a) Those built in the traditional 'Italianate' Classical Renaissance, exemplified by stations at Wykagyl, Mamaroneck, and Heathcob on the Westchester and Boston railways described on a following page.

(b) In this category we have those buildings erected to cope with a period of rapid expansion and replacement, severely practical from a planning and constructional point of view, whilst in character having a mainly 'domestic' flavour. We find here some examples which have their counterpart in certain rural stations in the Argentine, illustrated elsewhere.

ACCOMMODATION

For the service of the smallest communities, town or village, one finds a combination of passenger and freight station. Accommodation, arranged as indicated by the accompanying sketches, usually comprises a waiting room, ticket office, and a freight room, the latter also serves as a baggage room: occasionally separate baggage rooms and toilets are added. In larger towns it is usual to provide separate passenger and freight facilities. Here the passenger accommodation includes a main waiting room, women's retiring room, toilets, ticket office and baggage room. In

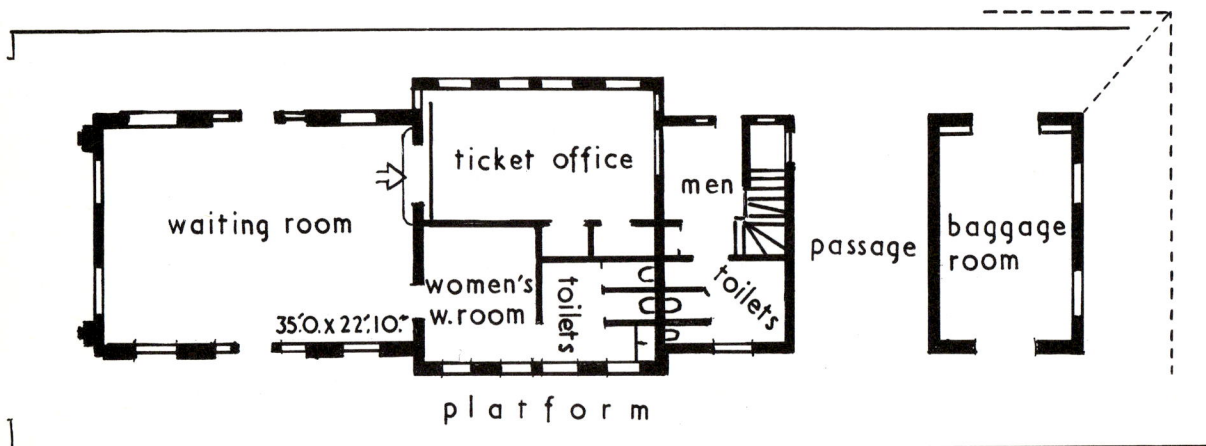

Layout of a typical 'wayside' station on the Pennsylvania Railway.

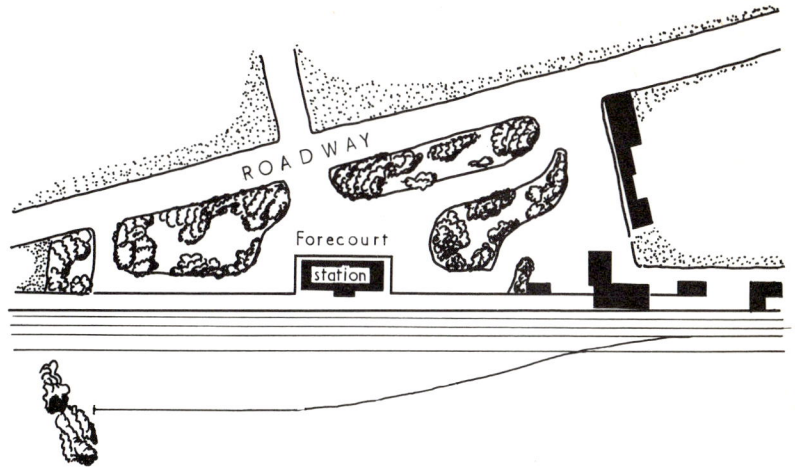

stations serving suburban towns, an interesting development in waiting space is sometimes to be found. This is in the form of a pavilion, adjacent to a drive at one end of the building, to accommodate, under cover, the large crowds attending sporting events (*e.g.*, racing or baseball, etc.). In the types above referred to, many of the smaller ones have a standardized arrangement of plan, and in most cases the siting and setting of the building have been carefully thought out, and it is not unusual to find the building surrounded by trees, shrubs, and other planting, set back from the roads and approached by driveways; a typical example of such a layout is shown here.

TYPICAL SIZES

Stations of the class above discussed are usually 20 ft to 25 ft wide on the Lehigh Valley line, the width being governed by the width of the right of way and the necessity

of providing a drive behind the building. On the Lackawanna Railroad 24 ft is the maximum width of building; this dimension applies generally on other railroads.

CONSTRUCTION

It appears that the use of framed structures, formerly quite common, now tends to be confined to new towns – for interior accommodation and for permanent buildings only – in the smallest communities. The wall construction for permanent station buildings of medium size is of brick or stone, while to a limited extent, concrete and terracotta are also to be found. An interesting building with external walls in cream, matt-glazed terracotta has been introduced by the Lackawanna Railroad, its quiet and somewhat severe Classical design here illustrated, reveals a characteristic departure from the 'domestic' treatment of the rural type of building, elsewhere

A station with brick facings and loggias at both ends (Riverside station).

This station on the Lackawanna Railroad is faced with glazed terracotta.

Three Italianate stations on the N.Y., Westchester & Boston Railroad. Wykagyl

Heathcob station.

Mamaroneck station.

found in a profusion of gables, eaves, and tiled roofs.

Situated at Lackawanna, this station is a quiet and restrained composition, having a central dominant feature with three arched openings, above which runs a strongly projecting cornice. The secondary elements of the composition consists of plain faced appendages having rectangular openings and a slightly lower roof. The façade is unified by a string-course at the level of the springing of the semicircular openings of the central feature, tying the whole together.

Other examples, also illustrated, show interesting variations in design, reflecting their appropriateness to the surrounding scene. Heathcob, a 'wayside' station on the Westchester and Boston Railway, was designed by the architects Fellheimer and Long, associated with Reed and Stem. This station building, while having a similar balance of masses, on the basis of Lackawanna, displays the charm of a rural Italianate exercise in design, the effect of which is heightened by sympathetic landscaping.

At Mamaroneck, on the same line as Heathcob, and of the same era, the railway has a small group of station buildings, similar in its basic design, but equally pleasing by its simplicity.

Almost contemporaneously with U.S.A., Canada considered the question of railway construction and development. In the year 1832, a charter under the seal of William IV was granted for the construction of a line from Laprairie to St Jean (Quebec). The first section between Champlain and the St Lawrence was completed and opened in 1836. As this section was constructed similarly to those early lines in the colliery districts of England before the advent of iron rails, when horses were the sole motive power and the life span of the wooden rails was just about one year. They were then replaced by iron rails and the tracks able to carry steam locomotives, thus the advent of the 'iron road' in Canada came about. The railway, as a railway, outlined in the above-mentioned charter, was completed about 1839 and formed the nucleus of the Canadian system.

CANADIAN PACIFIC RAILWAY

The Grand Trunk scheme was conceived in 1852 and seven years later, on December 17th, 1859 the Victoria Bridge over the St Lawrence, completing the line, was opened. The above bare facts, a mere outline sketch, do less than justice to the sublime courage, determination, and skill of the early 'pathfinders' who formed the spearhead of the survey parties on whom rested the responsibility for planning the route through the Rockies. The search for a path for the Canadian Pacific Railway began as far back as 1857, and Keith Morris in his interesting story of the development, describes it as an epic in adventure.

Following the construction of the C.P.R. the Canadian National Railway (C.N.R.) was laid out. One branch from Vancouver, followed the C.P.R. for part of the way along the Fraser River Valley, the other from Prince Rupert. The two lines join and pass through the main chain of the Rockies at Yellowhead Pass and then to Quebec. The third railway across the Rockies is the branch line from the C.P.R. from Lethbridge on the prairie to Vancouver, by way of Crows' Nest Pass.

C.P.R. TERMINAL AT VANCOUVER

It will here be appropriate to give some idea of the stage of development attained just prior to 1914. It became necessary (in 1912–14) to provide increased facilities for handling both passenger and freight business. Vancouver (port and rail-head), deals with the transcontinental business of the Canadian Pacific as well as the sea-going traffic to the Pacific coast ports and far distant trans-Pacific ports in Japan, Australia, and the Philippines, in addition to the joint transfer traffic with the various other steamship lines at Vancouver.

This station combines the facilities of a passenger terminal and a seaport. The passenger station is sited at the foot of Granville Street, which is extended over the passenger and freight tracks to a new steamship pier, and the buildings face on to Cordova Street and at right angles to it. Formerly the only means of access to the steamship piers was by way of a grade crossing, west of the old station. In the new layout the freight yard was rearranged with connexions to the present steamship piers.

The spaciousness of Vancouver's main waiting hall.

The new station buildings provided ultimate accommodation for several times the number of passenger tracks built under the immediate programme. The surrounding streets are about 30 ft above the track-level and these conditions imposed a two-level station. The principal public rooms are planned on the street-level, with the railroad facilities on the track-level below. Means of access to the train platforms and waiting shelters are provided by a bridge over the tracks; independent exits are provided for passengers to go directly to the street by means of a ramp without passing through the station. Luggage lifts are also provided to deal with passengers' baggage for the steamship pier.

At street-level are the following: ticket office, general waiting hall, refreshment rooms, women's waiting room, and toilet. The general waiting hall is 212 ft long by 56 ft wide. At the track level are the baggage, mail, and express rooms, together with rooms for the Canadian and United States Customs.

The station building is a steel-framed structure with brick exterior walls and Indiana limestone dressings. The principal façade to Cordova Street is frankly an exercise in Classical columnar architecture, comprising free-standing Ionic columns, 35 ft high, symmetrically flanked by end pavilions.

The waiting hall, immediately behind the colonnade is approached by vaulted corridors from each end of the building. An internal columnar order of Ionic pilasters and engaged columns in artificial stone, form the decorative treatment of this hall. The ceiling is 40 ft above the floor and it has a central continuous laylight; the laylight treatment is somewhat heavy with beams and deep coffers. The accompanying photograph gives some idea of the spacious feeling of this hall.

The services provided in the buildings are of a high order and very much in advance of their time. The architects for the passenger station were Barott, Blacklade and Webster of Montreal. The construction and equipment, general layout, etc., were under the direction of J. G. Sullivan, Chief Engineer of the C.P.R.

The design and construction of the pier, waiting rooms, Customs offices, etc., are items of further interest, but are outside the scope of this chapter; they will be referred to under the heading of 'North American Seaports' Chapter 13.

In that far-off republic, situated in the southern half of South America and extending to Cape Horn, details of the beginnings of railways, are somewhat undefined. What we do know is the fact that many of the lines were British-owned, and were administered by their respective boards in London, until late in 1949 when the Péron Government took over general control of their administration and finances.

Many of the railways stem from the capital, Buenos Aires, some running north-west by way of Rosario and Córdoba to the hills and lake district, others to the south-west and westward to Chile. As in India and Africa, the tracks are of varying gauges; both broad gauge and metre gauge. This and the geographical and climatic conditions exert their influence upon the design and construction of station buildings.

General layout: In all but a few towns the station is located on the main thorough-fares, this is natural since the railways were built first. A road borders the station yard on both sides with level crossings at either end. The goods yard is located on the side remote from the passenger station.

The classification of stations is interesting and simple: the three types are: main-line terminal and through stations; first-class country stations; and second-class country stations. Most of the examples date from the first half of the twentieth century, displaying unique variety and interest.

The Central Argentine Railway – referred to as Ferrocarril Central Argentino (F.C.C.A.) – provides a wide range of examples, and it will be appropriate to commence with the main terminal at Buenos Aires.

BUENOS AIRES STATION

This large terminal appears to bear the impress of European influence; it was opened in 1915 for main-line traffic, the electric lines serving the suburban commuter traffic were, at that time, in process of development. The project was initiated by Mr Charles H. Pearson, General Manager, and the architect responsible for the building was Mr Lauriston Conder. The building occupies an area of approximately 744,000 sq. ft upon ground reclaimed from the River Plate. The new terminal replaces a group of outmoded buildings which, for many years, the municipal authorities and the

The Retiro terminal, Buenos Aires, 1915. Lauriston Conder, architect.

Córdoba station, more restrained than the Retiro terminal, could serve almost any civic purpose, including that of a railway station.

company had regarded with extreme disfavour. The new station has a frontage of about 850 ft, which is greater than either New York's Grand Central or Pennsylvania terminals. The forecourt of the Retiro terminal overlooks the Calle Maipu, a wide, open, landscaped plaza.

Passenger and vehicular movement has been based upon the system in use on some of the lines in the U.S.A. and the European continent.

Externally, an orthodox application of free Classical Renaissance is the *leit-motif* of the elevations; the columnar order of which is Roman Doric. Internally the treatment of the principal concourse displays a vigorous character, the use of Ionic columns reflecting its Classical inspiration. The great concourse has much to commend its bold spaciousness, seeming to echo, as it does, the swelling contours of the vast roofs covering the platforms, even though the glazed faience and ornamentation may appear somewhat florid.

The impressive length of the external façade to the Calle Maipu, somewhat fails to convince by reason of the dichotomy in the use of the Classical orders, and the unfortunate incursion of adjacent buildings, this latter may be due to the fact that, at the time of the photograph, certain parts of the project were in process of completion.

By contrast, the major station at Córdoba, remote from Buenos Aires, by nature of its Classical Renaissance style, is more restrained, less fussy and, therefore, has more unity.

PROVINCIAL STATIONS—MENDOZA

South of latitude 33, and east of the Chilean border the station of Mendoza serves the district noted for the production of wine, wheat-growing and stock-raising. The line here[1] is metre gauge and links up with the city of Córdoba, to the north-east. As an example of a secondary terminal, Mendoza has some interesting features; built in 1943 it contrasts markedly with its counterpart at Córdoba, at the remote end of the broad-gauge line.

Architecturally its external elevational composition is disappointing. The grouping and proportional aspect are external lapses in control of composition which, however, are leavened by a masterly use of materials. This has been achieved by an intelligent application of new materials in an imaginative way. Climatic conditions have also exerted a marked influence upon the type of construction and upon the materials.

[1] Córdoba is at the end of the broad-gauge line in that province, but it is also served by the metre gauge which links up with Mendoza. Gauges of Argentine railways: broad gauge 5 ft 6 in.; standard gauge: 4 ft 8½ in.; metre gauge 3 ft 3⅜ in.

The long hours of bright sunlight and blue skies have created an excellent opportunity to use the clean sharp lines and plain surfaces in this modern idiom of expression.

The external surfaces are rendered in a special cement, with which is incorporated a large proportion of mica flakes, providing a perfect surface for reflecting the sun's rays and creating a luminosity in the shaded portions and sharp shadows of the deep projections. Internally, the structural elements are exploited in the broadly treated entrance to the main concourse.

The walls of the concourse and those adjoining the platforms are lined, to a height of two metres, with golden travertine marble.

An illustration of this treatment, which included some interesting details of booking-office windows and barriers, will be seen in the accompanying illustration, which displays remarkable sophistication and understanding. The floors of the entrance hall, concourse, and adjacent rooms are paved with granite mosaic, in polished squares of 0.40 metre, the general colour is Napoleon marble. The floors of the offices are finished with 'algarrobo', a hardwood parquet.

An external view of Mendoza station, built in 1943.

In the constructional members, local conditions have an important influence; the zone surrounding Mendoza being subject to earthquakes, it was found necessary to employ a special type of 'armoured' concrete embodying a special cement. The infilling between the structural members of the external walls is ordinary hard brickwork, with an outer rendering which produces the sparkling effect previously described.

As an example of a secondary station Mendoza's design is redeemed by the sophisticated use of surface materials and the bold sweep of the arch of the booking hall ceiling.

75

Mendoza's booking office is the outcome of careful study, both in design and in passenger control.

An interesting feature in the design of this station is the treatment of the long covered ways for passengers; these corridors are in the form of extended loggias of simple but convincing design. The simple lines and flush surface of the roof and canopy provide a very satisfying foil to the spacings of the vertical supports.

SMALLER ARGENTINE STATIONS

To conclude our brief review of Argentine stations, some widely differing types of somewhat smaller stations are here described and illustrated.

San Carlos de Bariloche is the terminal station for the State railway which runs from Carmen de Patagones, where it joins the Buenos Aires Great Southern Railway; Patagones being situated at the mouth of the Rio Negro and south of Bahia Blanca. The station illustrated is on the line which serves the famous Argentine lake district, a noted tourist resort.

The building contrasts pleasantly with the exterior of the station at Mendoza, in that it extends the atmosphere of the countryside in a sympathetic and human manner. It is a single-storey building, the long lines of its pitched roof, together with a dominant gabled entrance facing upon an open fore-court, presents the impression of an English farmstead or country club, almost in the traditional idiom.

About the same period – 1943, at Capilla del Monte, in the Córdoba Hill district, the station illustrated is some-what whimsical; while having a modern reinforced concrete structural frame, its outward appearance from the road, conveys the full-blooded romanticism of a Spanish *posada*. In fact, almost any film-set designer might be proud of its convincing realism!

In a more serious vein, the station at La Rioja, built in 1939, serving the same railway system as Capilla del Monte is situated to the north of Córdoba. In its

San Carlos de Bariloche station is a terminal serving a tourist district and its informality typifies the holiday mood.

Looking more like a country inn (posada) Capilla del Monte station, built in 1943 to serve the Cordoba hill district, is in reality a concrete-framed building.

design, it attempts in a more restrained and successful way to reconcile the Spanish traditional idiom with enlightened structural and local functional requirements. This will no doubt be evident from the illustrations; the view from the front indicates a less fussy and more pleasing exterior in a happy grouping with trees. The construction of the walls and main members is similar to that of Mendoza station, but in this instance the roof is covered with Spanish pantiles. Internally the entrance

hall and waiting rooms have a *socle* (dado) 1·80 metres high in white marble terrazzo and the walls above are plastered; the floors are paved with polished granite in 0·20-metre squares in mosaic form.

All in all, we may deduce that in these distant countries, remoteness is not one of isolation, particularly in the matter of design. Construction applied with sophistication places them in a position to compare very favourably with some European examples.

Two views of La Rioja station which successfully fulfills local needs and at the same time has the impress of Spanish tradition. It dates from 1939 and is on the same system as Capilla del Monte.

The railway systems of Africa.
Inset: Huguenot station in
Cape Province which is typical
of the architecture of South Africa
used for a country station.

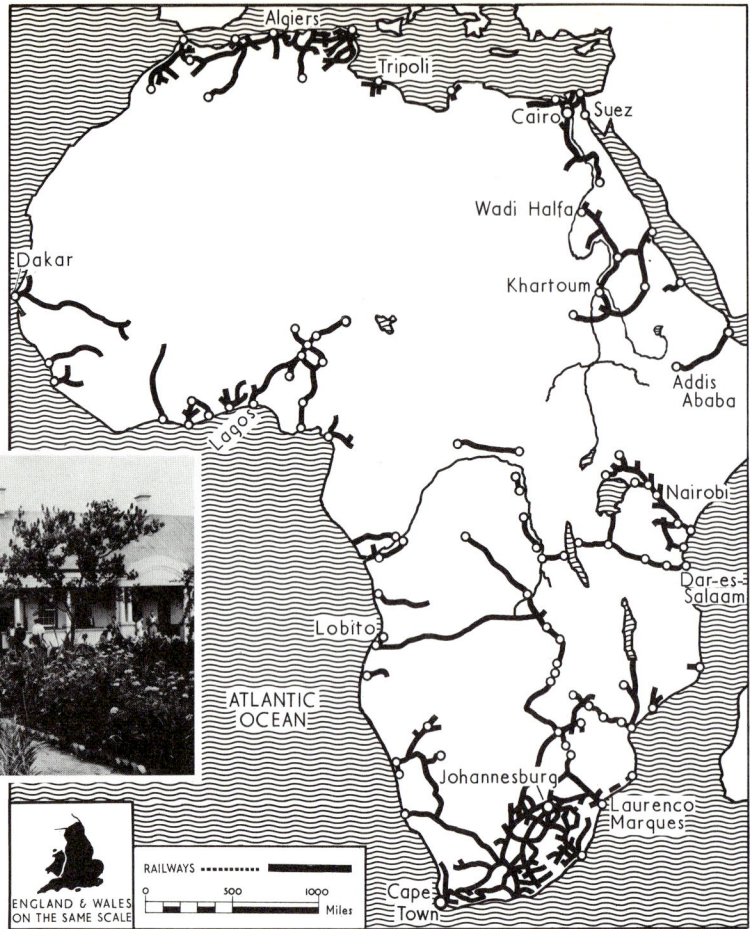

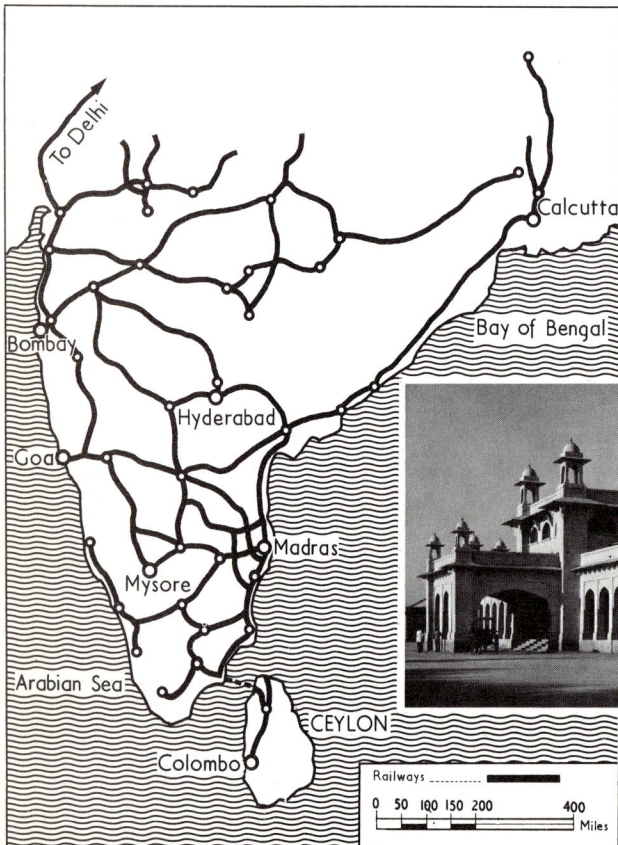

ENGLAND & WALES
ON THE SAME SCALE

RAILWAYS

0   500   1000
Miles

Algiers
Tripoli
Cairo   Suez
Wadi Halfa
Khartoum
Addis Ababa
Dakar
Lagos
Nairobi
Dar-es-Salaam
Lobito
ATLANTIC OCEAN
Johannesburg   Laurenco Marques
Cape Town

The railway system of Central
and South India. Inset: Gwalior
Railway station obviously
influenced by Mogul architecture.

To Delhi
Calcutta
Bay of Bengal
Bombay
Hyderabad
Goa
Madras
Mysore
Arabian Sea
CEYLON
Colombo

Railways

0 50 100 150 200   400
Miles

AFRICA

The first steps towards the realization of Cecil Rhodes' dream of the Cape to Cairo Railway were taken at Kimberley in 1889 northwards from Kimberley; by 1894 Mafeking was reached, construction having covered a distance of 223 miles. The next stage onward to Bulawayo was completed by the year 1897. The section southwards from Wadi Halfa, at the second cataract of the Nile, was commenced in 1896 and, cutting across the Nubian Desert parallel to the Red Sea, joined the river Nile again at Abu Hamed and then southward, the 305 miles of this section took some fourteen months to complete. In 1904, construction began on a 3 ft 6 in. gauge line from Lobito in Angola, reputed to be the finest harbour on the west coast, through Rhodesia to Beira on the east coast, some 2926 miles from its starting-point. This trans-African railway had many interruptions during its construction and was ultimately completed in July, 1931. One of the unforgettable facts about the great continent of Africa is that except for a few comparatively small areas, it has been developed principally by European powers.

According to figures published, there were about 59,000 route miles of railway in Africa, this mileage spread unequally over a continent about three times as large as Europe. Over the past century the mileage has obviously increased. There are two important facts which undoubtedly call for special consideration in station design in African railways, they are firstly the climatic inequalities, including intense heat, dust storms, and tropical rains, and secondly the terrestrial influence of geographical features, such as large swampy areas, deserts, and mountains.

As far as track gauges are concerned, although there would appear to be a great diversity, this diversity is more apparent than real, as the British standard gauge is concentrated in Egypt, Tunisia, Algeria, and Morocco. The 2 ft gauge is used in the two big systems in South Africa and Morocco.

All the railways of southern Africa may be said to be a gauge of 3 ft 6 in., whilst the metric gauge is the standard for most of the east and west coast systems – in addition to a large mileage in Tunisia. It is worth while noting that the 4 ft 8 in. is the widest gauge adopted, contrasting with India and South America's 5 ft 6 in. and Australia's 5 ft 3 in. Most of the line forming part of the Cape to Cairo route is in the 3 ft 6 in. gauge which, incidentally, provides the only link between the east and west coasts.

It will be apparent that owing to the wide range between extremes of geographical and climatic conditions, in conjunction with track variations, this vast continent poses many different problems for railway station design to resolve. One therefore would expect to find, as in India and South America, many interestingly different types. A typical station of minor proportions, built in the first half of the present century, is illustrated on a previous page.

INDIA

The first line in India was opened about 150 years ago. It was constructed by the Great Indian Peninsula Railway Company and extended for 21 miles from Bombay to

Kalyan, while in 1854 the East Indian Railway Company built a line 23 miles from Calcutta to Hooghly; subsequent developments broadly followed Lord Dalhousie's scheme of railways from Calcutta to Lahore, from Bombay to the same point in Pakistan, from Bombay to Madras and thence to the Malabar coast. On that framework of trunk lines the whole system of Indian railways has been built up. Progress was by no means rapid. It was twenty years later before the 5000-mile mark was passed, but in the next twenty years, by 1893, the mileage reached 18,000 and by 1913 the system exceeded 35,000 miles! By March 1929 the mileage had reached 41,000 with some 2400 miles .still under construction. Like in many other countries the railways are laid to a diversity of gauges: 50 per cent of the mileage being on the 5 ft 6 in. gauge and 40 per cent on the metric gauge, with less than 10 per cent on the 2 ft 6 in. and smaller gauges. A *map* here shows the distribution of the principal railway systems.

It will be appreciated that this country has posed some very special problems for the railway architect and it will be interesting to see, by the examples, how these have been resolved or ignored. Three of the problems we may assume are climatic, racial, and topographical.

AUSTRALIA

Prior to the year 1870 the railway idea in Australia developed in a somewhat leisurely manner, and for a few years later there is little evidence of hurry. The first locomotive appeared in the year 1855 and in the same year the first section of a line from Sydney to Parramatta (New South Wales) was completed, a track of a few miles only. The

Originally the Australian railway companies each had their own gauge which was the cause of much inconvenience in trans-continental travel.

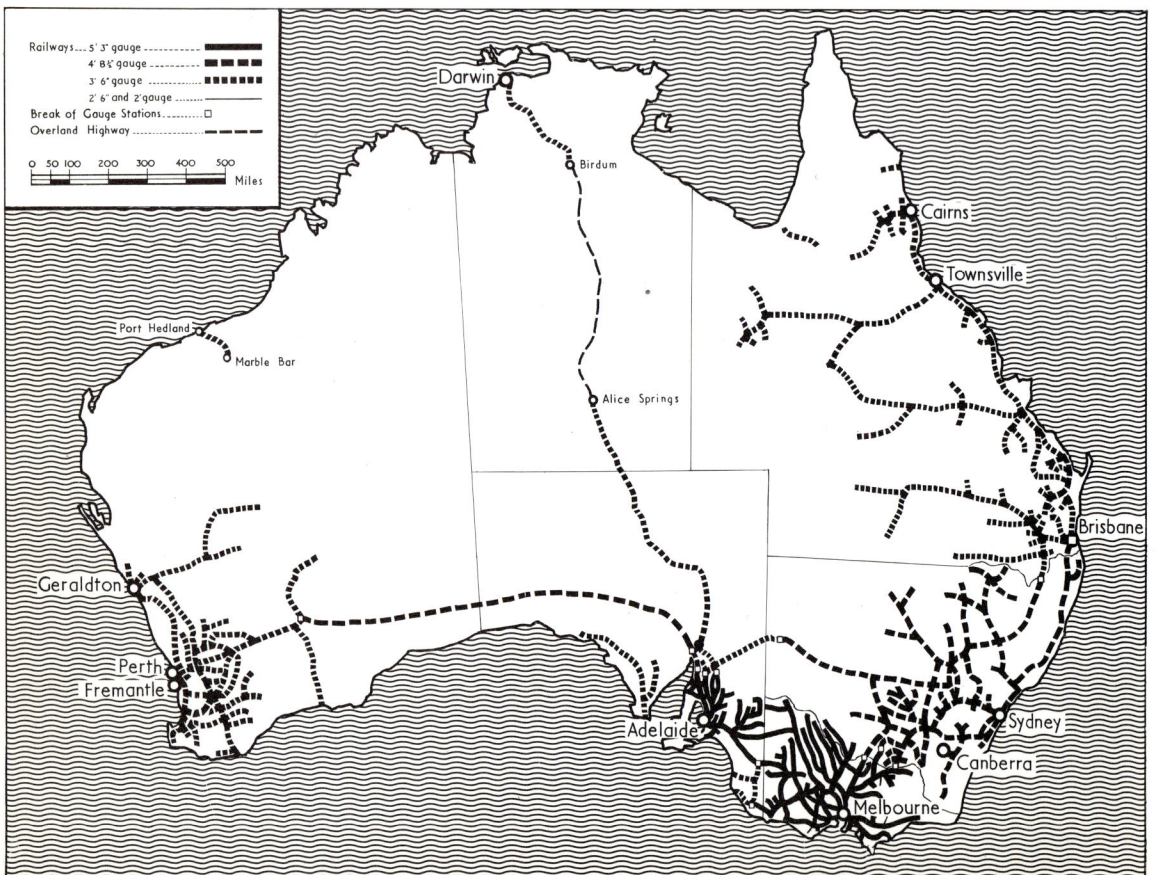

Sydney Central Railway Station.

first line constructed in Western Australia was completed in 1879. This, however, did not go very far towards providing transport in a country containing an area of nearly 3,000,000 square miles. It would be interesting to follow the development which provided the nucleus of the present system, but beyond indicating the background to the study of examples, it is not proposed to expand the historical sketch outside its proper limits.

Briefly, the principal routes brought into service were the following: in the north, from Darwin southward to Birdum; from west to east, Kalgoorlie to Fort Augusta and thence to Adelaide; in Western Australia, linking with Perth and the west coast line; and in the east with Canberra, Sydney, Brisbane, and northward, joining up the coastal towns of Queensland, where the gauge is generally 3 ft 6 in. It would seem from the passengers' point of view that the railways running from Adelaide, by way of Melbourne, along the coast of New South Wales and Queensland, provide transport through a belt about 300 miles wide, containing the heaviest population density of Australia.

The remainder of the country, excepting the coastal areas is, of course, very sparsely populated. That this vast continent has a great potential value as a future settlement of population seems evident. It has been computed by Mr George H. T. Kimble (in his book *The World's Open Spaces*) that Australia ought to be able to support at least four or five times her present population. The implications are, therefore, that Australian railways have in prospect an era of expansion, the importance of which should not be underestimated. An example of the architectural character of their large stations is illustrated in the photograph of Sydney Central station and, whilst it may not be typical of present-day standards, it will, at least, indicate that our Australian cousins have a right sense of the importance of their railway buildings.

The booking hall of Chichester station, 1961.
Architect: N. G. T. Wikeley.

INTRODUCTION

Having dealt with the growth of railways during the past century, having discovered the romance of their development, and having felt the thrill of those early achievements of such a grand and dramatic scale, let us now turn to the period between the years immediately prior to World War I to twenty years after the end of World War II, a period of STOP and GO, a period of research and hope, of frustration, followed by a New Order emerging from chaos.

Let us start, therefore, by studying the development of trends in the period under review by asking the following questions: What is Railway Architecture in its broadest sense? What is the ordinary traveller's idea of what railway architecture should be? And what are his impressions of the buildings provided by the older generation of railway companys' management? How far does the railway station of the twentieth century fulfil, in its design, the requirements of planned functional accommodation and national architectural character, or how far does it fall short?

Many interesting examples of nineteenth-century stations have been described and illustrated, sufficient to establish a 'railway style' in the reader's mind. Using these vintage examples as a 'touchstone' it is desirable to present a brief analysis of certain well-known mature examples, which may reflect in their character the central ideas of their authors, displaying in their planning, successful or not, the practical requirements of their time.

It will be appropriate to commence with our own capital city – London, where the great termini of the pioneer railway trunk systems are situated. Speaking in an expansive mood, and in general terms of that era, we may say that the great railway termini of London are the gates at which the metropolis welcomes the peoples of the world at large. The question, therefore, we should ask is: "Do these great termini suggest a welcome in a manner worthy of the City they represent?"

It is a canon of the rules of hospitality that we should extend to our guests, both on arrival and departure, either a welcome or a farewell at least as warm as the esteem in which we hold them. Custom, in fact, urges us to go further and we are not considered hypocrites if we enhance somewhat the tone and degree of our greetings. Can we, therefore, be sure that our London termini give travellers the impression of dignity and hospitality? Alas, examination reveals that generally they do not; their approaches and surroundings also leave much to be desired.

The best that can be said about our older surviving railway stations is that some are gloriously inconspicuous, few are conspicuously good and the remainder are conspicuously inglorious. And, quite apart from the larger question of general design, one of the prime sources of the dinginess so apparent to most travellers is the universal untidiness which hitherto prevailed. It has frequently been asserted that we are a nation of shopkeepers. In this business of shopkeeping, therefore, it would seem germane to include railway business.

The business of the Transport Commission is, *inter alia*, to sell travelling facilities to the public traveller, the railway station is their shop. Most shops of repute rely upon their inviting appearance to attract customers. In the past railway executives were a long time in realizing that by providing the public with better designed and tidier stations, they would not only be serving the public taste and comfort, but also they would advertise their services to far better effect; the gain would be obvious and solid. These facts were realized by the London Transport Board in the many excellent examples of their Underground stations.

There are few larger buildings in active use by the public than the railway station, and it should serve their interest more efficiently. This being so, it is essential that the building should from the outset express its purpose both in plan and composition.

Its essential function is to help the travelling public on its way in the pleasantest, easiest, and safest possible manner. This was realized much earlier by the American railway 'tycoons' and they made provision for the efficient transit of the passenger, who, after all, is the man who pays! In Britain the railway executives have now begun to think along these lines, the outcome of which will be more hospitable stations and better architecture; a policy which will bring its own rewards.

Before commencing broad comparisons it will be necessary to suggest an answer to the three questions formulated in the intro-ductory remarks. And we should not be very far wrong in saying that railway architecture is a highly specialized and complicated form of planning. This planning for traffic (freight and passenger) by railroad also includes the layout and design of structures, embodying, in some cases, many elements of engineering. This defini-

tion, however, falls somewhat short of what is actually involved beyond the mere outline, and we are concerned now with what it has come to 'mean'.

It is, primarily, the efficient and economical design and planning of the buildings and station layout, to satisfy all requirements of traffic, the circulation throughout the planned area, and the provision of all the necessary accommodation for passengers and railway staff, grouped in their related positions. The whole composed of materials of pleasing appearance which will be economical to maintain and easy to keep clean. Moreover, the siting of the station should be such that, strategi-cally, it will have full regard for the road systems of the particular areas which it serves.

Turning to the second question which deals with the 'typical traveller's' reactions to the older stations (the veterans of the iron road), the answer may well be negative in one sense, and the reason for this is suggested in the introductory remarks.

The generation, now long since dead, for whom these stations were built found this novel mode of travel a great improvement upon the stage-coach.

The present generation, emancipated and critical, regard these surviving stations as eclectic in their architecture, outmoded in their accommodation, overcrowded, and in their decrepitude.

The third question, which relates to 'fitness for purpose', can best be answered by comparing and evaluing some typical examples.

The year 1911 will be an appropriate starting-point to follow the twentieth-century evolutionary progress, starting from the time-worn stations striving to cope with the advance of an expanding social and commercial upsurge.

The principal London termini as they then existed have been referred to in the historical background. They will be referred to again in a later chapter for comparison, and reviewed as to their functions during the mid-century. Meanwhile, we may usefully consider the developments evolving from the period 1911 to 1914. It will be most appropriate to record what was happening at the terminal of Britain's premier railway, the London and North Western, at Euston. It will indicate the trends towards an adventurous future and will show the realization, by the railway managements, that the needs of the passengers have an importance, at least, equal to that of 'revenue receipts'.

The first important step carried out in 1912 was the provision of a new booking concourse across the front of the station, linking up the arrival and departure platforms; new dining and refreshment rooms were also provided. In subsequent years, right up to the time of its entire reconstruction, several extensive amenities were provided as further examples of this awareness.

Whilst other of London's great termini were, to a certain extent, carrying out improvements, outmoded 'route' stations were being rebuilt along the lines of the Big Four groups.

The field of discussion may be divided into three principal zones, representative of three types of stations – each performing its own particular function. The 'route' diagram illustrates the general relationship of many types, three of which are selected below: head of line, or terminal station; combined route-junction and terminal for branch lines; intermediate route or wayside station.

The above types may be sub-divided into high-level and low-level approaches, each having its own special problems; however, some of the varying types will be examined seriatim.

It will be appropriate here to refer briefly to London's location map p. 42, of principal main-line termini in order to be able to relate each famous rail-head station to the system it has served, in most instances, for over a century.

The placing of London's main-line termini was not pre-planned; it was the result of individual selection. The promoters

Various types of station buildings in relation to tracks:

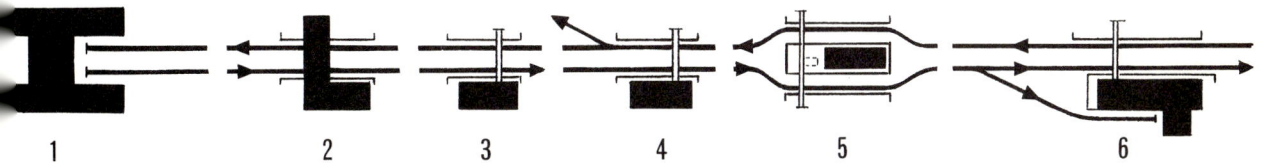

1. *Main-line terminal*
2. *Route station spanning tracks*
3. *Route lineside station*
4. *Route lineside station with branch*
5. *Route station on island platform*
6. *Combined route lineside branch terminal*

of railways following the London to Birmingham company, Britain's premier line, each selected the most convenient route in relation to its provincial starting-point.

DEVELOPMENT

London's main-line veteran terminal stations have been referred to, in some detail in an earlier chapter, as they existed towards the end of the nineteenth century; in the fullness of time, owing to the great increase of traffic expansion in the provinces, the original accommodation became inadequate and outworn.

As in the case of the former Euston buildings, rearrangement was possible within the boundaries of the termini; certainly Paddington was able to rehabilitate its booking and refreshment facilities, and to reorganize the layout of ticket barriers and concourse spaces.

ST PANCRAS

At St Pancras, however, the layout was not so fortunate, for, although it had a wide open train shed, its main concourse, south of the ticket barriers, was more constricted.

Behind Scott's neo-Gothic façade lies the station proper with a somewhat irregular concourse; on its north side are the ticket barriers, and on the south are entrances to the refreshment rooms, grill rooms, etc. Stepways down to the London Passenger Transport system also lead from it.

Owing to traffic expansion certain defects in the concourse and platforms have revealed themselves over the years. The result is an absence of demarcation and logical form, and a lack of sufficient space to deal with large crowds.

The narrow platforms, particularly those at the side, have numerous openings into flanking buildings which are one cause of interruption in the pedestrian traffic flow. On the west side, approached by a separate road, the main booking hall is sited. It consists of an oblong space with two openings to the concourse and west platform. Between which is situated the booking office, semi-elliptical on plan, and panelled in 'Tudor' linenfold. At the south end of the booking hall are the entrances to the enquiry bureau and the general waiting room respectively.

This completes, in general terms, the description of another fairly large terminal station in London and while the main station area is a fairly unified whole, it yet presents problems of circulation which will be difficult to resolve so long as the structural handicap of the old hotel building is permitted to set a limit on future large improvements.

KING'S CROSS

Adjoining St Pancras is the externally unique L.N.E.R. station, King's Cross, built by Lewis Cubitt, the engineer, in 1852. It has been both praised and condemned; described as a curious combination of boldness and timidity, it endeavours to reconcile the duality of two equal semicircular arched roofs by introducing a centrally disposed clock-tower, which so far from creating harmony introduces a disturbing element. It is, in fact, the result of the *application* of 'architectural features' by the engineer to an otherwise forthright piece of engineering construction. Had its designer adopted a three-span roof and discarded his trimmings, the result would have been happier. Not much latitude here for expansion.

The station and goods yard occupy about 45 acres of ground and, to prepare the site, an old hospital had to be demolished together with a number of houses on the west side of Maiden Lane, which was at that time widened considerably. The station platforms are entered through two main semicircular arches, facing Euston Road; each arch is 71 ft wide, and the dividing clock-tower is 112 ft high.

The plan is simple, with the main booking hall, waiting, and public rooms accommodated on the west side, adjoining the platform. The section view illustrates the bold sweep of the twin roofs, separated at their joint springing by a high parapet wall resting upon a series of arches for its entire length; the external parapet walls, east and west, are similarly supported along the line of the roof-springing.

As to the future, we may find that both St Pancras and King's Cross are subjects for a major redevelopment project.

WATERLOO

By some strange but subtle nuance the character of some of the Southern Railway stations on the south side of the metropolis reflect a continental influence. This can readily be understood from the fact that Dover and Southampton are linked to France and other European countries via the train- and car-ferry service across the Channel.

One of the larger sort, Waterloo is an interesting example of a station boldly enlarged from its original state. As far back as 1899 parliamentary powers were obtained for extending the old station and this involved rehousing approximately 1750 persons. The station now covers an area of about $24\frac{1}{2}$ acres, about $10\frac{1}{4}$ acres more than the old Euston. In the extension, completed in 1922, the work of the company's architect, Mr J. R. Scott, a laudable attempt was made to produce a great station and in many respects it is our nearest approach, in London, to a proper station. It has a spacious concourse with the public rooms and booking offices spread along its north side. The elevational treatment, particularly the 'Memorial' entrance, bears

The Memorial Entrance of Waterloo station (architect: J. R. Scott) was added to the existing building in 1922, together with a new rationalized layout, unique at that time.

witness to the architect's inspiration from overseas. In fact it is interesting to record that the planning and design of this station was based upon information supplied by a body of experts who had previously visited the Continent and America for the special purpose of studying examples of railway stations in those countries.

The underlying idea of the plan was to have all passenger circulation, from taxi, via booking hall and concourse, to platforms, all on one level, although the arrangement and grouping of waiting rooms, etc., could have been improved. There is a general air of lightness – the absence of the grimy and murky atmosphere common to most large stations is no doubt due to electrification. In the replanning of Waterloo the problem of passenger and parcels circulation was dealt with boldly by segregation, providing an ample concourse with direct access between the platforms and the entrance, exits, and the Underground system.

Before considering the final section dealing with future development, the basis of analysis may, with advantage, be broadened by a brief examination of examples from continental, Commonwealth and American sources: this will be dealt with in a later chapter.

The historical sketch will have provided a survey of the general development and romantic background of the overseas railways; whether the selected examples have fulfilled their functions successfully or otherwise. It is obvious that in each country national regulations and characteristics may impose some fundamental influence upon the orthodox railway plan and may provide some still more interesting variations upon the British examples already discussed.

SOUTH KENTON

During the period 1931–40, most of the new stations on the London Midland Region were constructed from the designs of W. H. Hamlyn, the company's chief architect at that time, in co-operation with the chief engineer, W. K. Wallace. The illustrations will indicate the interesting variations in design and construction.

One of the first new stations built since World War I was that constructed between London and Watford upon an island platform at South Kenton. Its purpose was to serve a new housing estate development in that neighbourhood, which lies midway between North Wembley and Kenton. In 1935 the new station was built to accommodate trains running upon the electrified lines. From the plan it will be seen that a long and narrow building is placed centrally upon the island platform. A short distance from the foot of the stepway a small passimeter booking office is situated within a screened and roofed enclosure. The platform awning is extended to the roof of this enclosure and thus provides continuous shelter from the stairs to the trains and platform buildings.

The plan clearly shows the position of the platform building from which it will be observed that its design is an interesting departure from the traditional example of earlier days. It is interesting to note that this station was built about three years before the reinforced concrete example at Apsley. The underlying motive at South Kenton was an essay in the reformulation of the essential requirements of accommodation and the experimental application of a material and form of construction not previously used in railway architecture. With regard to the planning arrangements, the passengers, having passed the booking

```
                                                                                    P
 ◀ UP          BOOKING                         WAITING ROOM                          L
               OFFICE                                                                A
                                                                                    T
                                                                                    F
                                                                                    O
                                                                                    R
                                                                                    M
```

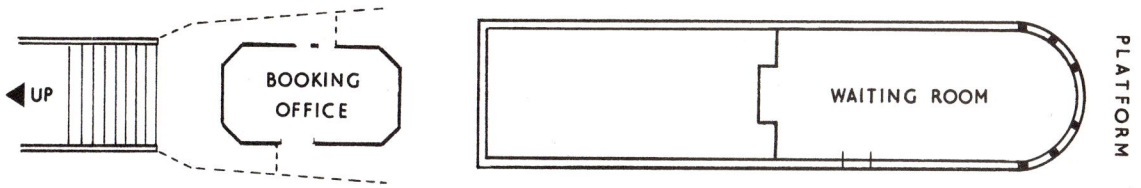

Plan of South Kenton station, 1935.

office and bookstall under cover, reach the waiting rooms. The principal buildings form a single block with the general waiting room sited at the end remote from the booking office, and having a semi-circular end window to provide an interesting and uninterrupted view down the platform.

The ceilings of the rooms are fixed at a 'domestic' level, not the lofty affairs of earlier examples, so that the proportions of the rooms are visually satisfactory. Internal wall faces are veneered in plywood finished with a natural wax polish. Furniture and fittings are all integral parts of the design.

In an endeavour to conform to the precept that reduction of maintenance costs is an essential prerequisite of design, the external cladding is in the form of stove-enamelled steel sheets, which also form the facing of the doors. The general colour of the enamel is light cream with a black recessed skirting, the doors being bright green. As the narrowness of the platform imposed restrictions on the width of the building, it was necessary to reduce the thickness of the walls in order to provide the maximum room accommodation. To achieve this the cladding was fixed to timber studding, and a certain flexibility in the form of construction provided slight tolerances in the fixing of the

enamelled iron sheets, particularly in curvature. It had been found that after about eleven years the surface of the stoved enamelling still continued to be unimpaired, and to show its freshness of colour which, with reasonable cleansing, should remain so for a considerable time.

At this station, for the first time, the problem of an ordered arrangement of poster panels was studied in relation to the window spacings. Moreover, the poster panels are constructed in such a manner that for reposting they can be removed and dealt with in the porters' room, thus avoiding the unpleasant effect of paste splashing on the surrounding structure. Another point about this station is the control of the design of all platform furniture, including seats and lamp standards.

Detailed view of South Kenton waiting room showing the external cladding of curved stove-enamelled steel.

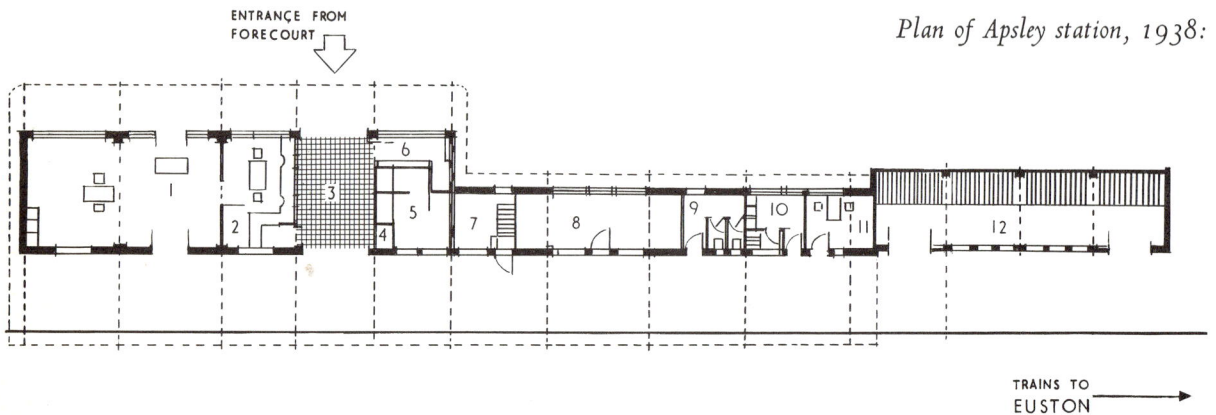

One of the first reinforced concrete stations was built at Apsley in 1938, and it is an interesting contrast with the earlier one at South Kenton in both layout and construction.

APSLEY STATION

About two years after the building of South Kenton, the new station at Apsley was commenced. This also is by W. H. Hamlyn. Situated between King's Langley and Boxmoor, it was built mainly to serve the large paper-manufacturing industry established in that area; the station was completed in 1938. In direct contrast to South Kenton, Apsley represents the first reinforced concrete station structure. It may be said that the point at which this new era in station design began to develop

is reflected in the influence exerted by active extensions of the London Underground railways under Sir Frank Pick.

The site of the station is a little over one and a quarter miles from Boxmoor on the London side. Its relation to the main road is somewhat similar to the conditions at Boxmoor, with the notable variation in that its greater distance between main road and new station enables the approach road to be brought up to platform level on an easy gradient. Another variation is that, whereas at Boxmoor the approach road has

Plan of Apsley station, 1938:

ENTRANCE FROM FORECOURT

TRAINS TO EUSTON →

KEY

1 Parcel office	5 Bookstall	9 Ladies' toilet
2 Booking office	6 Kiosk	10 Men's toilet
3 Booking hall	7 Heating chamber	11 Porters' room
4 Ticket collector	8 General waiting room	12 Cycles

ISLAND PLATFORM

double end connexions with the main road, there is only one end connexion for vehicles at Apsley, the other end is connected by means of a stepway. The fact of entering the station at platform level simplifies the problem of planning and construction in that it was possible to incorporate the booking and parcels offices within the building forming the waiting-room block. Like Boxmoor, the buildings and platform awning are unified in a simple entity. The plan and photograph illustrate the general arrangements and some of the details embodied in this station.

There is an island platform serving the up and down lines, and two single outside platforms. At Apsley waiting rooms, lavatories, etc., were confined to the two single platforms, the principal accommodation being located on the up platform adjoining the approach road. From the plan it will be seen that the passengers entering from the approach road do so under cover of an awning. Thence into the booking hall which has on one side the booking office and on the other a bookstall. On the platforms the entrances to the various rooms are sited; next to the booking office is the parcels office. There are no buildings on the island platform, the only structure being an 'umbrella' awning. All platforms are connected by a simple steel footbridge and stepways without roof covering.

In this station the principal unit of construction is a reinforced concrete frame with a cantilever extension to the awnings, the spacing between centres of the frames is approximately 15 ft. A reinforced longitudinal beam, back and front, ties the frames together. The infilling panels between the frames, which form the external walls of the buildings, are built with local facing bricks with the standard metal windows set therein.

On the platform buildings the roof beams are carried up above the slab construction, which thus provides a perfectly unbroken soffit to the platform awning. In the case of the island platform the construction is reversed and the cantilever beams forming the 'umbrella' roof are treated as supporting ribs below the awning. The thickness of the roof slab is uniform, but along the extreme edges the slab is thickened to form a beam which, projecting below the soffit, forms a stop for the end of the cantilever beams. This variation in treatment was experimental. The whole of the concrete faces are left untreated after removal of the shuttering, which was prepared to provide a smooth finish.

The treatment of the external elevations is governed by the unit of construction, but the spacing of the windows is arranged to provide for the intermediate accommodation of poster frames and notice boards, grouped in a comprehensive and ordered display. The booking-hall walls are faced with faience slabs up to a height of the top of the booking-office window, and the latter extends the full length of the booking counter. This window gives an unobstructed view into the booking office. Beneath the window is a horizontal bronze grille carried on cantilever brackets for travellers' hand luggage. The platform furniture – lamp standards, seats, litter receptacles, name boards, etc., were designed and arranged as part of a unified whole. The principal elevation, facing the approach road, is balanced about the centre line of the entrance with large display windows at each side of the entrance opening. A shelter canopy links together the elements of the composition.

Wembley High Street station as built in 1932–33, and incorporating a row of revenue-earning shops.

WEMBLEY CENTRAL

Having referred earlier in this section to the diagram of the various categories of stations on main-line tracks, and thereafter examining the two examples of small 'wayside' stations at South Kenton and Apsley – built in 1935 and 1938 respectively – we may now examine the larger and somewhat earlier station (1932–3) at Wembley; category 2 in the 'route' diagram, which is a high-level station.

The origin of the rehabilitation and reconstruction of Wembley's old station lies in the fact that it was an essay in exploiting the railway's unproductive land and property, to the betterment of the station itself and the creation of a commercial asset in revenue rentals.

The explanation is, perhaps, interesting. In 1930–1 during a recession of revenue from passenger and other traffic, the President of the L.M.S. group, the late Lord Stamp, initiated *inter alia*, a committee to examine, throughout the system, such sites and buildings as might contain elements for productive development. Of the many sites examined and for which schemes of development were prepared by

Plan of Wembley Central station showing concourse, booking office, and shops.

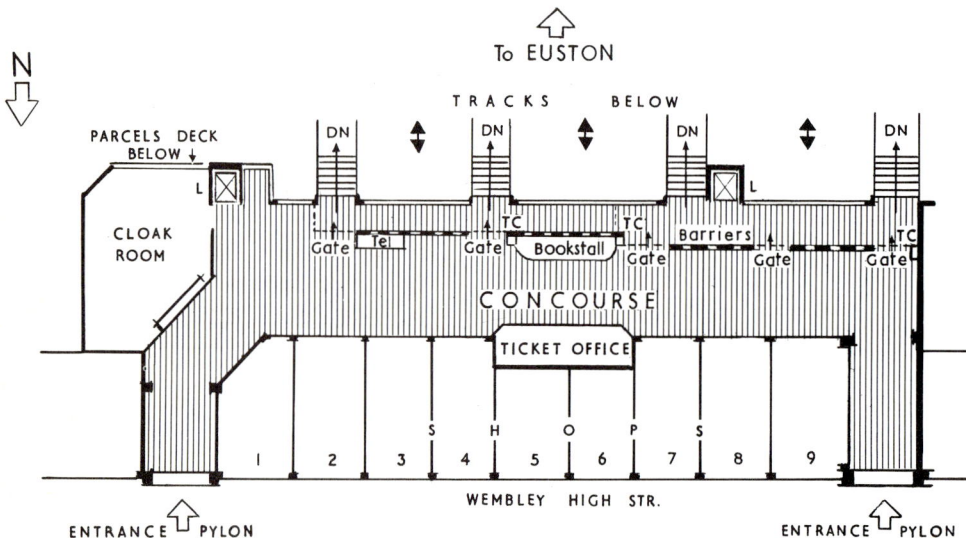

the architect seconded to the committee, Wembley is an example among others which justified its authorization.

At Wembley Central station, the High Street passes at right angles over the railway tracks. Formerly, the station entrance at street-level comprised two separate booking offices, one a simple brick rectangular booking hall serving the steam lines; the other gave access to the electrified lines and was of a later date. The two entrances were linked by a covered footbridge, the whole presented an untidy and neglected appearance. It will be appreciated that the continuity of shops and other commercial buildings in the High Street was interrupted by the bridge and parapet walls.

It was the introduction of electric traction into Great Britain which brought about a new approach to the planning and design of railway stations. The example at Apsley (London Midland Region), mentioned earlier, is typical and may take its place in the line of progressive development. Two years after the completion of Apsley, the reconstructions of the old station at Luton were opened.

LUTON

It will be instructive to examine in fuller detail this station, also designed by W. H. Hamlyn and of similar size to

Wembley, serving the old Midland Railway. The interest here lies in the fact that the town of Luton is in two parts, divided by the railway and connected by a high-level footbridge passing over the station about midway between the extreme ends of the platforms. A circumstance which imposed on the architect certain restrictions, for he had to integrate the footbridge into the elevational composition, particularly in respect of its approach road (Station Road) which passes alongside parallel to the railway at the approximate platform level. Parallel also to Station Road is the L.N.E.R. station, so that we have triple lines of traffic in parallel, crossed at high-level by the pedestrian bridge.

For many years prior to 1938 the old station, built in the style of the Gothic Revival, endeavoured to cope with the increasing traffic caused by the rapid expansion and development of industries in the town and surrounding areas. The accompanying illustration indicates the character of the former station buildings, symptomatic of the style of many of the old Midland stations.

In the planning and design of the new station it was essential to anticipate, as far as possible, the scope of industrial development of the area, and the future growth of passenger traffic.

The old Victorian Gothic station at Luton 1938 had become outmoded and inadequate for handling modern traffic. Its replacement is seen on the following pages.

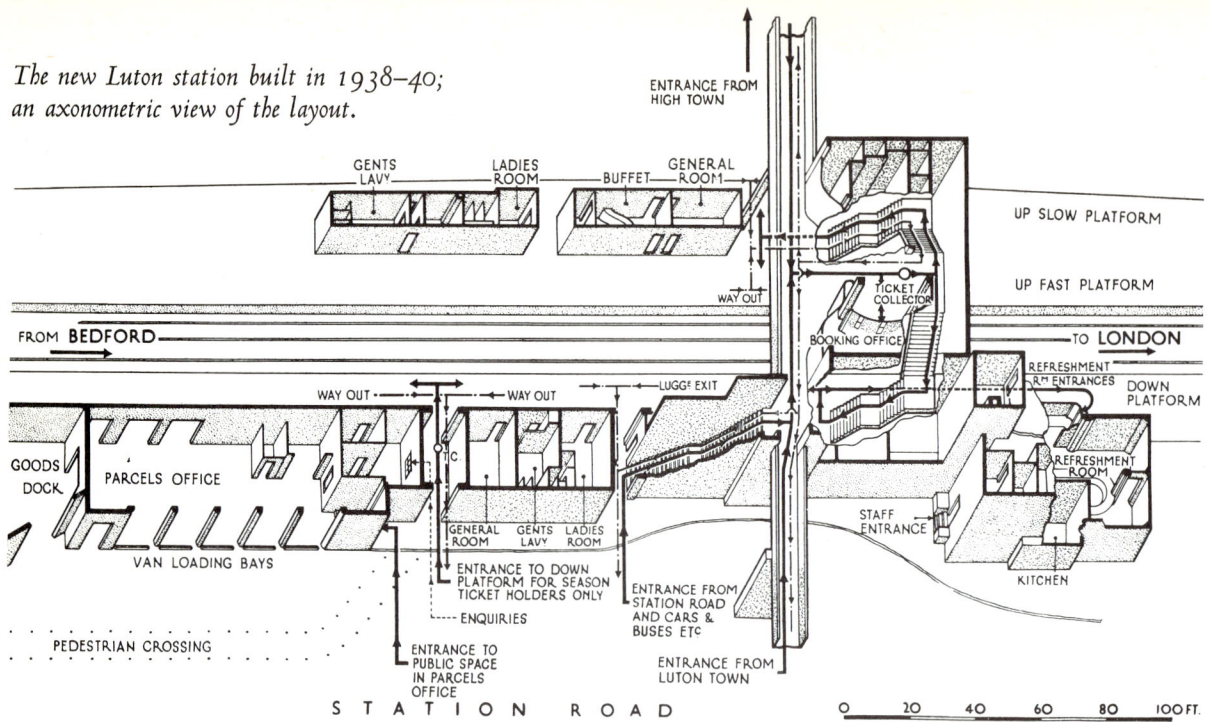

The new Luton station built in 1938–40; an axonometric view of the layout.

ENTRANCE FROM HIGH TOWN

GENTS LAVY — LADIES ROOM — BUFFET — GENERAL ROOM

UP SLOW PLATFORM

UP FAST PLATFORM

WAY OUT

TICKET COLLECTOR

BOOKING OFFICE

FROM **BEDFORD**

TO **LONDON**

REFRESHMENT RM ENTRANCES

DOWN PLATFORM

WAY OUT — WAY OUT — LUGGE EXIT

GOODS DOCK

PARCELS OFFICE

REFRESHMENT ROOM

STAFF ENTRANCE

VAN LOADING BAYS

GENERAL ROOM — GENTS LAVY — LADIES ROOM

KITCHEN

ENTRANCE TO DOWN PLATFORM FOR SEASON TICKET HOLDERS ONLY

ENTRANCE FROM STATION ROAD AND CARS & BUSES ETC

ENQUIRIES

PEDESTRIAN CROSSING

ENTRANCE TO PUBLIC SPACE IN PARCELS OFFICE

ENTRANCE FROM LUTON TOWN

S T A T I O N   R O A D

0   20   40   60   80   100 FT.

LAYOUT OF THE NEW STATION

The accompanying axonometric view of the new station will indicate the general arrangement designed to meet the special set of site conditions, mentioned above.

The main entrance and booking hall to the new station is logically placed on the level of the pedestrian bridge where it crosses over the track, and at this intersection a pylon provides a dominant note in the composition; this feature is shown by the adjoining photograph.

HIGH-LEVEL BUILDINGS

The high-level accommodation is contained in a rectangular structure on the London side of the footbridge, and it comprises a large booking hall with segmental recesses at each end, containing on one side the booking office and on the other a bookstall. On the side remote from the footbridge are the ticket barriers controlled by a central ticket-collector's enclosure. Beyond the barriers is the top landing of the principal stairways which descend to each platform. It will be

evident from the illustration that there is an unobstructed route across the widened footbridge from one side of the town to the other without interfering with railway passengers. A passenger embayment provides a subsidiary circulating area before passing into the booking hall. The booking hall is protected by a line of glazed swing doors, which prevent draughts caused by the

The elevated footbridge from Luton town leading to the station entrance is emphasized by a pylon.

The high-level booking hall seen from the platforms, with the refreshment rooms at platform level on left with staff quarters above.

suction of air down the stairs when express trains pass under the footbridge.

PLATFORM BUILDINGS

There are two principal platforms, one of which is an island, serving both up fast and up slow lines respectively. The other platform, adjoining the approach road, is considerably wider between the buildings and the platform edge, for it deals also with parcels traffic. The island platform has two blocks of accommodation comprising a general waiting room with a refreshment buffet adjoining, the other building contains ladies' waiting room and toilets and lavatories for men. These are separated by a small central heating plant serving the buildings on this side; the platform is covered by an awning.

The principal buildings at the lower level are sited on the down platform and occupy a frontage to the approach road of approximately 327 ft. Within this block are three groups of accommodation. At the end, remote from the bridge and adjoining the existing goods dock the new parcels office is sited, having five cartage bays on the roadside with an awning. Adjoining the parcels

office is a secondary booking office for low-level access to the building; this office is used for special events, such as football excursions, and serves also as an inquiry office.

REFRESHMENT ROOMS

On the London side of the bridge there is a combined refreshment room with dining annexe. The refreshment accommodation is approximately 85 ft long by 12 ft wide, the dining space occupying the return end. The photograph gives a general impression of the internal arrangements of the bar with its suspended ceiling. The entrance to the refreshment room is from the platform, and an external lobby, with doors at each end, obviates the unpleasant draughts and the noise frequently present in many refreshment rooms which open directly from the platform. A pair of glazed swing doors gives access into the room from the lobby, and the wide windows give adequate natural light; the end window gives a good view down the line and, incidentally, a slight advance notice of train arrivals. The service counter is elliptical on plan and provides service for the maximum area of the room with

Interior of the dining-room at Luton and the adjoining buffet.

minimum movement for the serving staff. Above the refreshment accommodation, the first floor is planned as residential accommodation for the manageress and domestic staff. Each bedroom has a built-in unit, comprising wash-basin, dressing-table, etc., and in these combination fittings radiators are accommodated.

CONSTRUCTION

The buildings facing the approach road and the high-level booking hall are constructed with a reinforced concrete frame and have flat roofs. The walls are in cavity brickwork. The principal beams carrying the high-level buildings have a clear span of 65 ft. The platform awnings consist of steel beams and cross-girders carried on steel stanchions, and the latter are cased in concrete. The roof covering is bituminous felting laid on boarding and wood purlins. All external walls are faced with Chesham brown multi-coloured brickwork; windows are steel framed and all parapet copings are reconstructed stone.

The construction of the station buildings is interesting inasmuch as it combines two forms of framing: the main buildings having reinforced concrete structural members, while the platform roofing and supports, the bridge girders, etc., are of steel.

GENERAL ELEVATIONAL TREATMENT

Externally the building groups naturally about the old footbridge, and the entrance into the high-level premises is emphasized by the wide opening and the mass of brickwork. Other points of importance, such as the loading bays, are emphasized by the architectural treatment. Where advertising posters are used, an attempt has again been made to arrange the display so that it forms part of the general scheme.

Internally, materials were selected having finishes which are pleasant in appearance, hard wearing, and readily cleanable. The surfaces of the high-level booking hall form permanent decorative treatment. The floors are paved with terrazzo slabs marked out with carborundum jointing lines. The walls are lined with faience. All joinery work is carried out in Indian silver grey-wood. The lighting fittings were specially designed and the trough fittings, made up in units, are fixed to the ceiling to follow the curves of the side walls. In the refreshment room lighting effects have been considered carefully with the general colour scheme. The walls are panelled to dado height with moulded plywood in french walnut, this is carried along the counter front. Doors are flush and veneered with cobalt blue plastic, the windows are provided with curtains with a blue ground and a dull gold pattern, and the floor is covered with cork tiles. In the waiting rooms the floors also have cork tiles and have a cellulin dado in natural grey. The furniture in the ladies' waiting room includes chairs of two types, the design of which has its origin in Finland.

CARNFORTH STATION

This Lancashire station of 1940 is of interest mainly from a structural point of view. The new island-platform building was designed as an example of co-operation between architect and engineer.

The general design and character was by W. H. Hamlyn, who co-operated with the chief engineer, W. K. Wallace; a reinforced concrete structural engineer assisted in the construction of the buildings and canopies.

The design of the structure here differed from Apsley in that, instead of using a series of unit frames, the station buildings comprised a structural 'shell' with a concrete lid extended to form a canopy. The internal accommodation is created by cross-partition walls; the external walls facing the platform have inset panels of frost-proof tiling arranged to conform to the practice of door and window units. Panels are provided for posters.

LOUGHTON STATION

A much more recent station is the L.N.E.R. and L.P.T.B. joint station at Loughton in Essex, with which is combined an electric sub-station. The buildings were designed by Stanley Hall with Easton and Robertson, and are sited amid playing fields, fringed with Lombardy poplars, which form an excellent setting in an otherwise open space. The tracks are carried on an embankment and the station abuts upon this at a near right angle; a long semicircular-ended road approach leads up to the station on the axis of the booking hall.

While the project was a joint undertaking, there appears to have been an expressed desire on the part of the L.N.E.R. management that the ultimate characteristics of the building should reflect its own style, rather than that of the L.P.T.B.

The entrance leading to the elevated track at Loughton (Essex) station. Architects: Easton and Robertson, 1941.

The platform canopies in relation to the ground-level booking hall. Loughton station serves both main line and London Transport service.

Consequently a barrel-vault form was adopted for the booking hall, the external treatment of which was reputed to convey an allusion to King's Cross station; an interesting whimsey, for those who can see it!

The general arrangement of the booking hall and its service rooms is compact and direct, yet there is about the overall layout an impression of detached, rather than grouped buildings, suggesting possible revisions in the programme.

The platforms and their awnings are well designed in reinforced concrete; a direct and clean piece of work, finished with grey-pink paintwork.

Loughton may be considered as the forerunner of the large Central London railway programme of extensions, with its many new and exciting types of stations.

OLYMPIA STATION

For many years the handling of parcels and passenger traffic at Kensington (Olympia) station presented a formidable set of problems, complicated by the outmoded and decrepit station buildings.

Power-house associated with Loughton station.

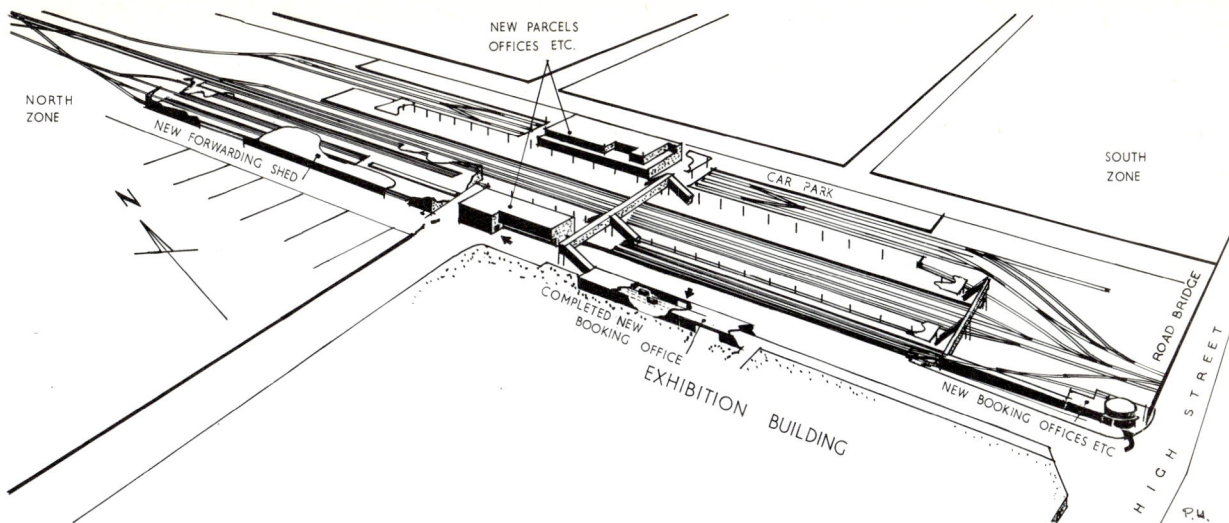

The reconstruction of 1946 of the station serving the Olympia exhibition centre and motor-rail terminal for British Rail and for London's Underground system.

The chief problem was to segregate these two types of traffic, to give ease of operation and provide for free expansion and flow. A scheme for full reconstruction was prepared in 1946, in collaboration with all the operating companies and the L.P.T.B., and the first stage was the construction of the concourse and booking offices, carried out as an urgent interim measure in November–December, 1946.

The new concourse occupies a site, formerly the unroofed forecourt between Olympia and the existing covered way, leading from the station footbridge to the entrance hall in Olympia. Visitors arriving by train pass over the footbridge and down the stairs into the covered way, now linked up with the new concourse. Facing the stairway and extending across the concourse are the checking barriers where passengers with rail tickets pass through to the covered way to Olympia Grand Hall. Visitors returning to the trains pass into the new concourse along the sign-posted routes, adjoining the booking offices, and thence through the checking barriers, before ascending the stairway to the footbridge. It will be clear that strong demarcation exists between the essential features of arrival and departure, the main basis of planning for passenger flow. Faced with the limitations of time and space the constructional programming of the work was a matter of first importance; it was resolved by the simple expedient of limiting the site work to a minimum and by prefabricating the booking offices, ticket stands, and barrier rails.

The construction comprises a roof-covering of wood-wool slabs supported on light steel tubular rafters, and having 'fins' welded to the underside to receive the edges of the slabs; steel channel purlins are at 6 ft centres, supporting the rafters; a cast fibrous plaster casing covers the purlins. Two lines of main supporting B.S. beams are carried on light steel columns. Natural lighting is provided in the roof by glass panels and clerestory sidelighting. The ceiling is plastered direct to the wood-wool slabs, which are covered on top with asphalt.

The prefabricated booking offices are made in six units: two sides, two ends, floor, and roof. The vertical units comprise dado, upper wall, and frieze – each unit is framed and welded with extruded

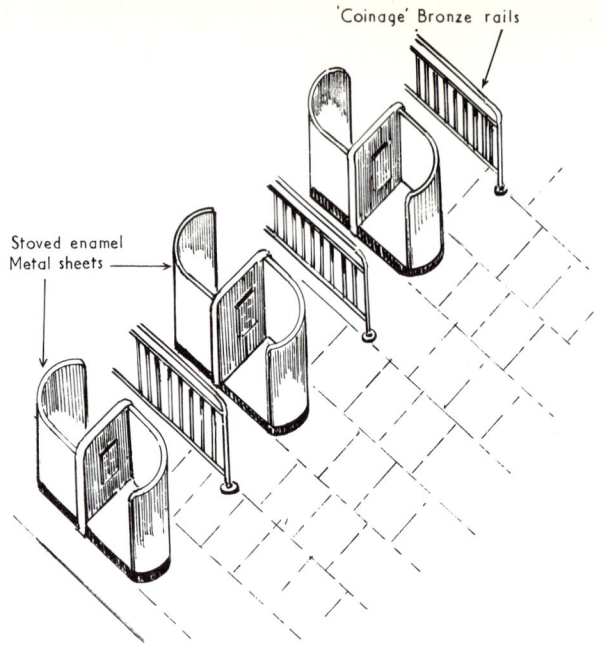

Detail of the ticket collectors' stands and check barriers at London's Olympia station. Below we see how these stands relate to the overall plan of the new booking hall, and how they regulate the passenger lanes, by their echelon layout, to and from the exhibition hall and trains.

manganese-bronze sections, with a toned satin finish. The dado cladding is stove-enamelled steel sheet, lined with insulating board. Above dado level the framing is filled with Gaboon ply-veneered sycamore outside and with teak face inside. Frieze panels are in polished plate-glazing, as also are the end units above dado level. Roof and floor units are light timber framings covered with birch ply and boarding respectively.

The ticket windows provide a special note of interest: each is a single sheet of plate glass with a narrow aperture at the base for the transfer of cash and tickets; at mouth level a 12 in. circular hole is fitted with a Pliofilm diaphragm in a bronze frame and protected by light metal gauze. The

object of this unit is to reduce draughts and infection, and to provide a measure of speech amplification for two-way conversation; it is fitted here experimentally. The Netherlands Railways employ this type of window as standard practice, in conjunction with a novel ticket-issuing device.

The maintenance of a steady flow in the passenger lanes is the measure of success in control at the checking-points. The collectors' stands are a modern version of the basic S-type barrier. They are constructed to conform with the design of the lower part of the booking offices; the sides being stove-enamelled steel sheets in extruded bronze frames; they embody also a tubular metal standard carrying a combined lighting and sign unit.

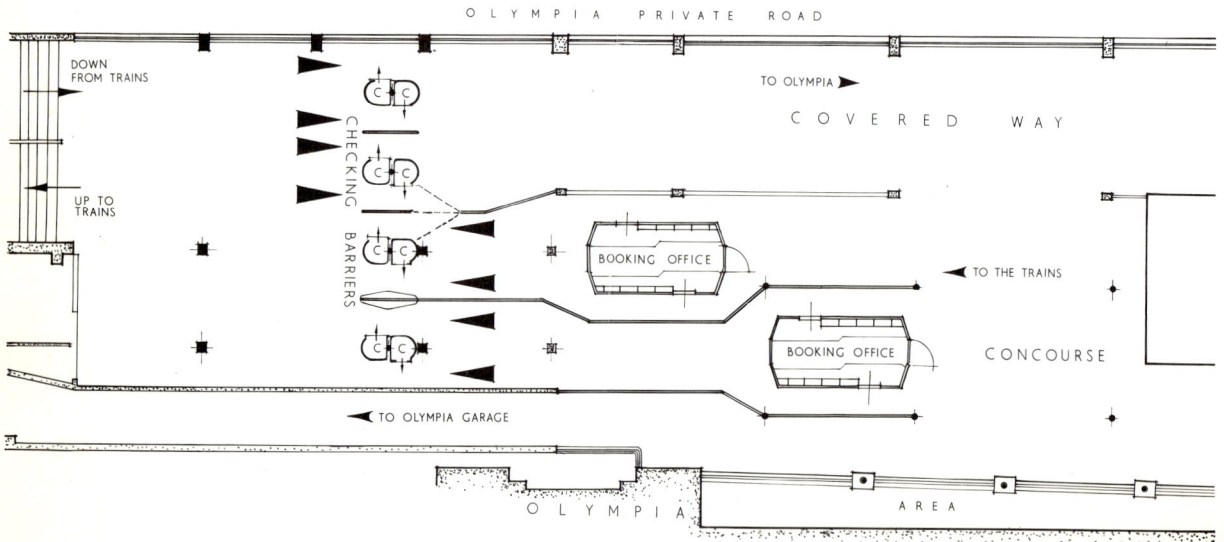

The trussed roof of the concourse of Leeds City station, by W. H. Hamlyn, 1937, with mouldings and Classical coffering, can be compared with (below) Uxbridge's similar concrete coupled trusses, which are treated in a more forthright manner, although only one year younger.

As a variation upon the project for the full reconstruction of Kensington Olympia, the development of British Rail car-carrying services radiating from London, a 'Motorail' terminal has been built upon the Exhibition Hall side of the station, leaving the opposite side available for further passenger amenity development should the Channel Tunnel materialize. In that event the reconstructed station may take on its prospective role of the London interchange point between British and Continental express passenger services. The recent opening of the Motorail terminal, May, 1966, allows incoming motorists to drive past a reception office, and proceed to a large covered park to await loading.

At the outer end, the parking area abuts upon the four platforms, three of which provide for end-loading, the fourth having a double ramp for simultaneous loading of the upper and lower decks of 'Cartic 4s', intended for Motorail service on the London–Perth trains, when that service becomes operative. So it seems that Kensington Olympia station (formerly known as Addison Road), so well known militarily during World Wars I and II as a through route for troops, will shed its timeworn timber buildings, such as remain, to become revitalized and rehabilitated in a modern idiom.

Uxbridge Underground station. Note the inward 'cant' of the upper part of the vertical members (Charles Holden, 1938).

SOME LATER DEVELOPMENTS

Thirty years of development in station design shows some fairly varied ideas and characteristics, influenced by local and imported concepts. But the importation of ideas from abroad, and no latent criticism is intended here, is no bad thing, perhaps. To lag a little behind other countries in new buildings gives advantages. The trial of new ideas in practice and the experience of others can prove most useful.

It was in 1937 that Leeds City station was largely rebuilt, together with a new office block and hotel. The illustration of the concourse in the rebuilt station designed by W. H. Hamlyn, emphasizes the dominant repetition of the structural frames and roof-coffers; this is balanced by the broad and uncluttered floor area.

An interesting comparison is the example in the station roof at Uxbridge, London Transport station designed by Charles Holden 1938 – where we have a similar 'format' but with coupled trusses spanning the tracks and platforms.

Manchester Oxford Road station, 1960, showing the bold 'coinoid' construction which provides an even distribution of loads and stresses. Architect: W. R. Headley.

MANCHESTER, OXFORD ROAD

At Manchester, Oxford Road, in 1960 a new station was designed by London Midland regional architect, W. R. Headley. The station is of medium size, situated upon a 'Y' junction serving the M.S.J. & A. line. The design is a clear breakaway from the traditional form of station building, and may cause many eyebrows to rise at the form of its 'conoid', arched, laminated timber roof. It has been sympathetically described as a more disciplined version of the Sydney Opera House; the latter, designed by Joern Utzon, appears to have had a somewhat unhappy and tangled sequence for the architect. By contrast, Oxford Road station, a bold essay in design, is not alone in successfully mastering its problems.

In the departure from traditional design and construction, several small stations, between Manchester and Crewe have been built. All are based on a unit-construction system, which is adaptable to varying local conditions, and which may be assembled on site with no conspicuous delay or disturbance to traffic. There is a distinct family resemblance in most of the smaller stations on the newly electrified line to the south of Crewe.

MANCHESTER, PICCADILLY

Manchester's larger station at Piccadilly, forms a punctuation mark among the new stations in this area, replacing the former London Road station, so well remembered by Mancunians!

The architect for the new station was R. L. Moorcroft, London Midland regional

The main entrance of Manchester Piccadilly station, although linked with a ten-storey commercial building, is obviously a railway station (R. L. Moorcroft, 1966).

The scale and unity of design of Manchester Piccadilly station viewed along the length of the concourse.

architect; the work was completed in 1966.

This is one of the more recent examples of site development for revenue, referred to earlier relating to Wembley.

At Manchester Piccadilly, however, the station asserts its own purpose in a forthright manner – partly by its lettered fascia in the modern B.R. idiom, and by the projecting canopy linkage across the space between the station and the ten-storey block of the developed site. Between the two buildings and placed at eye-level, as a compliment to Mancunians, the city's coat of arms is heraldically displayed.

The interior of the concourse gives an excellent impression of welcome and rightness in scale and unity; here, also, the design and placing of furniture and equipment in the avoidance of disharmony has been well appreciated.

COVENTRY

Four years antecedent to the new Manchester Piccadilly station, the long-deferred reconstruction of Coventry station was completed. During the years 1945–7, and in conjunction with the city's master-plan for a new Coventry – a scheme for a new station was prepared; obviously, so soon after the war, the fluidity of ideas could not readily be crystallized. However, with the advance of main-line electrification, and the inadequacy of the then existing station, coupled with an undertaking made in 1957 for the completion of a new station in time for the consecration of the new cathedral, the project had a special urgency.

The new station, completed in 1962, was designed by W. R. Headley, London Midland regional architect; it was planned in consultation with the city's town

Coventry station; general view from the forecourt showing the covered queue-stand for bus travellers (W. R. Headley, 1962).

103

The concourse of Coventry station expresses great simplicity and rightness of scale.

planning architect, Arthur Ling, to fit in with the regional layout. Its design provided for clear segregation of the various types of traffic, and the complexities of accommodation within the building has been skilfully contained in a simple yet expressive form.

The general arrangement of the layout indicates a roughly cruciform building plan; the main concourse and bridge block crosses the tracks and platforms and projects into the forecourt dividing it into two areas. The accommodation for waiting and refreshment rooms, also for station staff and luggage deposit, faces the forecourt, parallel with the tracks and platforms.

The architectural composition is dominated by the concourse block, projecting forward to the line of the bus shelters, its ceiling rising through two storeys;

ample side and front glazing enhances the spatial proportions of the interior.

It may be appropriate here to compare two recent examples of stations built to serve two well-known New Towns – Hemel Hempstead, Hertfordshire and Harlow, Essex.

HEMEL HEMPSTEAD

The new Hemel Hempstead station was also designed by W. R. Headley, and was completed in 1964, two years after Coventry. It is on the electrified line between Watford and Bletchley and replaces the nineteenth-century timber station, known as Boxmoor, and occupies broadly the same site. Here, as at Coventry, the local planning authority was consulted in respect of capacity and the general character of design. As a medium-sized station, having particular relationship with a New

Hemel Hempstead station; a view along the island platform (W. R. Headley, 1964).

104

The booking hall at Hemel Hempstead is an example of a New Town station which can be compared with that at Harlow (below).

Town, where traditional design and construction are respected, it would have seemed inappropriate to build a prefabricated 'system' unit station.

The adoption of a traditional basis has achieved pleasing results by reason of an intelligent appreciation of local surroundings; 'picture'-type windows in the waiting rooms provide wide-aspect views over the upland slopes of the countryside – as seen from the high-level platforms. The booking and entrance hall, at the lower level of the station forecourt, is well proportioned and airy. Its compact design in association with the well-ordered arrangements of furnishings, preserves a tidy appearance and ensures unrestricted circulation.

The external appearance is one of stability and permanence, by reason of the large amount of blue-grey brick walls with black pointing; a deep, horizontally boarded canopy, with a white-painted boarded soffit, ties the individual buildings together, and a frieze of long, narrow glass louvres provides light and ventilation at ceiling level.

HARLOW NEW TOWN

Harlow New Town station, Essex, completed in 1960, was designed by H. H. Powell, architect to the Eastern Region, British Rail.

As in the case of Hemel Hempstead's new station, the Harlow scheme was planned in consultation with the New Town Development Corporation. The new station has been considered as one of the best buildings in the New Town; the detailing is very consistent throughout and, although not a large station by ordinary standards, the overall impression is magnified by the powerful massing of its features, building up to the three dominant rectangular towers.

Harlow (New Town) station appears more massive than that at Hemel Hempstead, its junior by about four years (H. H. Powell, 1960).

Barking station, built in 1961, is reminiscent of Rome's famous terminal in the spacious effect of its concourse and the graceful cranked beam cantilevers of its roof and canopy.

BARKING STATION

Another interesting station on the Eastern Region, also designed by H. H. Powell, is that at Barking, built a year later in 1961.

The main entrance and concourse is reached from the bridge carrying the street over the rail-tracks. The profile of the canopy and concourse roof is reminiscent of Rome Central terminal station. Euston's vanished Propylaeum had its origin in Athens, upon the Acropolis.

At Barking, the cranked concrete beams provide a pleasing profile as viewed inside the concourse; the vertical supports comprise tall and slender concrete columns, finished in black. The whole is a very well-thought-out colour scheme. Work on the site commenced in December, 1959 and was completed in March, 1961.

PLYMOUTH NORTH ROAD

From the medium-size stations so far illustrated and described we may, by way of comparison of size (though not necessarily of quality), refer to a recent station of some magnitude upon the Western Region of British Rail. It is, perhaps, not unexpected that the railway system which initiated the

Barking station being on a 'bridge site' requires it to be of lighter construction, and this the architect, H. H. Powell, has achieved by supporting the cantilevered roof and canopy by slender pillars.

The south elevation of Plymouth North Road station faces the forecourt and is 520 feet wide. The distinctive 'trough' section roof of the station block effectively counter-balances the eleven-storey office block.

broad-gauge track and built Paddington station in the same bold manner, should, on setting out to build a new station in the blitzed Plymouth area, build big.

Plymouth North Road terminal was designed by the late H. E. B. Cavanagh, when the scheme was prepared in 1958; the building was completed 1962.

In a city where the whole post-war reconstruction has been somewhat disappointing in quality, the new station is an outstanding exception.

Apart from the eleven-storey office block, placed asymmetrically on plan, the station accommodation is quite extensive, with a building length of around 520 ft from east to west. The 'trough'-section roof, east of the tall office block, covers an extensive parcels hall, while the buildings westward, apart from the concourse, accommodate station staff.

The main entrance to the concourse on the south side, is protected from east winds by the tall office building, which projects forward; the entrance to the office block is adjacent to the concourse entrance and is likewise protected. The concourse, which is about 53 ft square, has a ticket office along its west side, and facing it a wide opening leads to a dispersal corridor and on to the ticket-collectors' barriers. On the north side of the main concourse, and adjacent to the dispersal corridor, the inquiry bureau is sited, with the refreshment rooms' entrance between it and the ticket office.

A plain and dignified appearance characterizes the well-proportioned interior of this extensive building; the same scale carries throughout, with main supporting piers spaced in double rows, upon a longitudinal grid of approximately 28 ft.

The concourse of Plymouth station reflects the bold, broad treatment of the main structure (H. E. B. Cavanagh, 1962).

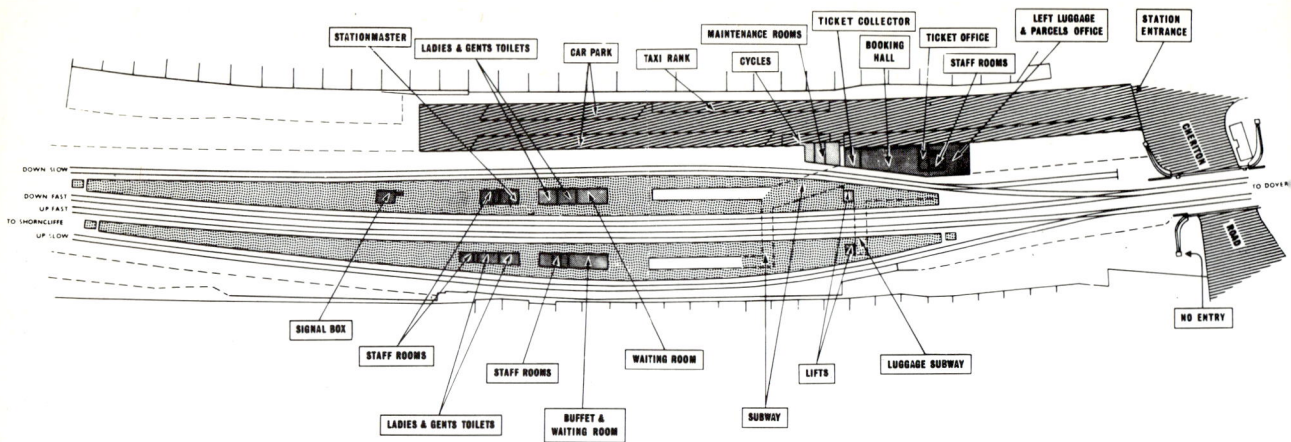

Layout of the new Folkestone Central station.

The clear, uncluttered entrance to the platforms at Folkestone.

FOLKESTONE CENTRAL

Folkestone Central station, designed by N. G. T. Wikeley, regional architect, Southern Region British Rail, provides a remarkable contrast with the immense scale of Plymouth's terminal. Built in 1962, it displays much delicacy of treatment throughout; its long line facing the approach road is contained horizontally by the deep projecting canopy, and the remarkable finely framed clock-tower provides a punctuation mark at the remote end of the canopy.

The general detailing is well studied, and there are two unusual features, simulated *baldacchinos* suspended from the soffit of the main canopy; these double canopies emphasize the entrances.

Internally, the delicacy of design extends to the entrance gates of the corridor leading to the trains.

The station entrance with its suspended canopies and unusual tower feature. A remarkable example of unfettered and imaginative design by N. G. T. Wikeley, 1962.

Chichester station built one year before Folkestone, has greater simplicity and purity of outline. An interior view is to be found on page 82 (N. G. T. Wikeley, 1961).

CHICHESTER STATION

An earlier and much larger example from the Southern Region is the station at Chichester, Sussex, built in 1961, also designed by N. G. T. Wikeley. The lofty rectangular concourse projects into the forecourt, forming an embayment, and from this embayment the passenger enters under a wide canopy. Above the canopy the whole face of the concourse is glazed; on the return side the canopy is cranked to a slightly higher level and the end wall of the concourse is in patterned brickwork.

The interior of the concourse is in sharp contrast to the restrained design of the exterior (see page 82). The main elements of the design comprise a strongly patterned ceiling formed by hexagonal coffers, which are painted a light colour in outline with centres in deep colour. The floor is also patterned with light and dark paving. Except for a lightly stencilled pattern on the dado below the ticket windows, the walls are restrained.

An interesting example of integrating a modern (information bureau) into an existing nineteenth-century structure: Bath Spa station.

Banbury station shows the influence of 'system building' on the post-war railway architecture of 1959.

A model of the new Euston Terminal showing the entrance façade.

The spacious concourse of the new Euston Terminal has underfloor heating to keep the grey-green marble terrazzo paving dry. The entrances and exits are cushioned by warmed air. This drawing, looking west, clearly shows details of structure that might not be evident in a photograph.

THE NEW EUSTON, 1969

In chapter 4 we referred to the historical background of the old station buildings as designed by the Hardwicks – father and son.

The elder, Philip Hardwick, produced the monumental classical gateway (page 38), with its magnificent ornamental cast-iron gates (cast by J. Bramah), and later the Great Hall, with its double-curved stairway leading up to the board room and committee rooms, was designed by the son, P. C. Hardwick.

From the simple plan with two platforms, Euston station developed from time to time to accommodate growing traffic, and by 1870 it covered upward of 10 acres. Extensions during subsequent years included four additional platforms and by 1892 it covered 18 acres. At that time a new class of passengers made its appearance – the commuters. London was still spreading and it became fashionable to live in the suburbs, which meant that businessmen had to travel to and from work each day.

After 1892 the first major alteration was the building of a new concourse, running east to west, on the south side of the great hall. New booking offices were added in 1912 and the former ones were converted to make dining and refreshment rooms.

The project for the entire rebuilding of Euston terminus, which had been under active consideration before both World Wars, was undertaken as part of the London Region's proposal for the electrification of its main routes linking London, the West Midlands and the North-west.

Former Assistant General Manager of the L.M.S. railway (1958), Mr A. J. Pearson, in his book *The Railways and the Nation* (1964) provides some interesting internal facts regarding this project. Regarding the total involvement, we should not be far wrong in saying that the New Euston is the culmination of what is virtually a new railway system; for it includes new tracks, signalling and main telephone exchange, power signal cabins, transformer substations, and the like. Additionally, ten major stations were rebuilt and fifty others were modernized.

The reconstruction was undertaken in two phases, the first of which was confined to those areas concerned with train working in and out of the terminus. The second phase comprised the construction of the actual terminal buildings. In order to maintain continuity, without interfering with passenger flow, a new overhead steel-framed parcels office was built during the first stage, in conjunction with the new platforms and track-layout. Work began on the first stage in April 1962 and was completed by April 1966 by the introduction of the new timetable of high speed services over the electrified routes.

The second stage began in May 1966 at the south end of the station site, and was based on the plan illustrated on pages 112 and 113.

The new building, which is 650 ft wide from east to west and 190 ft deep, is of concrete-frame construction and is sited over the maze of London Transport Underground tunnels – forming the Northern and the new Victoria lines. The proximity of the tunnels prohibited the use of piling and, to spread the load, a specially designed reinforced concrete raft was laid over the whole area.

Before referring to the main details of the plan, it will be appropriate to mention the important matter of circulation as it affects passenger movement. Initially, the guidelines of the plan embodied segregation of vehicular and pedestrian flows; with regard

Diagram of the concourse area of the new Euston Terminal:

1 *Travel Centre*	5 *Sprig Buffet, Waiting Room and Tea Bar*	8 *Toilets: Men*	13 *Telephones*
2 *Business Lounge*		9 *Toilets: Women*	14 *Shops*
3 *Station Manager's Enquiry Office*	6 *Concourse Bar and Snack Bar*	10 *Left Luggage Lockers*	15 *Access to Underground*
4 *Hotel Booking*	7 *24-hour Railbar*	11 *Lost Property*	16 *To Taxis and Car Park*
		12 *Left Luggage*	

STATION PLAN
AT CONCOURSE LEVEL

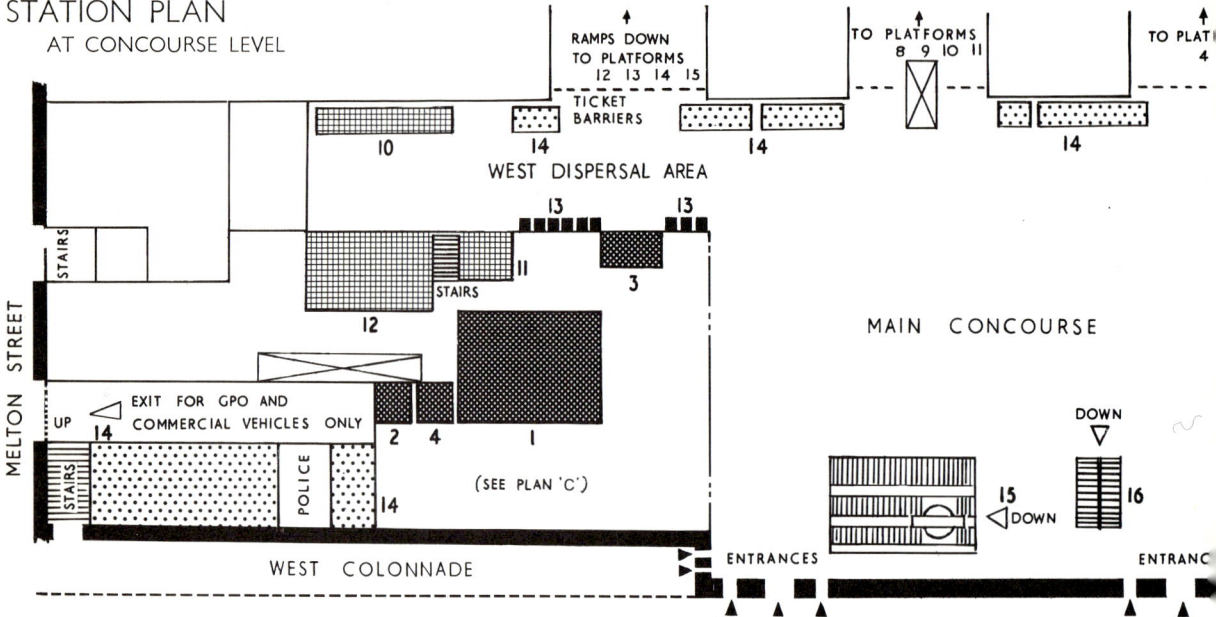

to the former, a further refinement is the separation into commercial, private car, and taxi categories, each with its own route. This is noted in the captions of the illustrations.

The new station was designed by the Regional Architect, R. L. Moorcroft, F.R.I.B.A., within the organization of the Chief Engineer, W. F. Beatty, A.M.I.C.E., and, for the detailed planning, a Travel Centre Planning Group was formed, comprising architectural, technical, and traffic personnel: the group functioned with a project manager.

In describing the new terminal, although we are pre-disposed to emphasize the architectural qualities and characteristics, it is obvious that we *ought* to consider it primarily from the point of view of the traveller, and the means to be provided for his comfort and safety. In an earlier chapter of this book, when discussing 'evolutionary progress' on railways, we referred to the fact that the passenger is the important person . . . *he is the one who pays.*

Having set forth this principle we shall doubtless recognize its influence throughout the planned area – and particularly in the Travel Centre accommodation – which is illustrated on page 114 in relation to the general plan.

It will here be appropriate to outline broadly the site aspects which may have influenced the architectural conception of the composition. The predominance of multistorey buildings along Euston Road and adjacent streets provided an opportunity to design a long, low composition which would establish an identity, uniquely contrasting with the heterogenous complex of tall buildings.

A wide and deep forecourt, free from vehicles, provides a satisfactory approach corresponding to some continental stations,

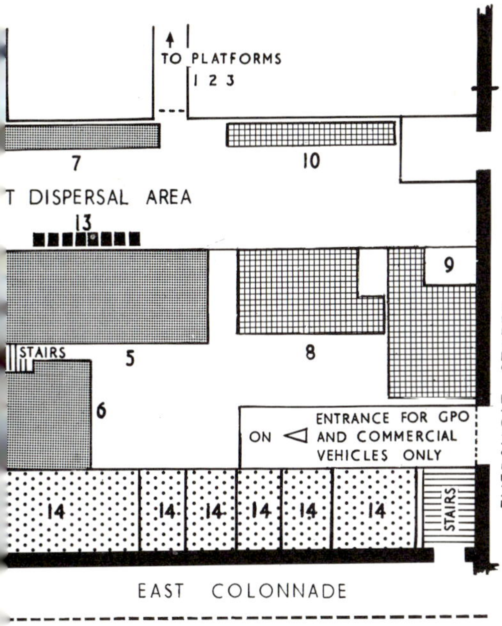

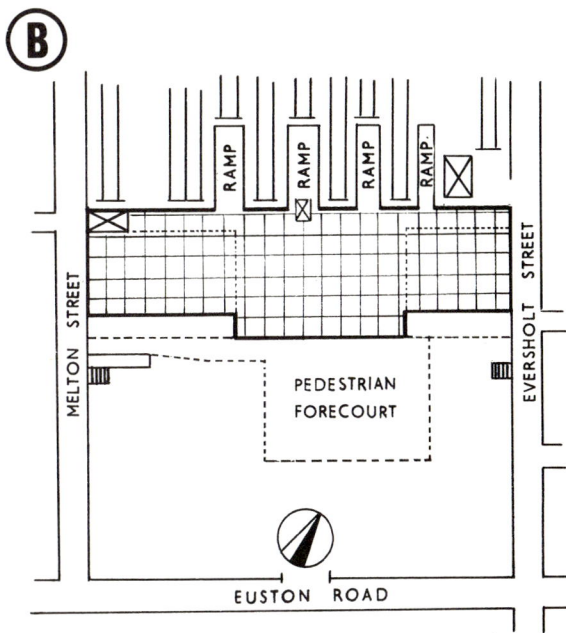

Block plan of Euston Terminal.

Plan labels (left diagram):

TO PLATFORMS 1 2 3

7   10

T DISPERSAL AREA

13

9

STAIRS   5   8

6

ENTRANCE FOR GPO AND COMMERCIAL VEHICLES ONLY

14 14 14 14 14 14

STAIRS

EVERSHOLT STREET

EAST COLONNADE

Plan labels (right diagram, B):

MELTON STREET

RAMP RAMP RAMP RAMP

EVERSHOLT STREET

PEDESTRIAN FORECOURT

EUSTON ROAD

for example, at the Rome Central Terminal facing the Piazza dei Cinquecento.

The accompanying plan of the New Euston illustrates the extent of the planned area with its main divisions of accommodation; it is hoped that this and subsequent illustrations may preserve the reader's patience by avoiding protracted descriptions in the text.

To relate the plan to the visual appearance from the passenger's point of view,

having entered the concourse, the accompanying photograph depicts the general scale of the structure.

The accompanying photograph of the concourse, by depicting the general scale of the structure, will relate the passenger's visual impression with the plan.

Referring to the plan at concourse level, the central feature is the main hall which affords access by escalators to and from London Transport Underground, also to

Eastward view across the concourse towards the waiting and refreshment areas.

113

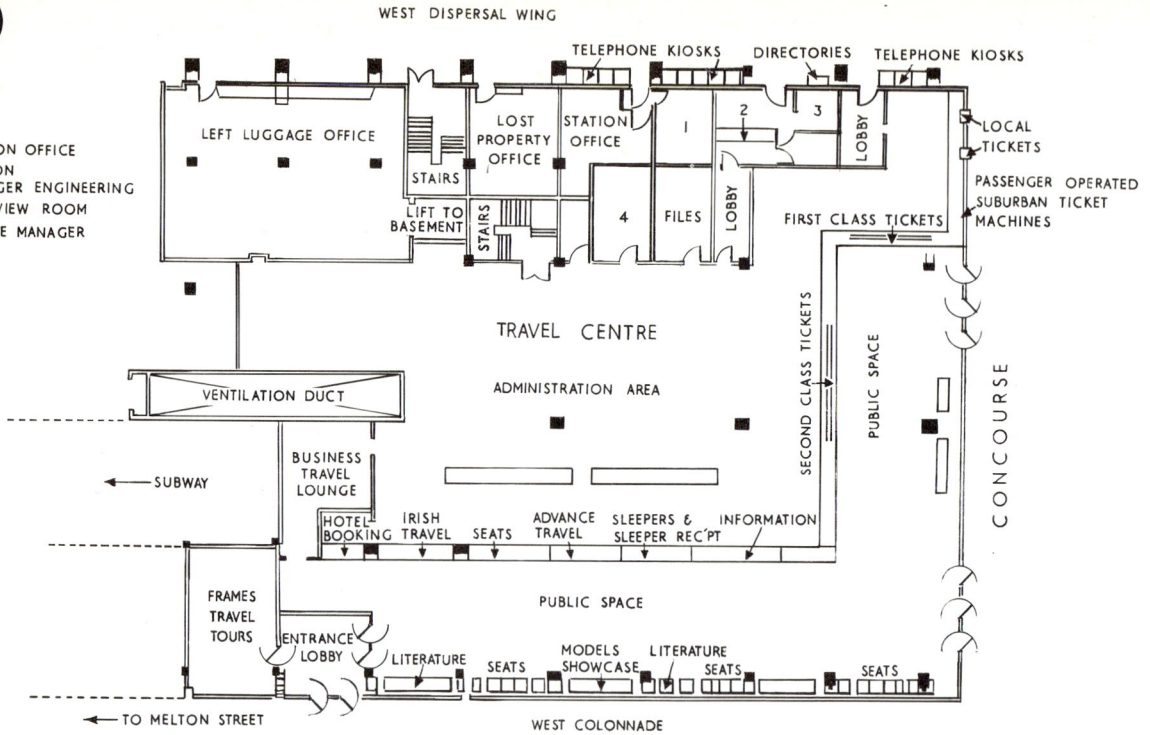

WEST DISPERSAL WING

LEFT LUGGAGE OFFICE

TELEPHONE KIOSKS DIRECTORIES TELEPHONE KIOSKS

LOST PROPERTY OFFICE

STATION OFFICE

STAIRS

LIFT TO BASEMENT

STAIRS

FILES

LOBBY

LOBBY

LOCAL TICKETS

PASSENGER OPERATED SUBURBAN TICKET MACHINES

FIRST CLASS TICKETS

1. STATION OFFICE
2. STATION MANAGER ENGINEERING
3. INTERVIEW ROOM
4. OFFICE MANAGER

TRAVEL CENTRE

ADMINISTRATION AREA

VENTILATION DUCT

SUBWAY

BUSINESS TRAVEL LOUNGE

HOTEL BOOKING IRISH TRAVEL SEATS ADVANCE TRAVEL SLEEPERS & SLEEPER REC'PT INFORMATION

SECOND CLASS TICKETS

PUBLIC SPACE

CONCOURSE

FRAMES TRAVEL TOURS ENTRANCE LOBBY

PUBLIC SPACE

LITERATURE SEATS MODELS SHOWCASE LITERATURE SEATS SEATS

TO MELTON STREET

WEST COLONNADE

Detail plan of the Travel Centre showing disposition of ticket issue, reservations and information services.

taxi and car parks below ground.

Situated to the left hand (west) of the concourse is the Traffic Centre, an entirely new concept in facilities for the convenience of the passenger, providing him with all the main requirements for his journey, such as ticket sales, general and special enquiries, and seat reservations.

On the right hand side (east) facing the travel centre, accommodation is laid out to provide waiting lounges, refreshment bars, toilets, etc. This accommodation occupies an area of about 3420 sq. ft, divided lengthwise by a glass screen and luggage rack into two sections; a feature of the waiting area is the Sprig Buffet Bar.

The information counter of the Travel Centre. The deeply moulded suspended ceiling assists acoustics and houses the ventilating system.

A feature of the waiting room is the sculptural group of Britannia
(by John Thomas, 1849) which is the only reminder of the
old station; its original site can be seen on page 34.
Beyond the division are the Sprig Buffet and the tea bar.

On the first floor facing the concourse are additional facilities which include grill room and snack-bar, licensed bar and high-class toilets ('The Superloo'). Baths and showers are also included.

Access from the concourse to the platforms on the north side is by way of the dispersal area, which is a buffer between the two, and passengers have their tickets checked at the head of easy ramps leading down to the platforms; the latter are under cover of a simple roof system.

Before leaving the concourse, it would seem appropriate to refer to a general impression made by the large areas of glass walling and open planning; this impression is one of light, space and movement.

All public areas of the concourse and the first-floor buildings are provided with

The first-floor grill room and snack bar has tables of elm-laminate tops on polished aluminium pedestals, the upholstery is in black leathercloth and the carpet is of brown tweed. The pine-slatted ceiling is repeated elsewhere at Euston.

background heating by means of warm air introduced around the high main concourse, and by radiant ceiling panels in the low-roofed dispersal area. Warm 'air curtains' also cover the main entrance doors and the openings at ticket barriers. A floor heating system and convector units near the main entrance keep the floor dry.

At the commencement of Section 2, we

The model of Wolverhampton station emphasizes its bold, logical layout.

referred to Britain's early railways, with particular reference to the London to Birmingham line. We described the old classical station at Euston in the days of steam-driven locomotives, which, while opening a new and exciting means of travel, had its own attendant discomforts of hissing steam, smoke, grime, and general untidiness in the stations.

NEW STREET, BIRMINGHAM

Having described the New Euston we should, as a postscript, refer to the provincial terminus of the former London and Birmingham railway. Birmingham New Street station, like Euston has been completely reconstructed – but unlike Euston, it embodies a large and complex commercial development project, covering approximately seven and a half acres.

Participants in the development comprise British Railways, the Birmingham City Corporation and a consortium of Industrial Building Estates, Capital and Property Development, with an Insurance Union.

This early model of the new Birmingham New Street station demonstrates an interesting arrangement of ramps feeding the various levels of the building and spanning the rail-tracks.

The open aspect of the information bureau invites the passenger to enter: Birmingham New Street.

Passengers at Birmingham New Street can reach the trains below this large concourse by means of stairs and escalators. The concourse deck is supported by about 200 pillars and is provided with all passenger amenities as well as a generous supply of telephone booths.

This picture of the concourse at Naples Central station, shows the impressively strong triangular lines of its roof members, which provide a lively contrast to the supporting columns. The concourse was designed by architect/engineer Pier Luigi Nervi, who with his son Antonio has contributed to the success of many fine buildings in Italy and in other countries.

Naples Central station, Piazza Garibaldi. A view from a point near the statue of the great patriot. Here we have a wide and open foreground as a setting for the outspread façade of the long low terminal, whose serried roofs recede towards the tracks beyond. Note how the canopy fascias are angled thus breaking what would otherwise be a long monotonous line.

GERMANY

A survey carried out in 1957 revealed the fact that, although a vast post-war programme for rebuilding had been prepared for West Germany, few completed stations had been built. War may destroy a railway station, for all practical purposes, but it is seldom completely flattened. Rebuilding is therefore a matter of starting afresh or adapting what remains as a basis. Demolition, as we have found out, can be exceedingly expensive particularly in the case where the station had been very solidly built.

The problem as to how stations should be adapted and how entirely new ones are to be built on the old site propounded serious consideration in West Germany, because of its significant position as a pioneer in the development of the *Autobahn* as a national road system. Therefore, competition tended to be very keen between the road vehicle

and the railways. The railways have met this competition in various ways; modernization of existing stations, a limited number of new stations and the electrification of main lines have all been attempted.

An outstanding example of the stations completed in the past decade is that of Stuttgart, designed by Paul Bonatz; this station represents a milestone in the development of railway architecture.

In some other European countries large new railway stations have been built during the 1960s, uniquely, without large-scale commercial development to pay for the cost, although proposals for the reconstruction of the twenty-five-year-old station in Milan may include property development as part of the scheme. The old station was reputed to be out of date by the time it was completed; it contrasts dramatically with some of the more

Urach (Wurttenberg) Germany, 1935, station designed for intense excursionist traffic.

GROUND FLOOR
1 *Booking Hall*
2 *Restaurant*
3 *Bar*
4 *Ticket Office*
5 *Baggage*
6 *Station Manager's Office*

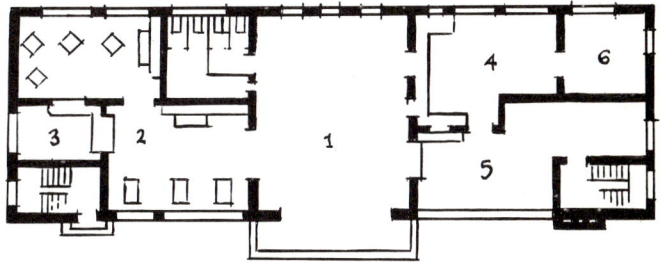

FIRST FLOOR
1 *Two blocks let as staff
living accommodation*
2 *Kitchen*
3 *Upper part of Booking Hall*

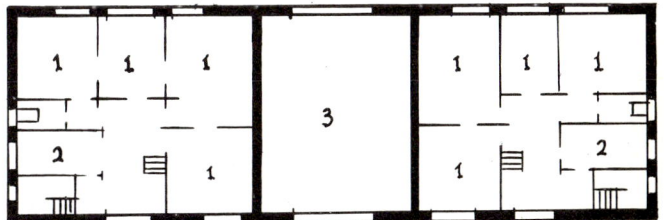

Berlin: Friedrichstrasse Station. 1939

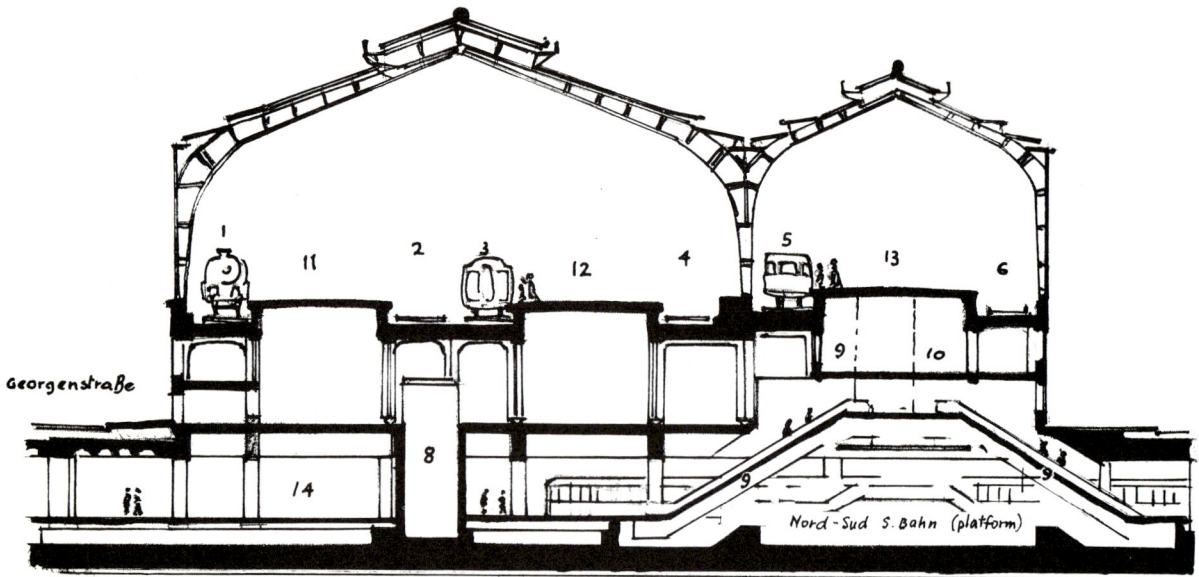

TRANSVERSE SECTION

REFERENCE
1 to 6 Rail Tracks. 8 Passenger Lifts. 9 Escalators.
10 Stairways. 11 Platform from West (main line).
12 Platform from East (main line). 13 Platform for
suburban lines. 14 Nord-Sud S. Bahn (underground).

ZONAL PLAN: *Showing main traffic arteries.*

Stuttgart Hauptbahnan (1911–28). Designed by Paul Bonatz and F. E. Scholer, this station replaced an earlier building (1863–68) designed by Georg Morlok. Its external treatment has a design combining the romantic with 'post-war-modern', this being expressed in a rough-surfaced stonework, and in the restraint of the ornamental detail.

recent stations, for example, the immaculate station in Rome, described later in the chapter, where several other interesting modern stations will be reviewed.

NETHERLANDS

A country where some buildings suffered drastically from invasion and damage throughout World War II was the Netherlands; yet, phenomenally and courageously, she commenced rebuilding and planning ahead soon after the war's ending. An interesting modern building is Amstel station, Amsterdam, designed by M. Schelling. It is a large 'commuter' station in the new part of the town, in an area of expanding development. It is planned on three levels, with particular attention being given to the segregation of the various types of traffic. At the lowest level are trams; cars, buses, and other road vehicles circulate at the middle level, while the rail-tracks are above all.

This recent station at Sloterdijk near Amsterdam, was designed by K. van der Gaast and Can des Grinton.

The unique 'bird-wing' type of roof of Rotterdam station, forms the platform awnings. Designed in the modern idiom by S. Van Ravistign.

The high concourse, with its glazed sides, is visible for a great distance. In its details we have evidence of fine appreciation which is indicated in several other examples in the long line of new Dutch stations. The plan displays a novel layout, based upon a plateau, under which the trams pass in a tunnel. The main feature is, of course, the concourse building.

A more recent station near Amsterdam is at Sloterdijk designed by K. van der Gaast, who in conjunction with Can des Grinton, designed the modern Schiedam station near Rotterdam, one of the most recent 'commuter' stations. The design was largely influenced by the unstable nature of the sub-soil, in that the overall roof is supported by four main vertical members, its chief characteristic is therefore functional; whilst all surplus elements have been

Versailles-Chantiers, France 1934. Architect André Ventre. An example of a European station with a high-level concourse.

A *Access ramp to high level*
B *Booking Hall*
C *Vestibule to exit stairs*
D *Concourse for trains*
E *Control Tower*
F *Vehicle Storage*
G *Local trains*
H *Ticket Office*

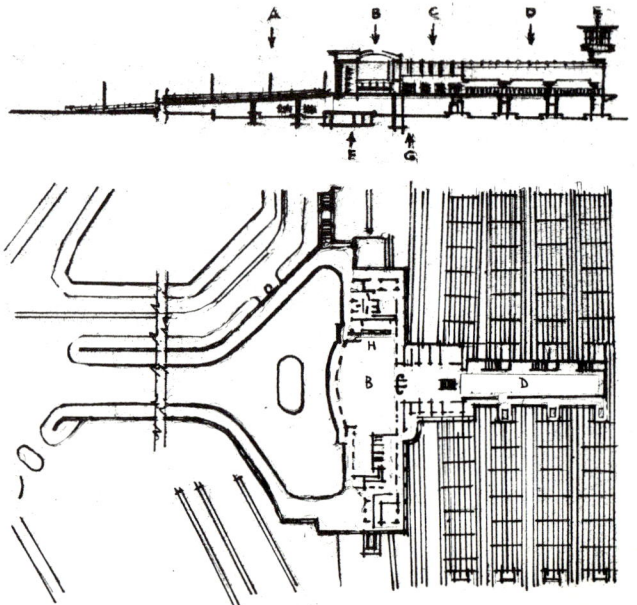

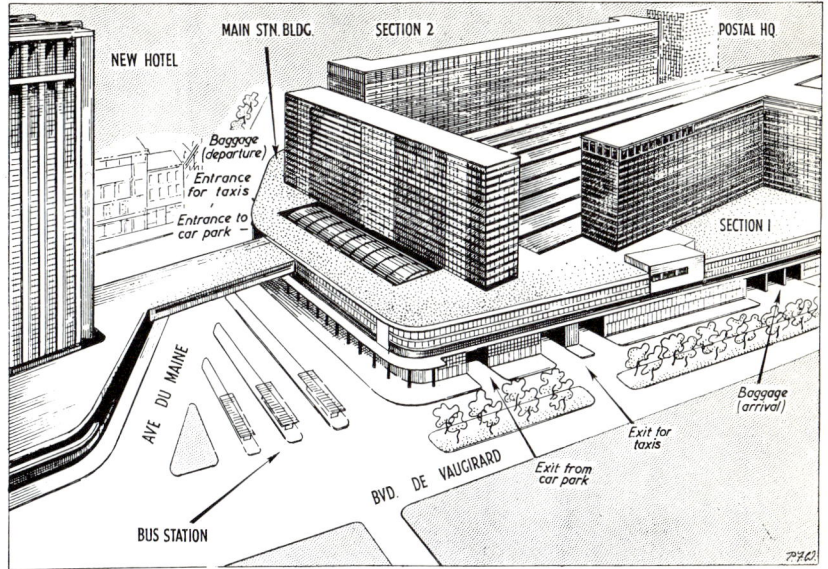

An artist's impression of the completed Montparnasse station, in Paris, with the new hotel on the site of the former terminus.

omitted the arrangement of its form provides a natural harmony.

At Rotterdam there is an interesting station designed in the modern idiom by S. Van Ravistign; the accompanying illustration demonstrates its unique 'bird-wing'-type roof which forms the platform awnings.

In 1960 work started on the new Metro line, from the Netherlands Railway station of Rotterdam, to serve the residential and dock areas south of the river. This scheme is long-term and forms part of a

Plan showing the reconstruction of the new Montparnasse station.

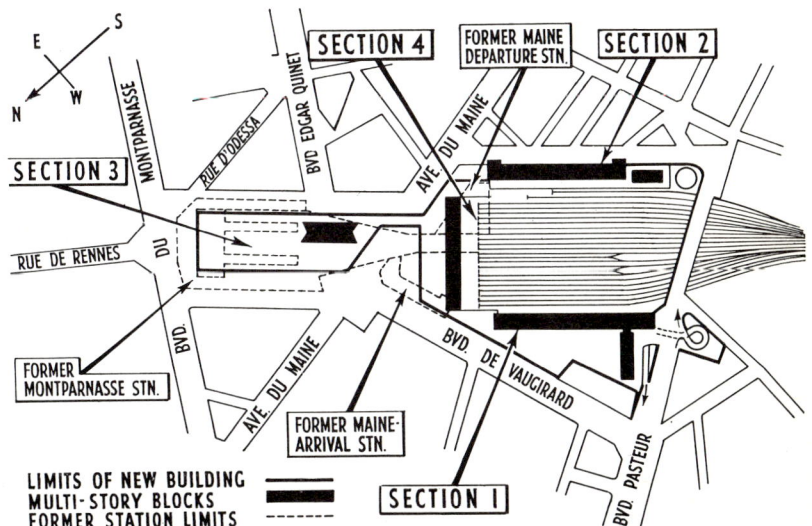

A drawing of the V.I.P. annexe at Florence station (1936). One of the main features of this remarkable station is its 'cascading' roof of glass.

wider undertaking to include the port of Rotterdam. The stations will be elevated to the height of the high-level tracks, while their concourses are to be below.

OTHER EXAMPLES IN EUROPE

The Chantier station at Versailles, built in 1934, which has a counterpart in the United States at Cincinnati, to be discussed later in the chapter. Both these stations have the same principle of passenger flow, but here with a more rectilinear layout and about half the size. A notable feature at Versailles is the control tower at the remote end of the gallery.

Italy provides a crop of interesting stations, mainly the product of the Department of Architecture, in the Ministry of Transportation. Typical examples are: Siena (1936) and Trento (1937). Better known, perhaps, is the remarkable station at Florence (1936) with its glass 'cascading' roof.

Of the many Italian post-war railway stations, which were rebuilt under the

A view of Rome Central terminal across the Piazza dei Cinquecento, showing the ample foreground approach graced by a grove of trees. To the left of the sweeping canopy is the 2,300-year-old city wall, which was incorporated into the design of this modern building.

financial aid of E.R.P. (European Recovery Plan), an outstanding example is the immaculate Rome Terminal, set in the Piazza Cinquecento.

Begun in the late 1930s, it was completed in 1951. Its designers included Montuori and Calini, as chief architects – with the associated architects Castellazzi, Fadigati, Vitellozzi and Pintonello.

Here is an example of contemporary Italian architecture in one of the brightest and most imaginative aspects; both in its setting and architectural composition, whilst providing a very modern and rational building – a respectful link with Rome's former greatness is provided by incorporating the 2,300-year-old stone wall, as a positive part of the design.

The wall is set in an enclave formed by a grassy bank – planted with Ilex trees; this romantic emblem acts as a foil to the huge wave-like sweep of the roof and canopy of the new terminal.

An interesting feature of the canopy is the deep aluminium fascia, which has a finely sculptured bas-relief throughout its length.

Behind the station façade, a 760 ft long office block presents a suitably reticent elevation, which is interesting mainly for its fenestration, which emphasizes the horizontality, by providing an upper and lower window to the rooms on each floor.

The interior of the vast concourse, by reason of its shaped ceiling – following the roof line, presents an expansive and unrestricted visual aspect.

Ten years later (1961) than Rome's terminal, the New Milan station, Porta Garibaldi was built; a forthright and restrained unfussy building with a widely projecting level canopy, supported at high level by nine sturdy beams, boldly displayed; truly, this is the antithesis of the former florid and out-moded station previously described.

The new station is principally a local

The spacious concourse and superb cranked-beam cantilever roof of Rome Central terminal give a feeling of exhilaration.

Venice, Santa Lucia terminal, as seen from the Grand Canal; the plain and simple façade takes on a 'landing stage' image, enhanced by a flotilla of canal-craft.

service terminal but it also handles traffic with Turin and Switzerland.

Before glancing at some of the many smaller stations, we should refer briefly to two recent stations of the larger order.

Naples possesses a strikingly unique modern station of 25 platforms; known as Central Station it is dramatically sited in the wide and deep Piazza Garibaldi.

Integrated with the terminal, and set at an angle is the city bus terminal, whilst facing, on an adjacent side, a multi-storey block of offices – occupied by the Ferrovie dello Stato, Divisional management. Also incorporated is the Station Hotel.

The interior of the station concourse is impressive with V-shaped supports in concrete, multi-grouped and carrying geometrically arranged concrete beams. The

whole effect is reminiscent of Pier Luigi Nervi, whose work abounds in Italy.

Venice provides us with a new station in the Santa Lucia, which faces the Grand Canal; it embodies landing stages along its forecourt. It is a plain and simple building, whose façade towards the canal is appropriate to its surroundings.

Examples of the modern secondary stations on the Italian State railways are many – and of several types: it will be appropriate therefore to refer to three representative types.

Maratea, on the main line from Naples to Messina has a solidly built appearance; an end block of two storeys is topped by a deep fascia which bears the station's name. The single storey platform buildings have widely projecting roofs – whose deep chunky

Maratea is a 'route' station situated in hilly country between Naples and Messina. The character of this station is reflected by the rugged surroundings of the nearby mountain and tunnel frontispiece on the left.

Acquafredda is another example of an Italian 'route' station, and this view, from the forecourt, shows its interesting 'cranked' roof and fascia, the outline of which is indicated by the 'cut-out' windows on the otherwise plain two-storey block.

beams match the sturdy piers – characteristic of the hilly country in which it is situated.

Acquafredda, near Benevento (north of Salerno) in contrast to Maratea – has a cranked roof, the edges of which are turned down to form valances lining with the platform edges. Here, the two-storey block is severely plain and has no trimmings.

The third example is at Fiumicino – a suburb of Rome; whilst having some similitude of Maratea, as to projecting beams carrying the roof; the higher level of the latter, in relation to the glazed room-bays of the building (having a lesser height) gives the impression of a 'floating' canopy over the buildings. By way of contrast the station at Stuttgart provides, in its principal entrance, a remarkable combination of strength and grace.

Fiumicino station, near Rome. The platform building has a straight and thin roof slab resting upon 'chunky' cross beams, the strong deep shadows between the slab and the top of the long windows give it a 'floating' appearance.

127

STATION MASTER — LEFT LUGGAGE — WAITING ROOM — TICKETS & TELEGRAPHS — HALL — STORE

12·00 — 18·00

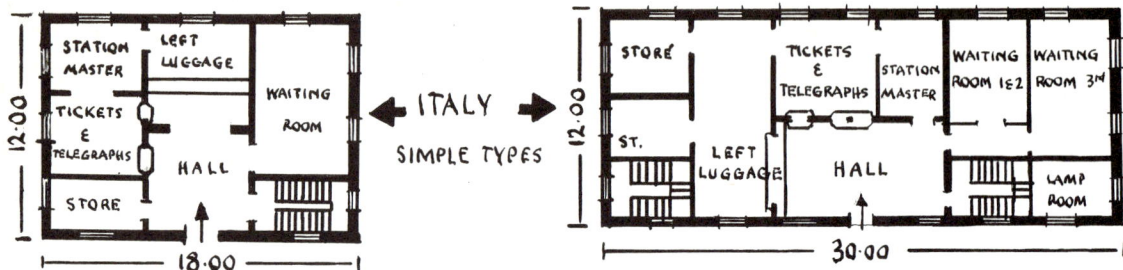

ITALY
SIMPLE TYPES

STORE — TICKETS & TELEGRAPHS — STATION MASTER — WAITING ROOM 1 & 2 — WAITING ROOM 3rd — ST. — LEFT LUGGAGE — HALL — LAMP ROOM

12·00 — 30·00

A selection of European Continental small 'wayside' stations in Italy, Germany, and Bulgaria, which offers an interesting comparison.

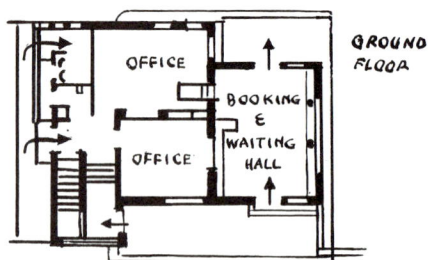

OFFICE — OFFICE — BOOKING & WAITING HALL — GROUND FLOOR

TORINESE ELECTRIC RAILWAY STATION AT ORBASSANO

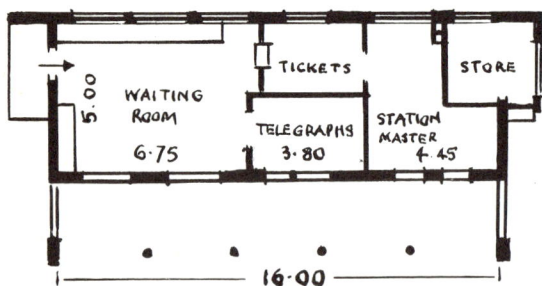

WAITING ROOM 6·75 — TICKETS — TELEGRAPHS 3·80 — STATION MASTER 4·45 — STORE

5·00 — 16·00

S.M. FLAT — FIRST FLOOR

0 1 2 3 4 5

ARCHITECT: N. MOSSO (Project 1934)

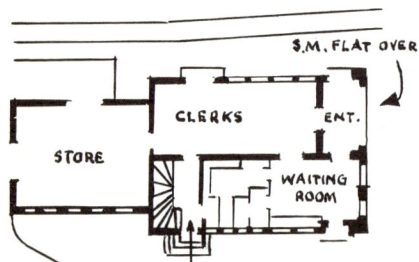

GORNA OVEHORITZA, BULGARIA. ARCH: V. BRANECOFT, 1936

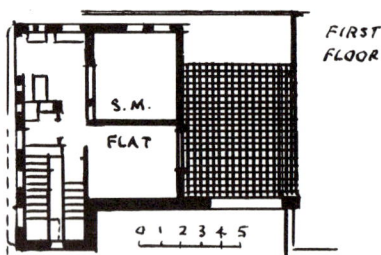

STORE — CLERKS — ENT. — S.M. FLAT OVER — WAITING ROOM

BAERENSTEIN: GERMANY

NOTE: STATION FOR LIGHT TRAFFIC, TICKETS ISSUED ON TRAINS

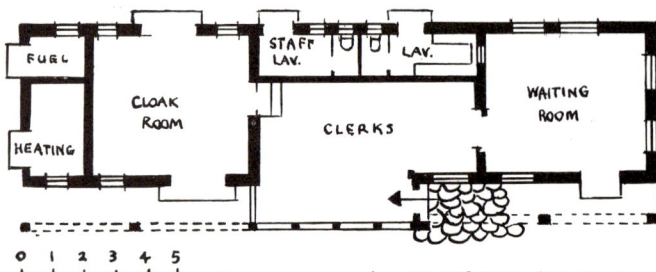

FUEL — CLOAK ROOM — HEATING — STAFF LAV. — LAV. — CLERKS — WAITING ROOM

0 1 2 3 4 5

HEIDENAU: in the ERZGEBIRGE, GERMANY. Example of small mountain type.

Helsinki station, Finland 1904. The architect, Eliel Saarinen, later exerted a great influence upon American skyscraper design.

FINLAND

Helsinki (Finland), 1904, has similar characteristics, but the giant pairs of figures adjoining the entrance somewhat upset the scale. Perhaps it was this Gargantuan urge which led its architect, Eliel Saarinen (1873–1950), to exert his influence later upon American skyscraper design.

Tampere station, Finland 1937, architects: O. Flodin and E. Seppala. A view from the forecourt of this very modern station.

Bussum station, Netherlands. One of several post-war stations, designed by H. G. Schelling, which heralded the beginning of revitalized designs in railway architecture.

Many more railway stations on the Continent might be described, as for instance the very modern one at Tampere (Finland) 1937, whilst Dutch railways display some interesting products of a planning policy, vigorously pursued, even during the late war. Some of these are now arising at Amsterdam: Amstel, Muiderpoort, whilst at Bussum, H. G. Schelling has provided a simple and pleasing modern city gateway. Space, however, sets a limit to the number of examples that we may select from this fertile field.

CANADA—MONTREAL

A comparatively modern example of a medium-sized station is the reconstructed Canadian National Railways' station, Montreal Central, opened in 1943. The project was commenced prior to 1931, after which it was suspended for about eight years, recommenced in 1939 to enable war-time requirements to be achieved, and ultimately completed and opened for service on July 15th, 1943. The architect was John Scholfield.

Bâle railway station, Switzerland, architect, Karl Moser.

This unusual view of Montreal Central station, as seen from the north, provides a somewhat more lively grouping of buildings and platforms than the more formalized façade of elegant neat brick and stone facing the forecourt. Architect: John Scholfield.

The C.N.R. had, at Montreal, the problem of providing at street-level a station concourse and booking offices designed to service the railway which runs at low level. Below the tracks the parcels depot is laid out with a series of escalators, ramped roads, and other connexions.

The site is roughly rectangular, approximately 24 acres (about twice the size of Rockefeller Center, New York) and it is bounded by Dorchester Street on the north, by Lagauchetière Street on the south. Taxis and cars approach the station by roads and ramps on north and south sides, parking areas are provided for them in separate areas, termed 'plazas'. At the western end there is a lead-in road to garage accommodation. The entrances to the station are numerous – there is no main entrance in the accepted sense.

The basis of the plan is an extensive concourse, running east and west at about street-level, spanning the tracks and the platforms below. Down the centre of the concourse there are seven stairways leading down to the train platforms. Four of the stairways are supplemented with reversible escalators. This spacious hall is reminiscent of the Frankfurt Market Hall, the scale is in the same sort of relation. At the western end of the concourse the offices, bureaux, and ticket booths are grouped together with the restaurants. At the eastern end, waiting rooms and lavatories for men and women are situated in the less busy part of the station where the long-distance trains arrive. A special feature of the accommodation for women is the inclusion of a children's nursery fully equipped with cots, toys, and the like, also a room for nursing mothers and a private ward for emergency cases. This section is under the care of a medically qualified matron. The standard of fittings and equipment, including baths, showers, etc., is on a high level.

At this station facilities are provided for

travellers' hand luggage by the 'locker' system of temporary storage, a form which is labour-saving and queue-eliminating. This system has, of course, been in use at London termini for about twenty years.

One of the outstanding characteristics of this concourse is the simplicity of the arrangements and the direct routes for travellers arriving and departing. The passenger has a clear comprehensive view of the whole layout. Stairheads are clearly marked and numbered, each having affixed thereto the principal destination indicator; in addition special roller indicators can be fitted, giving intermediate stopping-places. Linked up with these arrangements there is a loud-speaker address system; the speakers are neatly accommodated at intervals along the ceiling, which is acoustically treated with tiles.

The main structure is a steel frame, with splayed piers at 25 ft intervals carrying the cross-beams and reinforced floor slabs; overhead are two floors of offices. In order to lessen vibration the structure is isolated from the streets and tracks, and in the case of the latter, stanchion bases are separated by cork slabs.

The external architectural character has a certain masterly directness in its set-up and grouping. Built with grey-brown facing bricks it seems to reflect the influence of some of Willem Marinus Dudok's work in Hilversum, and the general mass of the brickwork is relieved by the introduction of stone dressings and sculpture in a natural and successful way, even though with a somewhat heavy hand.

It will be obvious from the illustration of the view from the north-west that something more than a railway station concourse composes the buildings. As in the case of the Grand Central terminal in New York, where the development of overhead sites for revenue – during the financial boom of 1929 – covered all 'carrying charges'. The buildings which have been described were the first stage of a still more comprehensive scheme, which provides for extensive building development for

Cincinnati Union station 1929–33. Architects: Fellheimer and Wagner. An impression of the façade, viewed from the central avenue approach and marked by central fountain. The bold arch is reminiscent of Buffalo Central station designed by the same architects, 1927–29.

revenue, in addition to further station accommodation. We have referred earlier to development for revenue in the case of several of the large stations on the British railway system.

UNITED STATES—CINCINNATI

In 1933 the architecturally spectacular Union Station at Cincinnati, Ohio, designed by the architects A. Fellheimer and G. Wagner, took twenty years to build and involved uprooting five existing stations in the vicinity, together with the regrouping of the whole track system.

The general architectural composition is typical of the North American stations of the larger sort in that it boldly proclaims its presence, taking for its precept that it stands as an enduring advertisement for the railway company in the city. Placed in a liberal setting, for a large terminal forms an eddy in the flow of traffic

through the city, the grand upward curve of the concourse roof which, like the boldly ramped approaches, presents a fitting climax to the avenue approach. Internally the main concourse continues the same broad and bold treatment and has a deep frieze, about half the height of the hall, and is decorated with figures of Homeric stature.

The plan is a remarkable example of the outcome of passenger movement study, and can be compared with its more rectilinear counterpart at Versailles. The shape of the plan conforms to the natural sequence of traffic densities; the maximum space is provided in the vast semicircular concourse at a high level from which the streams flow onwards, by way of a covered gallery and thence by ramps to the platforms, the areas diminishing as the densities thin out.

INDIA—BOMBAY

Before returning home to our own modern contributions, two widely separated examples of types may be compared in the Eastern and Western Hemispheres. First, the new station at Bombay (1930) in a vast sub-continent having over 41,000 miles of railways. The Central station, whilst catering for a large population, is a clear breakaway from the traditional Saracenic style, it has commendable restraint with a sense of scale and breadth of treatment.

The railways of India have been described briefly and in general terms in the Historical Sketch. The remote geographical position of India renders it difficult for Europeans to appreciate the magnitude of the railways linking up the many provinces of that country. Europe and America have provided some well-known examples of railway stations, of the larger sort, but in the case

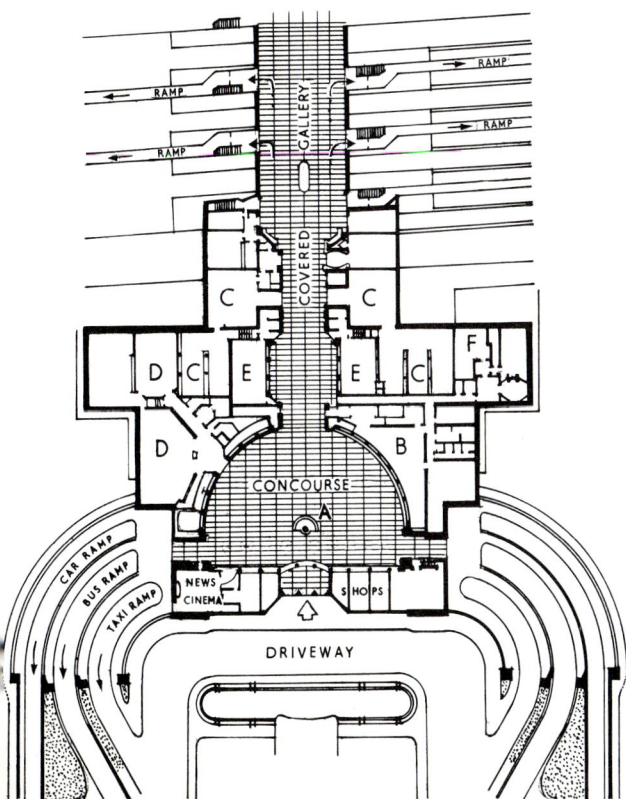

Cincinnati station plan.

A *Enquiries*	C *Waiting & Toilets*	E *Baggage*
B *Ticket Office*	D *Refreshments*	F *Offices*

Bombay Central station, 1930. Architects: Gregson, Batley and King. The monolithic effect of the large plain surface is given central emphasis by the strongly shadowed 'porte cochère' of the main entrance.

of India, whilst towns such as Amritsar, Calcutta, Bombay, Cawnpore, and Delhi are fairly familiar as place-names, their railway stations are less well known.

One of the more important examples is the new Central station at Bombay, terminus for the Bombay, Baroda, and Central India Railway.

It is interesting to note that the inception of this station arose out of conditions, similar in character, if not in degree, to those bearing upon our own post-war planning. The first terminus of the system in Bombay was formerly Grant Road. Following World War I, housing conditions in the Bombay area were difficult, and the Bombay Government initiated a number of development schemes to provide the necessary houses. Part of the scheme was contingent upon the acquisition of land over which the surface line of the Bombay, Baroda, and Central India Railway operated. In February, 1927, the Railway Board sanctioned the scheme for a new terminus, to be known as Bombay Central; the work on the scheme was immediately put in hand. The station was formally opened on December 18th, 1930 by the Governor of Bombay. The architects for the buildings were Messrs Gregson, Batley, and King

who, in the general conception of the composition, have relied almost entirely upon scale and proportion for its general effect. The opening of the station marked the virtual completion of the largest railway terminal executed in India during recent years.

The station is bounded on the south by Bellasis Road, which gives its name to that portion dealing with the suburban traffic on the electrified lines; on the east side, by Lamington Road, from which latter road the main 'in' and 'out' gates open into a large forecourt, which is axially sited with the concourse and entrance hall.

Among those who have seen the station, it is generally conceded that the Bombay Central could not be mistaken for anything other than it is, and the illustration confirms this. It fulfills the first canon of good craftsmanship, the true expression of purpose. There is also an air of spaciousness and a sense of scale in the general outline which are at once pleasant and effective. That it is so effective is due largely to the wisdom of the railway management in realizing that the treatment of the precincts of a monumental piece of architecture is no less important than the building itself. The vista through the central main gate, with the station entrance as its focal point, the extensive lawns on each side, and the 'quadrangle' effect given by the flanking wings, strike a new note in railway architecture not previously attempted in India.

The elevational treatment stands as a striking example of restraint, a characteristic rarely found in other examples of modern architecture in Bombay. The limited extent to which ornament has been incorporated in this building, therefore, enhances its significance. The external walls, following the trend of the time, are constructed of concrete; scale and proportion providing the controlling elements of the design. The main central block, embodying the entrance, is monolithic and it makes no attempt to appear as other than a vast pylon; contrast is obtained by constructing the walls of the flanking buildings with coursed pre-cast concrete slabs. Whilst the predominant lines of the composition reflect a severely Classic predilection, the architects have, in the treatment of the *porte-cochère* and the larger windows, introduced subtle nuances associating the building with its Indo-Saracenic background in a delicate but nevertheless convincingly successful manner.

SOUTH AFRICA—JOHANNESBURG

Johannesburg calls to mind images of diamonds and gold. The city's history has been romantic and distinguished. With a population of over one million its development has been lateral, spreading over the yellow soil of the Transvaal and growing outwards rather than upwards. Its tallest building is 23 storeys high; the trend is towards a complex of buildings, two theatres and a great office building for the Transvaal Provincial Administration, which is to be 45 storeys high and 5 ft taller than the Hertzog Tower, a television transmitting tower, standing on the Witwatersrand, the long ridge of earth and stone, which is a background to the city. Future prospects for the city seem to suggest that the ultimate trend in building will be upwards.

One of the finest buildings of recent times is the new (1957–8) railway station, designed by the architects Kennedy, Furner, Irving-Smith, and Joubert. It is a finely proportioned building of great distinction and masterly composition. The site is an open one, facing a well laid out forecourt, as will be seen from the accompanying photograph.

Johannesburg station, South Africa, 1957–58. Architects: Kennedy, Furner, Irving-Smith and Joubert. A finely proportioned building of great distinction and composition.

Customs House, King's Lynn, 1683. Architect: Henry Bell. An elegant little building designed for Sir John Turner, who was a patron of Merchants and Traders. The Customs Offices were on the upper floor, the arcaded ground floor being later filled in.

CHAPTER 12 EUROPEAN SEAPORTS

We may consider it probable that the first human inhabitant of this country walked over a 'land-bridge' from the continent of Europe. However, throughout the times of which written records exist the whole story of British history has been dominated and conditioned by our island situation. For about 2000 years we have depended on an ever-increasing degree on sea communications and overseas trade.

From the days when Roman merchantmen sought the shelter of Southampton Water or, negotiated, not always successfully, the treacherous channels of the Thames Estuary, the ports and harbours of our shores have played a large part in our national life. Ever since that time, Dover, commanding the shortest sea passage, must have been the favourite landing and embarking place for sea travellers to and from the Continent. No other major port, save only London, can trace so continuous a development from the earliest times to the present day of continental travel.

Other Channel ports have their historical association. Were this a history of transport it would be interesting to follow the early sea voyagers' progress in their 'tall ships' from Bristol, Plymouth, and many other seaports, as they sailed to the South Seas or to the New World.

In Britain the elements of the early seaports were simple – a harbour and a Customs House. Among the latter the best-known example is at King's Lynn, a relic of a bygone style. It was built in 1683 by Henry Bell, and is a rectangular structure with a steeply pitched roof; its pedimented turret forms a notable landmark in the old market town.

EARLY DEVELOPMENT

As in the case of railways, the steam-engine was the deciding factor in the development of passenger-ship service, but here the paddle-wheel and later the screw-propeller were the dominant feature. Modifications in the construction of ships followed the introduction of new fuels, and these were reflected in the changing layout of seaports. The increasing size of ships also demanded new-style berthing piers and port buildings; all requiring careful planning and thought.

In considering the layout of a seaport and its essential buildings, we are faced with the obvious fact that the geographical aspects of the coastline, the tidal facilities, and the landward approaches for road and rail services will determine the shape and linkage of the buildings. The harbour board also has its requirements. In this connexion it will be convenient to review briefly the main types of business operating at the port, with particular reference to sea-routes and cargo; together with the manner of passenger arrivals.

We are here mainly concerned with those ports whose main activity is to provide facilities for passengers – incoming and outgoing. Many ports in Britain deal with exports and imports of cargoes of all descriptions, which are the life-blood of our commerce in our trade relations with the world. While the planning of those ports and docks involve warehouses, tranship sheds, and the like, which are also within the province of the architect, it is obvious that we should select our examples from those ports which are of interest primarily to travellers. It will therefore be both useful and convenient to compare two of the major seaports on the south coast; Southampton and Dover.

They represent two varieties of sea travel; Dover is mainly for local Channel services to France and Belgium by the short routes, while Southampton is the gateway for trans-ocean travellers. Since Dover is the most important and busy port for the continental traveller, both for businessmen and tourists it will be appropriate to refer to its main characteristics here.

THE PORT OF DOVER

The volume of traffic at Dover is intense, and the services for its passengers threefold; for in addition to regular pedestrian travellers, for whom the cross-Channel service is provided, the alternatives of car-ferry and train-ferry are provided.

Dover Harbour block plan showing the harbour area in relation to the Passenger Terminal Building and Car-ferry.

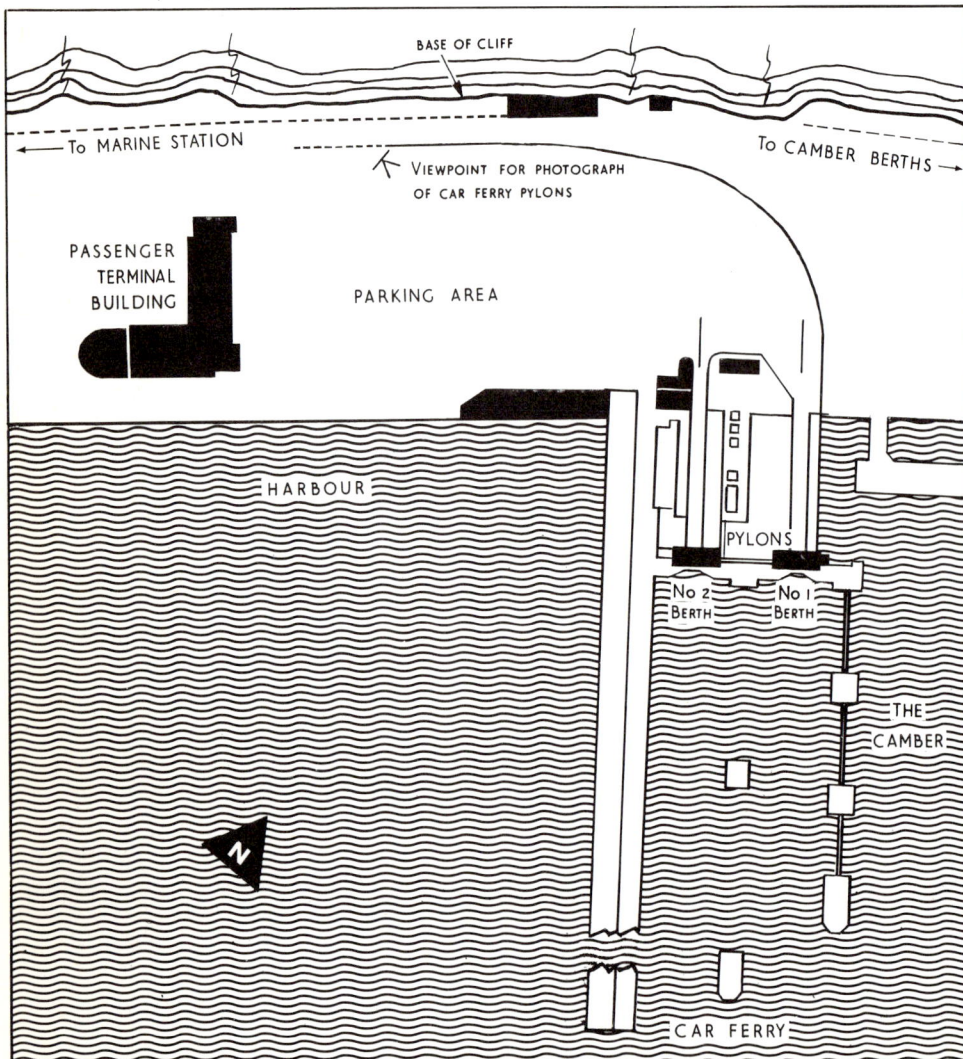

Dover Car-ferry terminal. View towards the entrance pylons through which cars pass to the boat-ferries.

The docks at Dover were opened originally in the early part of the nineteenth century; for a long time they continued as the single place for the embarkation of passengers at that port. As ships increased in size, and the volume of passenger traffic grew, the size of the port became inadequate. The accompanying layout plan of the harbour indicates its present accommodation, and includes the post-war reconstruction of the car-ferry buildings, adjoining The Camber on the East side of the harbour.

In the latter half of the nineteenth century the Admiralty Pier, at the western side of the inner harbour, and the Prince of Wales Pier, dividing the inner and outer harbours, were both built; this increased the berthing space and, for the first time in the history of the port, the easterly drift of shingle was effectively checked. The landward end of the Admiralty Pier was subsequently widened to 350 ft and the former narrower pier was extended 2000 ft seawards to line up with the south breakwater. In 1914 the Southern Railways

Marine terminal station was constructed on the widened Admiralty Pier. It is from this pier that the train-ferry services operate; normally a night service of sleeper cars, leaving Victoria, are conveyed across the Channel to Dunkirk or other continental ports.

THE TRAIN-AND-CAR-FERRIES

With the completion of the large marine terminal station, with its two island platforms capable of serving four trains, the long-suffering Channel passenger's stock grievance was removed or alleviated. Adjacent accommodation included waiting and refreshment rooms, toilets, and concessions for kiosks of the usual order. The four steamer berths on the Admiralty Pier, screened from the weather, serve the Marine station.

As part of the Marine project, a concrete viaduct was built to cross the railway, immediately adjoining the seaward side of the tunnel-mouth, which provides a clear run to the station quay; the viaduct has provided easement for the continuously increasing number of motorists, proceeding to the car-ferry.

At the north-eastern corner of the outer harbour, lie The Camber and the car-ferry terminal, established prior to World War II; it links Dover with Calais, Boulogne, and Ostend. In 1939, approximately 31,336 motor vehicles, both cars and coaches, were ferried by specially constructed ships across the Channel from Dover; by 1952, the numbers had increased to 100,993. This spectacular increase made necessary a new layout of the associated buildings, which were built in conjunction with the Dover Harbour Board who had established the car-ferry.

GENERAL LAYOUT

Several new conditions predicated the layout of the new accommodation. Firstly there was the need to regulate traffic between the incoming car park, the main reception building, and Customs. Secondly it was necessary to provide protection at the main public entrance of the reception building, and this was achieved by placing it to the leeward, in the angle formed by the two wings of the L-shaped structure. The main axial lines run roughly north and south for the office block, and east to west for the public waiting hall, refreshment room, and buffet. In line with the latter axis is a long 'island' petrol filling-station, the long sweeping curve of which greets the incoming driver on his way to the reception car park sited in the shelter of the two wings of the main building.

The architects of the general site were J. M. Wilson, H. C. Mason, and Partners, who also designed the first group of ancillary buildings; these comprise the reception area and the petrol filling-station.

The second group, mainly devoted to the Customs Examination Hall, was the work of the Chief Engineer of the Dover Harbour Board.

The reception buildings provide accommodation on three floors; access stairways are naturally placed adjacent to each of the entrance porches; the principal entrance from the car park is at the north-west junction between the two wings; the subsidiary entrance is at the northern end of the office block.

On the ground floor, the public enters through the principal porch, sheltered from the south-west winds; it gives access, both to the large vestibule and hall, as well as to the long lobby serving the offices of the operating companies. The main hall is the circulating area for the ground floor, in conjunction with the large vestibule; it provides access to the buffet wing. A feature of the main hall, is its sense of space – achieved by its ceiling height of 30 ft – and its full-height glazing on one side. At the east end of the hall, screened by telephone booths, is sited the toilet accommodation. Opening out of the hall, on its north side the wide, long lobby, mentioned above, extends along the wing.

On the first floor each wing contains groups of offices; the northern wing accommodates harbour officials, landing officers, immigration and surveyor's departments; there is also a suite for water-guards. A central corridor runs the length of this wing, joining the stairs at one end and linking the offices over the buffet block, by way of wide balconies overlooking the main hall. In the buffet block the stairs ascend to a second floor.

The internal layout on the ground floor creates an impression of fluidity and spaciousness throughout; this is achieved,

Dover Marine station for the train-ferry. Customs Hall interior.

partly by the floor treatment providing continuity with the long counter in the operating companies' lobby, and partly by the immense area in the hall fenestration with the mural relief-map, adjoining the balcony at first-floor level.

The structure is steel-framed, with the stanchions carried down to individual foundations.

The cladding to the steelwork is concrete, fair face; the walls are cavity brickwork, with brick or artificial stone facings. Reinforced concrete is used throughout in the construction of floors and roofs, the latter being insulated and asphalted. The ceilings are boxed down to conceal the main constructional beams in the important public rooms, an arrangement which enables recessed lighting-fittings to be used.

The general external character of the reception building is a well-balanced composition, where the structure is emphasized by the fenestration, whose rugged simplicity is appropriate to its situation – facing across Dover Harbour. The end wall of plain Hammill facing bricks, contrasts well with the adjoining elevation, and acts as a respond to the glazed apsidal end of the refreshment buffet.

Axially aligned with the refreshment buffet wing, and adjacent to the reception car-park, are the clean sweeping lines of the filling-station, whose mushroom-shaped ends, echo the adjoining wing of the reception building. This island filling-station stands upon a wide base, which follows the line of the overhanging roof. The construction is reinforced concrete; the roof-form is of 'butterfly' section. The total length is 128 ft, the width is 38 ft.

CUSTOMS EXAMINATION HALL

Cars, with their passengers, pass from the reception park to the Customs hall, where immigration and other formalities are completed prior to embarkation. The building in which these inspections are carried out, is approximately 218 ft long and comprises two bays of a width of 95 ft.

Dover Car-ferry passenger reception buildings 1952, designed by J. M. Wilson and H. C. Mason. The bow-fronted restaurant abuts against the two-storey main building, beyond which is the Customs building.

The span is formed by galvanized steel trusses at 12 ft 6 in. centres, supported on steel stanchions.

The examination 'islands' are arranged on the floor in a herring-bone pattern, which allows the cars to flow through the hall, and avoids both reversing and congestion.

The Chief Engineer's Department, Dover Harbour Board, was responsible for this building.

SOUTHAMPTON

Before entering the Harbour from the landward side, it will be appropriate to refer to the railway terminal station, as designed by Sir William Tite in 1839 – to serve the Port, in its earlier form and contrasting remarkably with the spectacular development since the great shipping lines transferred from Liverpool to the Channel ports.

The town and port of Southampton are of ancient lineage, though much of the old has disappeared through war damage. Still remaining are some stretches of the medieval wall and the fourteenth-century Bar Gate, the Norman House, the Wool House, and

Southampton Railway terminal, designed by Sir William Tite in 1839, still survives in a new and expanding era.

142

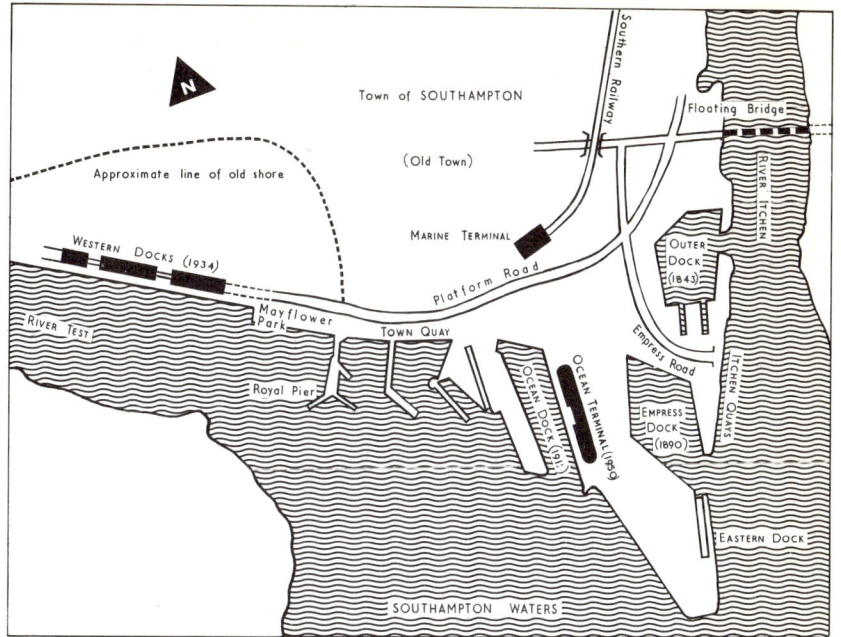

N

Town of SOUTHAMPTON

(Old Town)

Southern Railway

Floating Bridge

Approximate line of old shore

Marine Terminal

Platform Road

WESTERN DOCKS (1934)

Outer Dock (1843)

River Itchen

Mayflower Park

Town Quay

Empress Road

Itchen Quays

River Test

Royal Pier

Ocean Dock (1911)

Ocean Terminal (1950)

Empress Dock (1890)

Eastern Dock

SOUTHAMPTON WATERS

Southampton Harbour. The block plan shows the general layout of the harbour facilities, from the docks and wharves at the western end, by the river Test, to the river Itchen at the eastern end. This adjoins the spectacular Ocean Terminal serving continental and transatlantic sea routes.

a few other ancient buildings. It is interesting to recall that in 1620, from the West Quay, the Pilgrim Fathers set sail for Plymouth in the *Mayflower*, on the first stage of their voyage to America.

Just as Dover is pre-eminent in cross-Channel passenger traffic, so Southampton has a near monopoly of ocean-borne passenger traffic. Maps of the harbour, published before 1927, show a broad tract of mud-flats to the north-west of the Royal Pier, two miles long and half a mile wide.

The growth of shipping required more accommodation for the expanding numbers of ocean liners; consequently the Southern Railway management decided to extend the port of Southampton by reclaiming the area of the waste mud-flats. As a first step, a sea-wall was built, behind which millions of tons of the mud, dredged from the river Test, were deposited, so that an area of about 400 acres, on a frontage of one and a half miles, was reclaimed over a period of about six years.

It will be appropriate to refer here to the sketch layout map of the port area. The position of the docks, piers, and quays are

shown in relation to the landward rail terminal and the river Itchen. The lines of the main sea-routes are also indicated.

The King George V Graving Dock is sited at the western end of this extensive wharf. Eastward along the wharf the Union Castle Line operates ships to the port of Cape Town, South Africa. As an indication of the volume of traffic on the western wharf there are about eight large tranship buildings. At the eastern end of the wharf, and about 400 yards from the break in the line of the sea-wall, the Royal Pier projects its odd, irregular shape. It was originally constructed in 1833 to accommodate the steam-packet boats, operating to and from the French coast, the Channel Islands, and the Isle of Wight. More than 600,000 passengers use the pier annually. The Harbour Board owns and operates the Royal Pier and the adjacent Town Quay, but not the docks, these are owned and operated by the British Transport Commission.

The Town Quay attained its present size at the end of the nineteenth century; it deals with a considerable amount of coastwise traffic, special boat-trains run from

The Ocean Terminal building at Southampton, opened in 1950. Built for the 'Queen' class of leviathan liners.

Waterloo to connect with these Channel steamers. Throughout the year, at least three services a week link Southampton with the Channel Islands and the French coast (with le Havre throughout the year and with St Malo during the summer season). The dock-side buildings are well equipped with amenities for the travellers; these include comfortable reception and waiting halls, apart from the regulation offices.

The transatlantic traveller embarking on the 'Queen' class liner is provided by the Southampton authorities with accommodation comparable with that he will have on his journey across the sea. Inevitably the arriving passenger's impressions are influenced by the means provided for his easy flow through the official formalities, the comfort and convenience of the refreshment rooms, the spaciousness of the greeting area, and the efficiency of transfer to road and rail transport.

TERMINAL BUILDINGS

The Ocean Terminal was planned and constructed to meet all these needs. The preliminary idea was outlined in 1907, when the White Star Line transferred its New York services from Liverpool soon after the closing of the Liverpool Cotton Exchange, caused by a business depression. After four years, in 1911, a dock was constructed and was designated the White Star Dock, and remained so called till 1922; the location was between the Town Quay and the river Itchen wharves.

Owing to delays caused by World War II, and the subsequent amount of reorganization of port services, so essential a preoccupation in the shipping world, four years had elapsed before the new Ocean Terminal was opened, in 1950. The capacity of the new terminal is such that the largest ships afloat can be accommodated; approximately 2000 passengers are received, together with their luggage, at one time, and ninety minutes from the time of berthing the first boat-train of passengers is normally ready to leave for London. Two full-length trains can be available at the platforms, adjacent to the quay, where all the

The passenger reception hall of the Ocean Terminal conveys an impression of 'ship architecture' and decor.

facilities for handling luggage, mail, and cargo are distributed to their required positions. For passengers departing by car, access roads, car-parks, servicing, etc., form part of the layout.

Accommodation has been planned in a building two storeys high and has public facilities, similar to those at airports, which will be described later. On the ground floor at dock-side level are the baggage room, bonded stores, cargo berths, and the railway terminal; also, of course, there are garage accommodation, car-parks, and road connexions for vehicles.

On the upper floor, the main circulating areas and Customs examination halls are situated; adjacent to them accommodation is provided for both passengers and visitors. For the use of the latter a visitors' balcony extends the whole length of the terminal. Lateral and vertical communication between floors and ship is provided by means of six telescopic gangways, which are both flexible and mobile, and can be so aligned that passengers may enter the ship doorways from the building at first-floor level. Vertical travel between floors is facilitated by four escalators and twenty-one elevators.

The passengers' accommodation at first-floor level is planned upon a natural sequential grouping. The traveller enters by the gangways either of two large waiting

The quayward façade of the passenger reception hall, used principally by P & O liners, was opened in 1960. The overall impression is of deck lines, emphasized by the balcony at the 2nd floor, and by the wall treatment which suggests a 'system' design layout.

The most recent addition (1967) to the Port of Southampton is the passenger waiting hall at Princess Alexandra Dock. The roof rises in a parabolic curve, supported by laminated timber frames which spring from floor level.

The interior of the main hall, with its clear and uncluttered floor space, contrasting with the strong structural lines of the roof ribs.

halls, around which are grouped writing rooms, telegraph offices, banking facilities, and information bureaux; other amenities including refreshment rooms, comfort rooms, etc., are provided. We have already referred above to the vital nucleus of the Customs examination hall, adjacent to the main circulating areas.

The general character of *décor*, furnishings, and detailing has been motivated by the high standard set in the ships of the 'Queen' class. Here the traveller has the opportunity to appreciate the fitness of purpose of the planning, as well as the more personal welcome of the terminal staff.

Newhaven Car-ferry Terminal building, designed by N. Wikeley, 1965. A modern building with all the characteristics of 'system' design; being plain and severely rectangular it relies for contrast on vertical boarding bound together by broad bands at floor and roof level.

*Genoa Maritime Terminal, designed by Luigi Vietti, 1933. The plan is
'U'-shaped, with the Customs hall forming a link between the two arms, one
of which is for passenger and the other for office accommodation.*

*Block plan showing the layout of Genoa harbour. The city has retained its
Roman and medieval importance, and is still the foremost Italian port serving
Algiers, N. Africa, and New York via Gibraltar.*

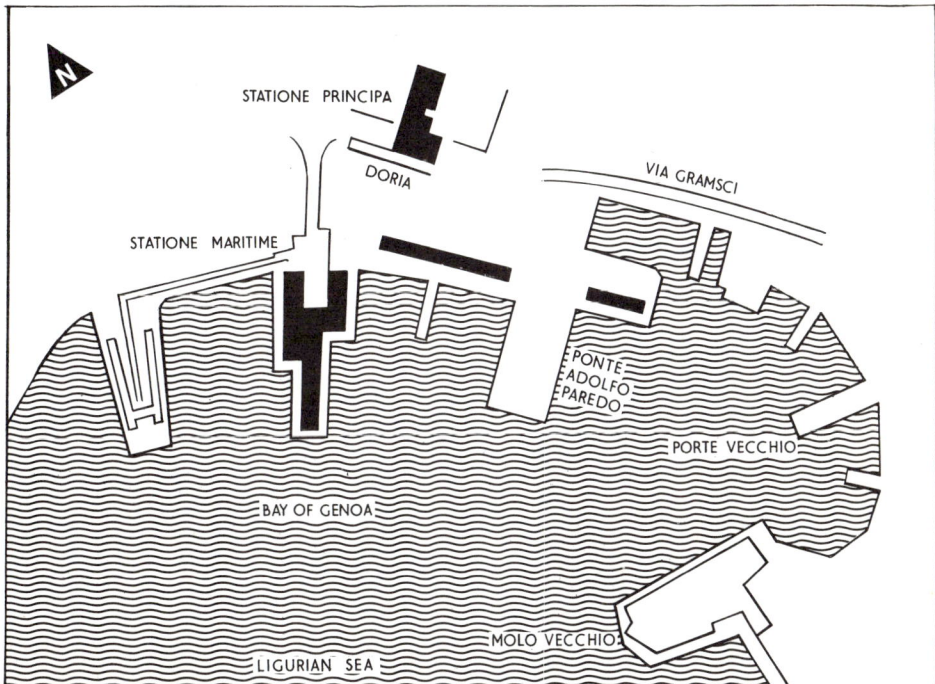

N

STATIONE PRINCIPA

DORIA

VIA GRAMSCI

STATIONE MARITIME

PONTE
ADOLFO
PAREDO

PORTE VECCHIO

BAY OF GENOA

MOLO VECCHIO

LIGURIAN SEA

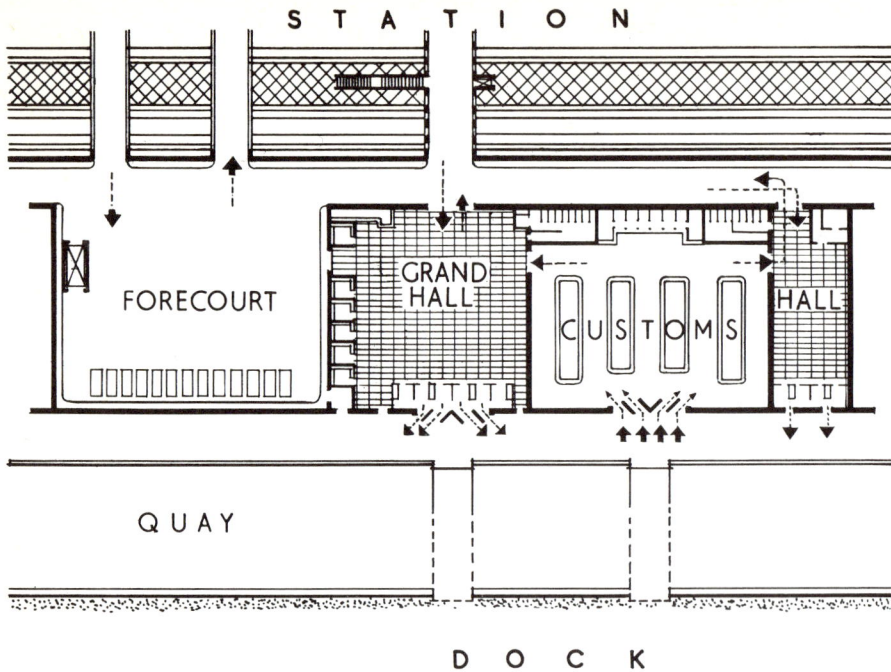

STATION

FORECOURT

GRAND HALL

CUSTOMS

HALL

QUAY

DOCK

Le Havre Maritime Terminal, designed by Henri Pacon, 1933. The rectangular layout indicates a straightforward co-relation between the rail link and port transit operations.

Block plan of Le Havre harbour, France's main transatlantic seaport adjacent to the river Seine, linking the ocean with Rouen and Paris. After extensive World War II damage it was reconstructed to the plans of Auguste Perret, and includes an offshore heliport.

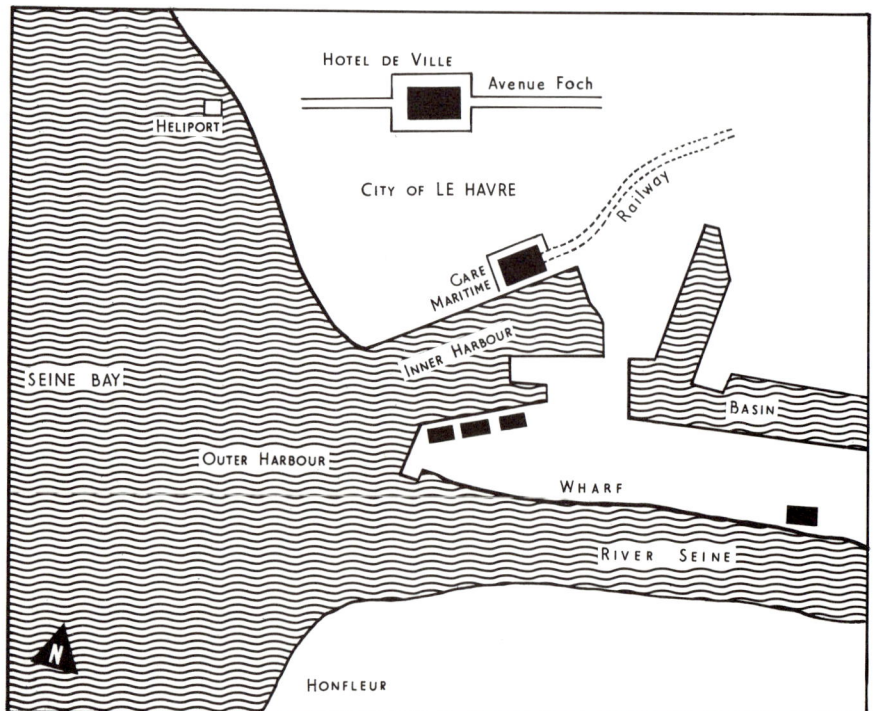

HOTEL DE VILLE
Avenue Foch
HELIPORT
CITY OF LE HAVRE
Railway
Gare Maritime
Inner Harbour
SEINE BAY
BASIN
Outer Harbour
WHARF
RIVER SEINE
N
HONFLEUR

BOSTON

We have examined some of the seaports of Britain and examples from two other European countries; it is logical, therefore, that we should follow the sea-lanes of the big ships to their destinations in the western hemisphere, and particularly those in the United States.

It will be appropriate to commence with Boston, whose location holds an advanced position on the American seaboard.

Historically, the first recorded mention of this harbour relates to Samuel de Champlain, who sailed into the 'Baie de Isles', during his early seventeenth-century explorations of the northeastern coast. Since its earliest days as the focal settlement in the Massachusetts Bay Colony, the fortunes of Boston have been linked closely with commerce. Its importance is that it has easy access to Connecticut, Rhode Island, New Hampshire and Vermont.

The block plan indicates the strategic features which contribute to the successful functions of the port, and with the adjoining airport of Boston-Logan (International) it emphasizes the wisdom of integrating road, air and sea services.

At Boston all marine terminals shown on the plan are served by railroad with branch tracks on the wide wharf aprons. The port is also linked by an expressway road system, bringing direct communication to the Far West to Chicago, and to the southwest via New York and Philadelphia.

Among the numerous piers shown on the harbour plan are the more important examples – such as Castle Island Terminal (formerly built by the U.S. Government during World War II) and now modified as

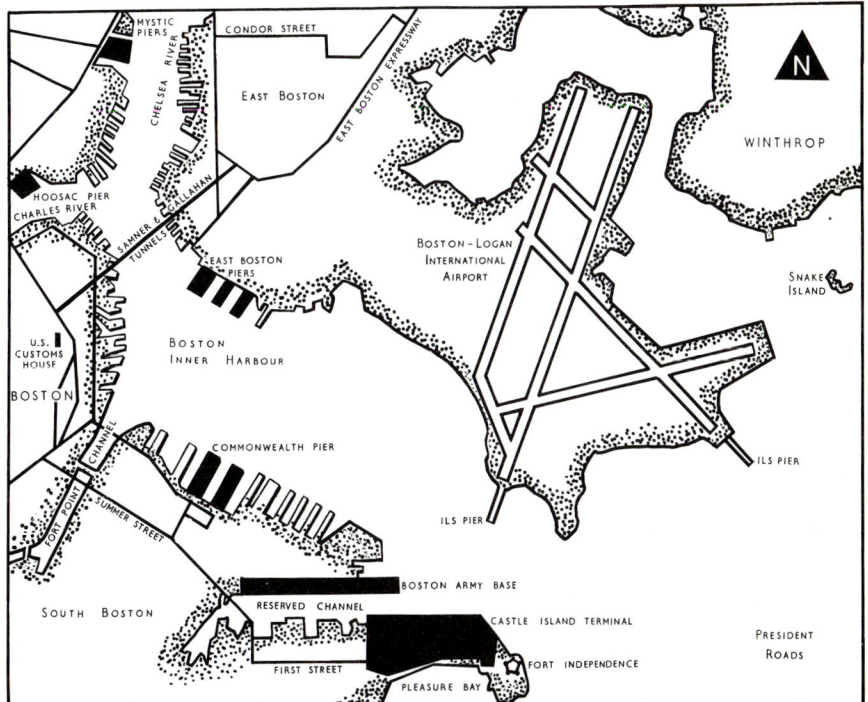

The block plan of Boston harbour showing its relationship to airport and road systems.

Commonwealth Pier 5, Boston, built by the state in 1912. Here the S.S. UNITED STATES *is being manœuvred by tugs into its berth.*

one of the busiest in the 'Hub' waterfront, and the Boston Army Base, now embodying a large dry-dock.

On the west side of the Inner Harbour, Commonwealth, Hoosac, and Mystic piers are the principal and outstanding examples. On the north-eastern side, the three East Boston piers are sited adjacent to the Boston-Logan International airport; apart from the influence of the Airport, they serve as important railway connections to the Penn Central.

We may now refer particularly to the large Commonwealth Pier 5 built by the State in 1912, with a second-level viaduct and continued development by the Massachusetts Port Authority. Its most recent acquisition is the large $75,000 passenger lounge illustrated by two photographs, one of which shows the fine view over the harbour skyline.

The Port of Boston is in the process of transition, keeping in step with the changes in concept and design to meet the progressive needs of reawakened maritime traffic, both passenger and commercial. We shall find a similar condition present in the Port of New York, to which we will now refer.

The passenger lounge on Commonwealth Pier 5, was built and opened in 1967. Vinyl-covered walls and wall-to-wall carpeting are provided in the lounge which is adjacent to the area dealing with tickets and customs inspection.

An excellent panoramic view of the Boston skyline, harbour and Logan International Airport may be enjoyed through the large glass windows of the passenger lounge.

The port of New York from the air. Manhattan separates the Hudson (left) and East rivers (right). Governors Island is in the foreground.

NEW YORK

We can now describe briefly and illustrate the collateral seaport of New York, famous Atlantic terminal for leviathan liners passing to and from European ports.

The geographical position of New York, at the entrance of the Hudson-Mohawk Gap, is conditioned by the only complete opening affording access to the Great Lakes and to Montreal to the north.

From the point of view of interior transport communications, no less than two canals and four main railways run down the Hudson valley, with the Expressway road system extending to and beyond Kennedy Airport, to serve both the city and seaport of New York.

An appreciation of the extent of New York's harbour and dock facilities will be stimulated by the adjoining view from the air. The usefulness of many piers and docks which have served shipping lines for several decades, has diminished through deterioration. This condition was apparent to the authorities in 1966, and revealed by expanding passenger and commercial pressures.

A new interest has been stimulated by the port's activities in September 1968. The Port of New York Authority announced the project for building a consolidated passenger ship terminal on the Hudson river from 46th to 50th streets. It was planned to start work by the end of 1968 or early 1969, with an anticipated completion in three years.

Among the main provisions are six new berths for liners and super-liners; and a modern system for processing baggage

Plan for the new consolidated Passenger Ship Terminal on the Hudson river mid-Manhattan.

through Customs. The buildings include a new lounge and other accommodation for passengers and visitors, with direct vehicle access to the piers, together with large parking areas.

The main plan embraces three 'finger' piers, each with four levels, linked by the main mass of the 'headhouse' at the shore end to provide one large consolidated terminus.

The accompanying photographs show both the lateral layout and a 'cut-away' drawing of the structural build-up of the units of accommodation, with the means of access for passengers and vehicles.

By way of contrast to the Atlantic ports of America, it will be interesting to compare the layout and facilities of the land-locked port and harbour of San Francisco on the Pacific coast.

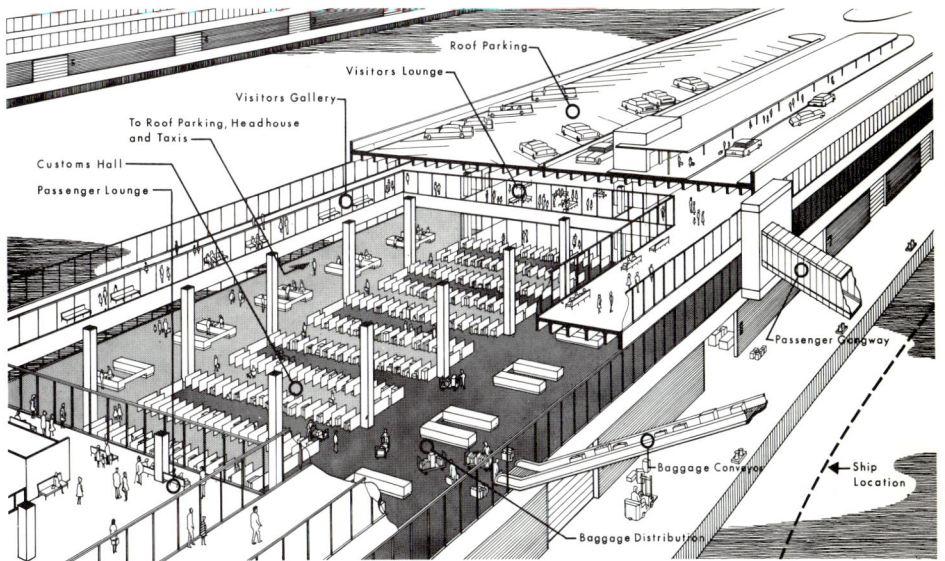

A cutaway view of passenger and customs facilities, for the new Ship Terminal in the port of New York.

An aerial view of the port and city of San Francisco, with its famed Golden Gate bridge, upper left. Mission Rock Terminal, and one of the port's largest piers are shown at lower left.

SAN FRANCISCO

The coastal area of San Francisco has been referred to as the Mediterranean Region of America; the estuarial waters contained within a landlocked deep-water bay, with a series of subsidiary bays, forms a very large natural and safe harbour.

The principle approach to the bay from the Pacific is through a strait, well known as the Golden Gate – its mile-wide passage is spanned by the celebrated bridge.

Historically San Francisco dates back to 1769, when it was sighted by the Spanish Captain Don Gaspo de Portola; later, in 1775, Lieutenant Juan Manuel de Ayala of the Spanish ship SAN CARLOS sailed into San Francisco bay through the Golden Gate and anchored off Yerba Buena Cove.

From that time the harbour developed slowly until 1849, when the discovery of gold in California stimulated its rapid expansion. In 1863 a Board of State Harbour Commission was set up to administer and expand the harbour.

Studying the aerial photograph of the port and harbour, one is impressed by the eight-mile long waterfront, and the numerous 'finger' piers and wharves, all served by the State belt railway – whose branches traverse the wharf aprons. The Freeway road system from the mainland provides looped and ramped connections.

154

Architecturally, the landward entrances to the piers are unified by a façade, the central feature of which is illustrated by the drawing on the following page.

At San Francisco, as with the Atlantic ports, the need for reconstruction and development to cope with expansion exists, and, in this respect, at Ferry Building, the Port Authority has a project for the construction of an office building-garage complex which is being developed for providing accommodation for 1,000 cars.

The roof of the building will provide a landing and take-off terminal for the San Francisco helicopter service. Other features of the project include restaurants and the landscaping of the waterfront.

In the above consideration of some of the foremost American seaports we have referred to their neighbouring airports, and as a natural sequence, in Section Four of this book, we shall be dealing with air travel and the buildings associated therewith.

Army Street Terminal, San Francisco, a 68-acre site providing more than a million square feet of covered storage space. Note how the road and rail services are integrated into the design.

Typical entrance to pier
buildings, Port of San
Francisco.

The new Islais Creek Grain Terminal at San Francisco. The storage and loading capacity
is 2,000,000 bushels and 1,200 tons per hour, respectively.

Vancouver C.N.R. Terminus, Canada

The inter-relation of sea, rail and road services is easily appreciated from this layout plan of Vancouver Ocean Terminal. Passengers proceed between the port and the railway station by way of Granville Street. Vehicular traffic makes use of the same approach. There is plenty of room for future expansion, either of the existing pier or by building a second one to the south.

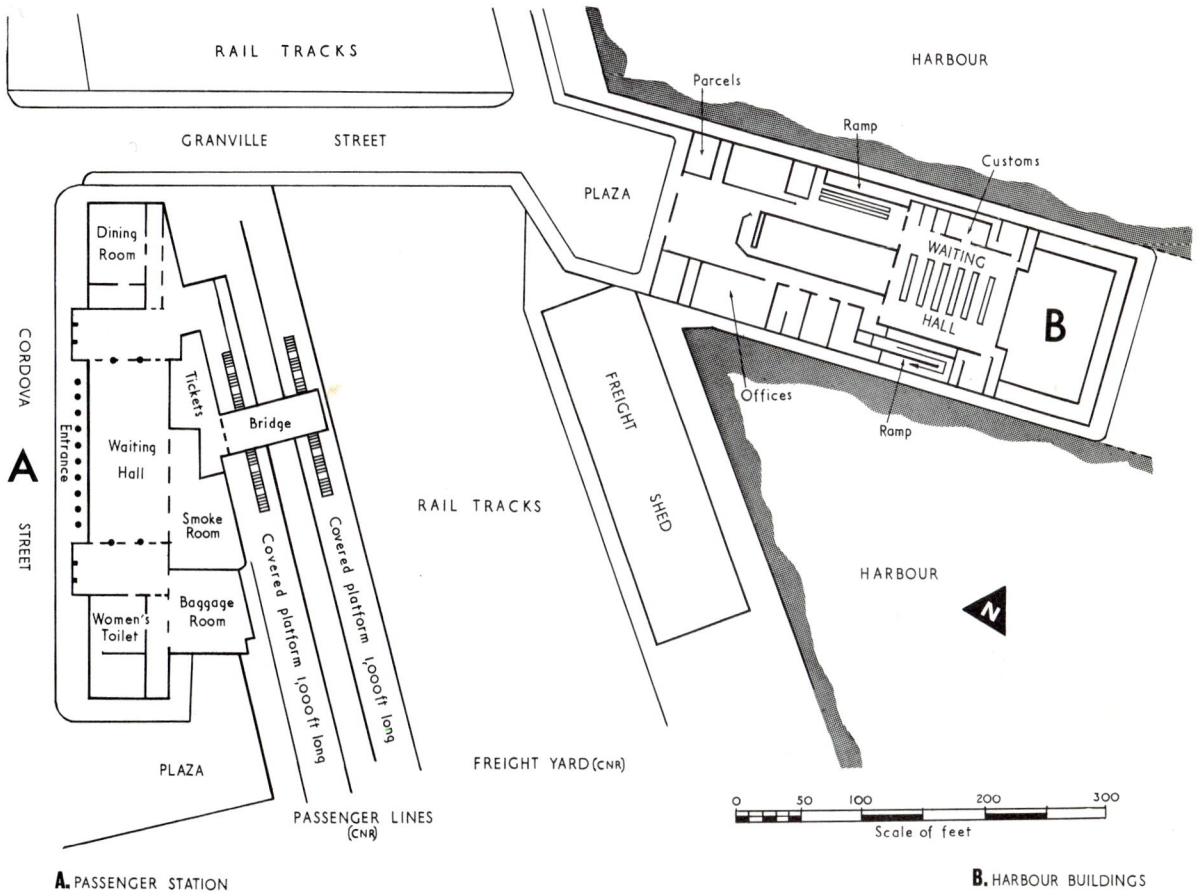

RAIL TRACKS

GRANVILLE STREET

HARBOUR

Parcels

Ramp

Customs

PLAZA

WAITING HALL

B

Dining Room

Tickets

Bridge

CORDOVA STREET

Entrance

Waiting Hall

Smoke Room

RAIL TRACKS

FREIGHT SHED

Offices

Ramp

HARBOUR

A

Women's Toilet

Baggage Room

Covered platform 1,000 ft long

Covered platform 1,000 ft long

N

PLAZA

FREIGHT YARD (CNR)

PASSENGER LINES (CNR)

0   50   100   200   300
Scale of feet

A. PASSENGER STATION

B. HARBOUR BUILDINGS

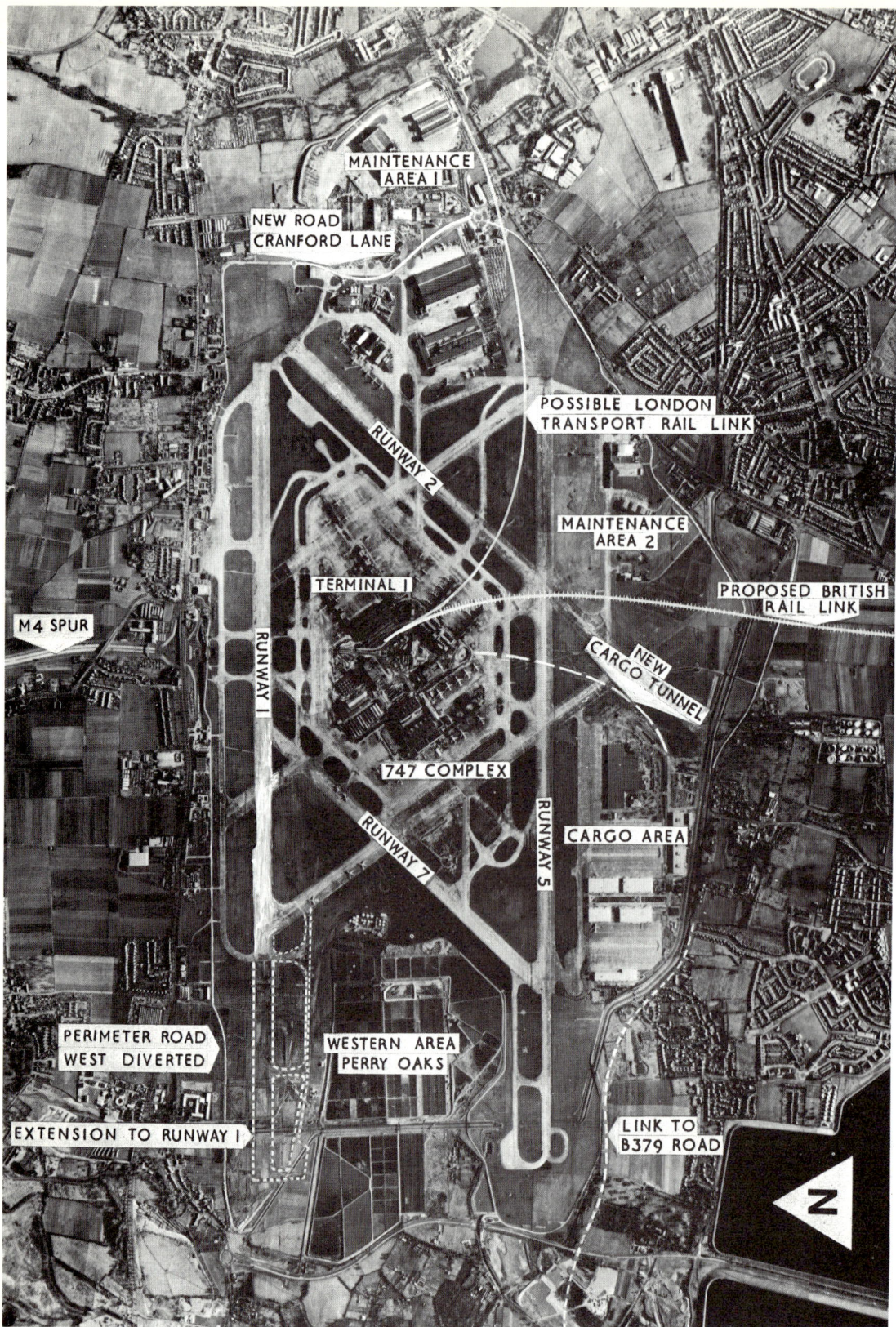

London Airport, Heathrow, from the air showing the central area complex, runways, and the subsidiary buildings, with the proposed new road and rail links superimposed.

CHAPTER 14 AIRPORTS IN GREAT BRITAIN AND THE CHANNEL ISLES

INTRODUCTION

Airborne . . .! What a thrill – those first lurching leaps into an unsteady glide – for a furlong, then for a mile or more in the days when the American brothers Wright, in their bamboo-and-wire contraptions, were making essays into flight, in that far-off time before World War I. Following these pioneers, the intrepid Frenchman, Louis Blériot soared across the English Channel in 1909, and thus initiated an 'air bridge' over the sea. Today, in a very real sense, the aeroplane knows no barrier.

Travel and exploration have long been fruitful subjects upon which to dream and speculate, and much that we now take for granted must once have its origins in an idea to 'span the globe'. Fortunately, perhaps, men have constantly wanted to know what lay beyond the horizon. In flying, however, soon after we take off our horizon is no longer a defined line closing our terrestrial field of vision. As we ascend, below and ahead, a panorama of 'land-forms' and sea falls away into mistiness, and we pass through the cloud base into the stratosphere on our way to a distant airport.

ESTABLISHMENT OF AIRPORTS

The development from wartime and strategic flying to civil-passenger and commercial purposes posed many planning problems – not the least being the siting of airports. From 'take-off' to 'touch-down', a whole series of pre-planning schemes was generated. It embodied the combined efforts of the operating companies, aircraft designers, airport control and 'met' stations – far and near.

The problems of road and rail links with airports had to be resolved in a manner which would not heighten the growing congestion in road transport, and to do something towards bridging the time-element, which may be the deciding factor for the air traveller, relying on speed for the whole journey. In Britain in certain instances overhead mono-rail links with British Rail terminals may provide an answer.

When an airport is being designed many kinds of 'land-form' conditions, quite apart from the direction of prevailing winds and other meteorological considerations, will influence the choice of site. The most necessary being that it should be level in two dimensions, a requirement obviously not demanded in road, railway, and canal planning. Topographically the selection tends, of course, to be very restricted in the neighbourhood of large cities.

The airports of Britain may be classified broadly under two headings: coastal and interior. Briefly, the coastal land-form is the more general, and examples may be found on Islay (Port Ellen), and on Tiree, both off the west coast of Scotland, and at Ronaldsway on the Isle of Man.

The 'land-forms' are of various kinds; at Liverpool (Speke) for instance, it is built mainly on blown sand; at Blackpool (Squires Gate) it is entirely so. Prestwick is virtually confined to a raked (shingle) beach. By contrast, Cardiff (Rhoose) and Lympne are both coastal sites, yet they are separated from the sea by cliffs of 200 ft and 300 ft respectively.

In the case of inland (interior) airports, London (Heathrow) is the most notable; it occupies one of the broadest stretches of the 'Taplow Terraces', the type of terrain considered most suitable.

METEOROLOGICAL CONDITIONS

Whilst meteorological conditions in the vicinity of airports are held to be of paramount importance, many of the problems they can introduce – e.g., high-altitude siting and high-temperature take-off are not normally encountered in Britain. On the other hand, local climate does play an important part in airport location, particularly so where visibility is affected by the incidence of fog and industrial smoke. It is generally found that the prevailing south-westerly winds make a situation in the south or west of a large city preferable to one in the north or east. This is confirmed by London, Croydon (now disused), Manchester (Ringway), Glasgow (Renfrew), and Edinburgh (Turnhouse). An exception to this is Elmdon, sited to the east of Birmingham. Here the reasons are two-fold; the southern and western environs of the city are much more hilly, and in places they are affected greatly by industrial smoke.

Of the London group of airports, only Stansted lies outside the south-western sector and is situated about 33 miles in the opposite direction from the centre. The land communications between airports and the urban centres which they serve are of the greatest possible importance. Inevitably, unless rail and road transport connexions can operate upon a fast and efficient time schedule, the value of air travel as a time-saver would be cancelled out. Obviously also, economic efficiency at airports will be influenced by the means provided for rapid and comfortable ground transport.

CONDITIONS FOR PLANNING

Past experience indicates that no airport has yet been built which provides efficiently all the services required of it. It therefore follows how vitally important it is that all future airports benefit from the short-comings of their predecessors; they must be planned with the utmost care and foresight. Such features as take-off and landing safety, passenger comfort and convenience, ease of access and transfer, increasing traffic in all media, and technical advance in aircraft design, all must be taken into consideration.

While an airport is generally planned as a complete unit, it will obviously consist of two main elements. Primarily, the main runway and the tracks linking the take-off and landing path with the service buildings. Secondly, the arrangements for the control and loading of the aircraft, the maintenance, and the Customs facilities which will form part of the group of 'service buildings'.

There are naturally different permutations between these two main elements. On the one hand one might find simple aerodromes with the minimum of ancillary buildings. On the other, larger airports affect much greater areas of land outside their immediate perimeters – land for roads and for railways, not to speak of areas suffering from the widespread curse of noise from giant aircraft.

AN EARLY EXAMPLE

One of the most widely known of early aerodromes in Britain was that sited at

Croydon in Surrey; built by the Air Ministry between the years 1926 and 1928, it was a massive and inelastic structure. Although the Ministry was roundly criticized for building upon so great a scale intended to meet expected future development in air travel, the critics were, however, confounded.

In actual fact, traffic expanded beyond expectations, so that about six years after the airport was opened it was endeavouring to cope with traffic far beyond its planned capacity. To alleviate its shortcomings, it became necessary to provide increased facilities for passport and Customs examination, for office accommodation, and additional hangars. It was here that the defects of the inelastic, massive nature of the structure became more apparent.

Croydon having outlived its usefulness as an airport is now being devoted to housing and urban development.

THE NEW APPROACH

During the comparatively short period of seven years, following the building of Croydon aerodrome, a very considerable amount of thought and investigation was expended upon the subject of the layout and design of buildings to accommodate new types of aircraft, and providing for the development of expanding air-routes, both in global travel and on interior services. It will, therefore, be appropriate to examine and compare the development of various types of airports in Britain.

THE FIRST GATWICK AIRPORT

One of the first of the new types of design, was the novel circular layout at Gatwick, built in 1935 adjacent to the Southern Railway, with a subway connexion. The chief point about this plan, here illustrated, was its flexibility; it

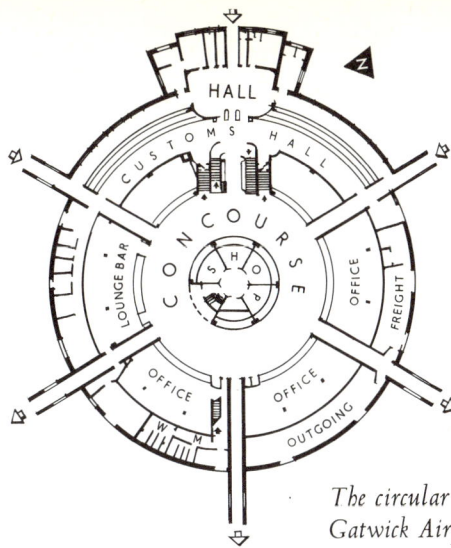

The circular layout of the first Gatwick Airport, 1935.

embodied a series of five, radiating, telescopic covered ways or corridors (known as 'fingers'). These fingers moved on rails, so that the aircraft could be manœuvred into an easy position for disembarkation. Passengers proceeding by train passed to the railway subway by way of the main concourse.

After serving its purpose for nearly twenty-seven years, it became outmoded and a new structure was built in 1962 – designed by Yorke, Rosenberg, and Mardall; this time, a rectangular block, to be illustrated and described later.

It will be very interesting to compare the shape of the first Gatwick Airport with that of Helsinki built in 1938, three years after. The similarity will be apparent, having regard to a slight variation in the projecting wings indicated in the Finnish design, on the adjoining plan.

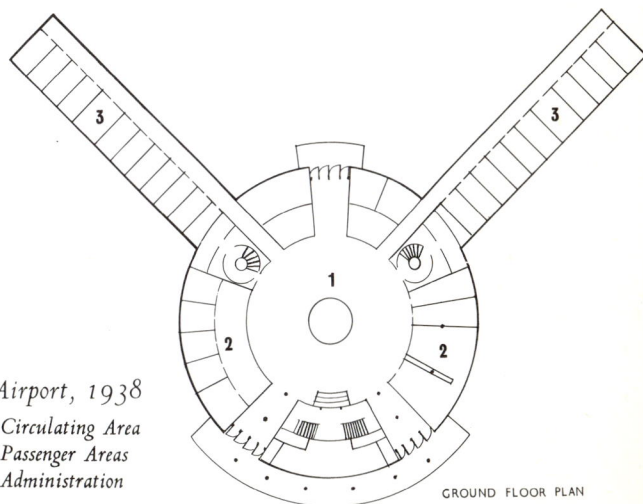

Helsinki Airport, 1938

1 *Circulating Area*
2 *Passenger Areas*
3 *Administration*

GROUND FLOOR PLAN

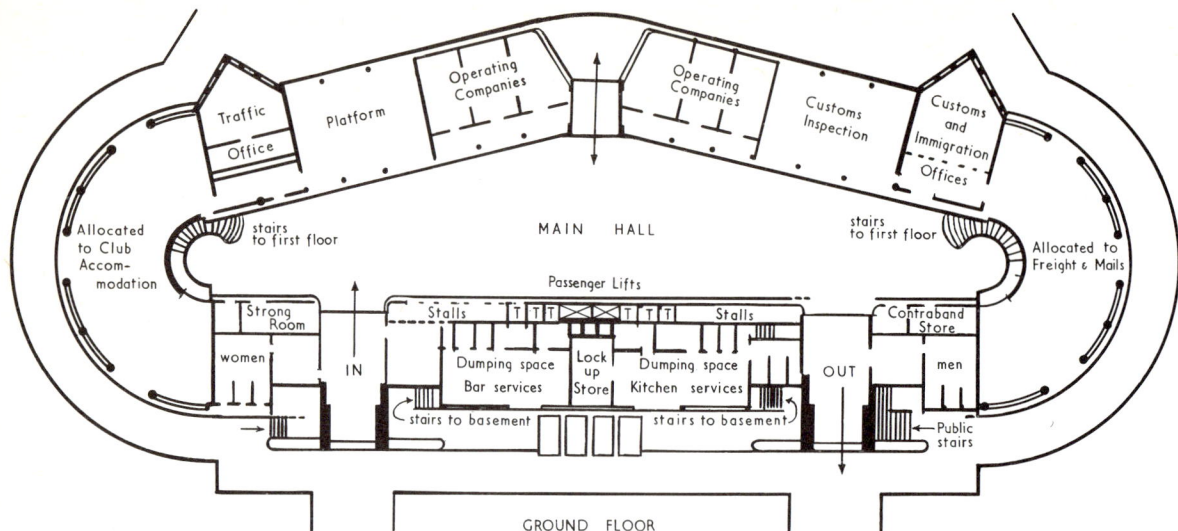

Plan of Elmdon Birmingham Airport Terminal, 1936.

ELMDON AND JERSEY AIRPORTS

Two medium-capacity airports, both similar in shape, were built in 1936, one year later than Gatwick, upon a plan which was mainly 'linear' as opposed to circular. Both these airports were designed by Graham Dawbarn; one is on the outskirts of Birmingham, at Elmdon, the other in the Channel Isles, on Jersey. A comparison of the two plans indicate some elements of the layout, whose outlines are reminiscent of the wing of a plane of an earlier age, with the pre-jet profile.

In the case of Elmdon, the simplest in outline, the overall length is about 250 ft ('wing tip'), with a maximum depth of 90 ft along the central axis. The central area on the ground floor, comprises a large waiting hall, which rises up through the first floor; surrounding it are the airlines' offices, etc. At each of the ends, which are semicircular, there are staircases leading to the galleries at first-floor level, which in turn give access at each end to a covered way and an open terrace on the air side; on the land side, suites of office accommodation link the two galleries, which latter also give

access to toilets at each semicircular end.

On the second floor a centrally placed restaurant has at one end a lounge and, at the other a café; on the land side of the restaurant are sited the kitchens and services. Passenger lifts, centrally placed on the land side of the office block, serve all floors.

Jersey Airport, which to a large extent caters for holiday traffic, has a somewhat more rectilinear layout than Elmdon, particularly in respect of the central administrative block. On the ground floor, the main hall is disposed centrally upon the axis of the principal entrance, which is flanked by the main staircases, and which forms a link between the incoming and outgoing flow. On one side are grouped the Customs office with its examination and immigration hall, fitted with a long baggage counter; in addition there is a waiting room and further accommodation to handle freight, mail, and stores. The other side of the waiting hall is devoted to incoming traffic. Facing the Customs office are those of the operating companies.

A secondary hall leading into it is used for

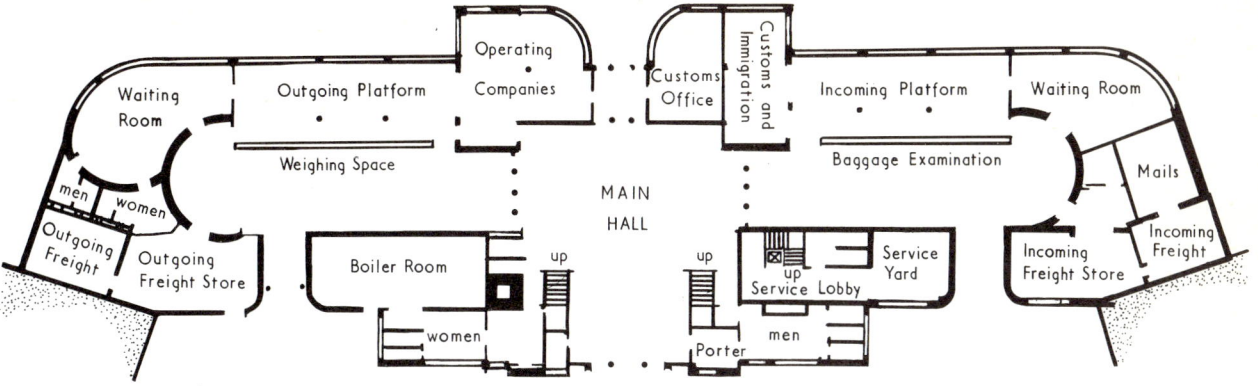

Plan of Jersey Airport Terminal, 1936.

the outward flow and has the weighing counter; the platform has its attendant waiting room and toilets. Finally, adjoining the entrance are outgoing freight office and store. The overall dimensions of the central block of the terminal buildings are 230 ft long and 70 ft from back to front.

THE NEW GATWICK AIRPORT

The earlier Gatwick circular airport extant in 1935, after serving its purpose for nearly twenty-seven years, was unable to cope with the rapid development of air travel.

The New Gatwick, designed by F. R. S. Yorke, E. Rosenberg, and C. S. Mardall in 1958, in an entirely different form as shown on the layout plan, (p. 161); it is in the form of rectilinear blocks linking the Southern Railway station and projecting a long two-storey 'finger' 900 ft out to the airfield apron.

In the first stage of the development it was intended to be used for Channel Island services, the flights of various charter companies, and as a relief to London Airport whose weather is frequently adverse, while at the same time is favourable at Gatwick. Later all tourist-class European services could be transferred here.

Although 27 miles from central London, Gatwick can be reached quickly by train, in about the same time that airline coaches from the West London Air Terminal take

Platforms and stairways of Gatwick Airport railway station, which lead directly to the Airport Terminal.

An aerial view of the New Gatwick Airport, designed by F. Yorke, E. Rosenberg, and C. S. Mardall, 1958, showing the closely connected railway station, the partly constructed Terminal building, and the ramped roads with open 'roundabout' leading from the motorway to the first-floor entrance (concourse).

to reach London Airport. The railway station adjoins the new terminal building, and the main London–Brighton road passes through it, a fly-over giving direct access to the entrance at concourse (first-floor) level.

The system of Customs control is similar to that operating at the Paris (Orly) Airport whereby, on arrival passengers give up their baggage to the Customs officers, but do not themselves pass through the Customs control until immediately before boarding the aircraft. During that period of waiting they are able to avail themselves of the various 'comfort' facilities in the building, such as restaurants, shops, etc., in the company of their friends or relatives who may have come to see them off.

TERMINAL BUILDING

The terminal building is a simple rectangular structure, about 350 ft long and 130 ft wide. The ground floor, pierced by the main road and the airport perimeter roads, is occupied by the baggage-

New Gatwick Airport. First-floor level, main concourse.

The enquiry desk and departure hall at the B.O.A.C. Victoria Air Terminal, London.

handling area and G.P.O. block. At concourse level are the check-in desks and airline offices, the Customs hall and search rooms, the immigration hall, departure lounge, bank, post office, and various shops and inquiry bureaux. The Customs waiting hall occupies the mezzanine floor; on the second floor a restaurant is situated, where it overlooks the apron on the air side. Adjoining the restaurant, *en suite*, are a lounge and bar, together with a lounge and café overlooking the concourse.

Basically the terminal building consists of a floor at concourse level carried upon large reinforced concrete columns; the roof is of steel construction supported by lattice girders in spans of 80 ft.

The cladding of the building was designed to provide for the combination of flexibility in layout and speed in construction. To achieve this a system of steel mullions, with glazing in wood frames, was employed.

With the exception of the topmost storey of the control tower, the basic

B.O.A.C. Terminal building, Victoria, London.

structure comprises a reinforced concrete framework, the surface of which is textured with a fair finish left from the shuttering. The infilling panels are of local stock brickwork. The upper (octagonal) observation storey is constructed in welded steel frames, carrying two skins of heat-absorbent glass in the form of an external skin of 'antisun' glass, and an inner skin of double-glazing hermetically sealed glass, the inner and outer glazing separated by a space of 4 in.

The glass-covered walk-way from the terminal building is virtually a series of bridges with spans of 40 ft between welded steel portal-frames, an arrangement permitting flexibility for ground operations.

DEVELOPMENT AT GATWICK

From the completion of the first stage in 1958, when the terminal building became operational, the rate of increase in traffic revealed that an acceleration of the building programme had become necessary and, six years later, towards the end of 1964, the size of the airport had doubled.

Apart from the progressive design of the buildings, a noteworthy fact, in respect of co-ordination, was that the Ministry of Works and the Ministry of Transport and Civil Aviation were persuaded that the architects should also be responsible for the design and control of all furniture and fittings, to ensure that the whole and all its parts should be related and reflect the dominant character of the project.

NEWCASTLE AIRPORT

As part of a programme to assist development in the north-east of England, the Woolsington Airport at Newcastle has been reconstructed and enlarged. The limited runway of 5300 ft was, as a first step,

enlarged in 1964 to prepare for the new airport. The project, designed by York, Rosenberg, and Mardall, the architects of Gatwick Airport, have at Newcastle provided a very comprehensive layout, compact in design, to meet a probable demand for 500,000 passenger movements a year in the 1970s. The design has many of the characteristics of Gatwick, but lacks its direct rail connexion, although its road approaches are comprehensive. Similarly the concourse is at first-floor level, which is also the level of the approach road. Passengers enter through automatic sliding doors.

A covered pier, or 'finger', projecting from the centre of the terminal enables passengers to proceed to and from the aircraft on the apron. The runway is one of the few in Britain where centre-line lighting has been installed as a landing aid, in addition to edge lighting.

At second-floor level restaurant, buffet lounge-bar, and viewing gallery are provided; also rooms for business meetings and conferences. On the roof, as is customary, an area for spectator viewing has a buffet attached.

Externally the new buildings, like the control tower and ancillary buildings, is faced with white ceramic tiles, contrasting with the background slopes which have been landscaped with trees. This £2,250,000 airport was opened in February, 1967.

LUTON AIRPORT

The outdated and overworked airport at Luton was, in 1966, enlarged to three times its original size and became fully operative on May 3rd of that year. This airport provides relief from pressure at Heathrow and opened up tourist air travel to Corsica and the Adriatic Riviera. Its cost was a little less than half that of Woolsington.

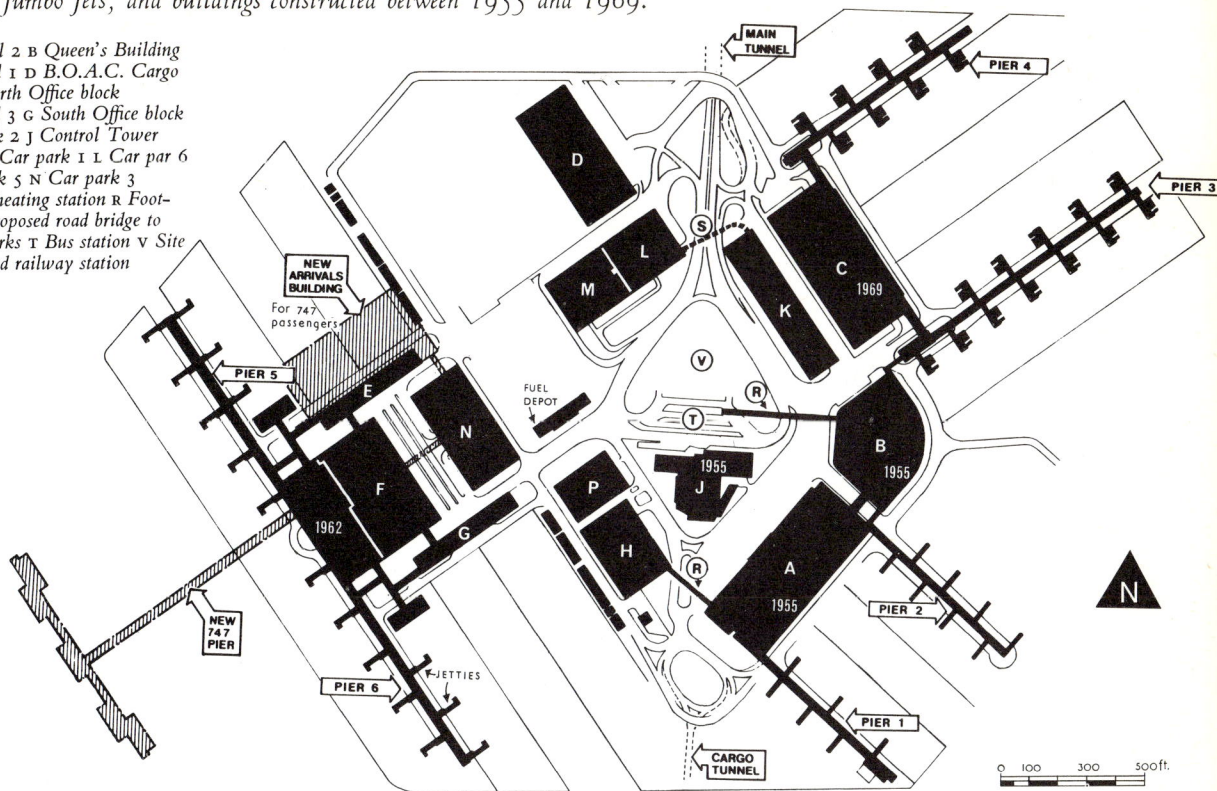

The central area of London's Heathrow Airport. The plan shows the new accommodation for 747 Jumbo Jets, and buildings constructed between 1955 and 1969.

KEY
A Terminal 2 B Queen's Building
C Terminal 1 D B.O.A.C. Cargo
depot E North Office block
F Terminal 3 G South Office block
H Car park 2 J Control Tower
building K Car park 1 L Car par 6
M Car park 5 N Car park 3
P Central heating station R Foot-
bridge S Proposed road bridge to
link car parks T Bus station V Site
for proposed railway station

LONDON AIRPORT (HEATHROW)

In the introductory section on 'land-forms' the reader will remember how the site of Heathrow Airport occupies one of the broadest stretches of the Taplow Terraces – the topographical conditions which could be considered mainly suitable for the purpose of runways and airfield.

The development of the airport had been pondered over ever since the aerodrome first existed in 1914 on part of Hounslow Heath, once familiar to stage-coach drivers and highwaymen.

The airport, designed somewhat hurriedly, was opened for civil aviation on January 1st, 1946; it now covers an area of over 2827 acres south of the Bath Road.

Until the spring of 1955 the conditions for passengers using the airport were not attractive; the accommodation was unbalanced, consisting of an untidy range of buildings along the north side of the aerodrome.

THE NEW AIRPORT

The scheme of the architect, Frederick Gibberd, for the development of this site, as a major airport, envisaged a series of units capable of being brought into use progressively in step with the demands of air traffic expansion. The major initial operational service buildings, comprising the passenger and 'apex' buildings on the centre site, were opened by Her Majesty the Queen in December, 1955.

London Airport is unique among the major European air terminals by the fact that its buildings are centrally disposed. A roughly rectangular site, interpenetrated within by equilateral triangles which are formed by the runways. The plan diagram above will indicate the general placing of the central control buildings and passenger-handling blocks. An access tunnel connects the building areas, north and south to accommodate vehicular traffic.

The Control Tower (1955), from the south-west, at Heathrow Airport; in the foreground is St George's Chapel (1968). Background right, Queen's Building (1955); left, Terminal 1 (1969).

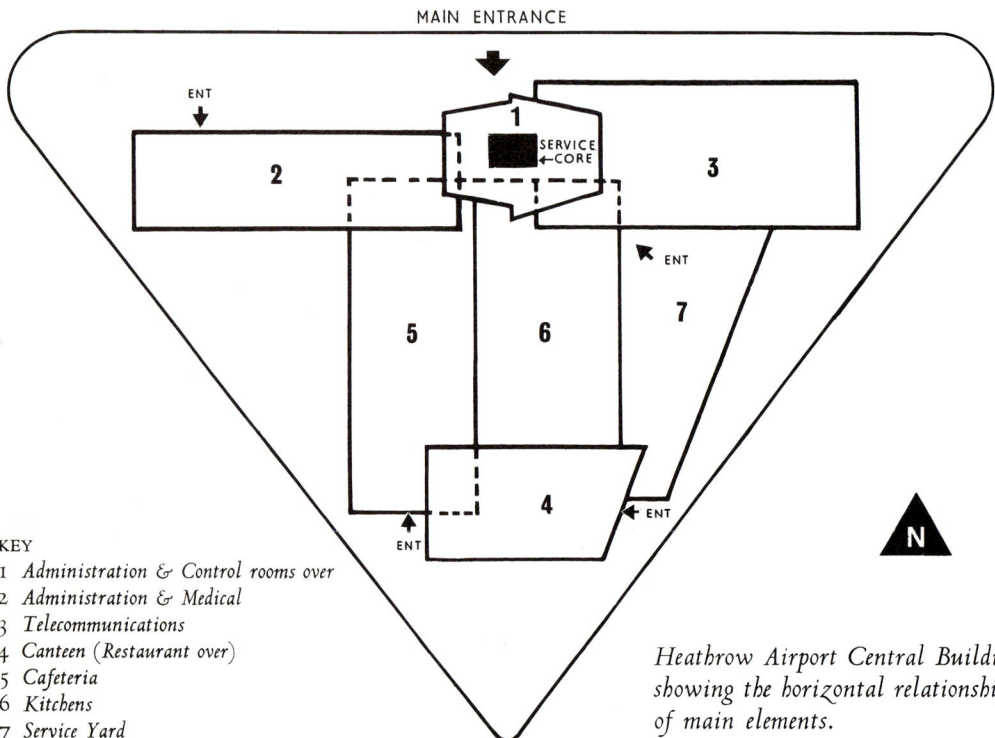

KEY
1 *Administration & Control rooms over*
2 *Administration & Medical*
3 *Telecommunications*
4 *Canteen (Restaurant over)*
5 *Cafeteria*
6 *Kitchens*
7 *Service Yard*

Heathrow Airport Central Building, showing the horizontal relationship of main elements.

PRINCIPAL BUILDINGS

While the control tower is centrally placed, various other blocks occupy the 'faces' of the perimeter; for instance, that on the south-east face is the passenger-handling building, and that on the south is the apex building. The positions for future extensions are shown by shaded outlines on the plan.

The dominant feature of the airport is the control tower, rising as an independent structure. Its principal function is, of course, aerodrome control administered and accommodated in the 'operations' rooms. In the glass dome are two radar sets which indicate not only what is happening in the air, but also on the ground; they are known as A.S.M.I. (Airfield Surface Movement Indicators). Their function is to inform the ground controllers exactly where each aeroplane is. Also in the dome is another radar set whose 'scanner' follows aircraft for the first 15 miles after take-off.

Three storeys below the dome, the approach control officers are located; their duties entail watching the pattern of the airliners queueing up in the air spaces, 15 miles away and waiting their turn to come in to land on the airfield.

To appreciate the extent of these operations we have to remember that air traffic into and out of the airport has to fit into the whole flying pattern over southern England. We are thus presently aware of the difficulties inherent to decisions upon the development of a third London airport around the area of Stansted, or some other site in a less populated area of flat, 'estuarial' character.

SOUTH EAST FACE BUILDINGS

The completed building on the south-east face is possibly the largest and most complex 'passenger-handling' installation in the world, but built around a mainly

View over part of Queen's Building Roof Gardens, Heathrow; in the background stretches the pier serving the air jetties, each of which has a forward assembly area.

Terminal 1 Building was designed to give an extensive frontage for vehicles setting down and picking up passengers. The interior layout is split-level, the lower for arrivals and the upper for departures. On the left of the picture is the integrated twin-deck car park, adjacent to the sweeping ramp-road.

two-level processing diagram, basically similar in pattern to be found in many modern airports. The building may be divided into its two principal levels; the lower floor for passengers' baggage, the upper for the travellers themselves. Along its length it can be divided into twelve 'processing' channels; and, from the land side to the air side it comprises concourse, Customs, immigration, health, waiting halls, and ramps down to the aircraft.

This processing of a passenger (as if he were an animated parcel!) takes him up by escalator to the main concourse and into the Customs hall where he meets his baggage to be checked, after which it goes down to ground-floor level for transit to the aircraft. The passenger continues at the upper level and emerges into the waiting

rooms on the air side of the Customs barrier. The apparently regimented movements of the traveller are softened and diversified on the air side, by the provision of such humanizing features as restaurant and lounge for transit-passengers, and a grand central concourse on the land side. On the second floor is a smaller central concourse, overlooking the main concourse below, with offices, another restaurant, and access to roof gardens, one of which is a 'waving base'; at the highest level of all there are more terraces and gardens for visitor-spectators.

Generally, the structural layout is a regular 12 ft grid; floors and roof are mostly reinforced concrete precast units. Walling is mostly brick (the facings are of pink bricks) except for glass panels

The ramp-road vehicle exit from Terminal 1 Building at departure level.

with some areas of stone dressing. The Customs halls have a roof carried on exposed steel portal-frames, with monitor lights.

SERVICES

Runs of services are carried in deep ceilings, many of which, on the air side, are faced with acoustic tiles and most rooms in the control tower have double-glazed windows to reduce the effects of aircraft noise.

It has been estimated that global air travel expands at the approximate rate of 10 per cent a year; this estimate would appear to be on the low side. At Heathrow, in the late autumn of 1965, a further stage of the programme was achieved in building new accommodation for travellers arriving on British internal air-routes; this building became operational towards the end of October of that year.

Interior view of Terminal 1, departure level on upper floor; severely practical and utilitarian.

Multi-storey Car Parks Nos. 5 and 6 at Heathrow Airport, sited on north-west side of proposed railway station (see plan on page 167).

The new Arrivals building at Heathrow, shown under construction, is to serve the 747 Jumbo Jets in the 1970s. This development will be referred to later in section 5.

Renfrew Airport, Glasgow, designed by Rowland Anderson, Kininmonth, and Paul. The great arch helped to support the interesting roof construction before the building was superseded in 1968.

RENFREW AIRPORT, GLASGOW

The medium-sized airport at Renfrew performed the functions of a 'feeder' connecting Glasgow with the great international airlines. Renfrew, designed by Rowland Anderson, Kinimonth and Paul, had, nevertheless, its own Customs facilities and thus provided in miniature the services of a major airport.

It is interesting to note that the outline of the plan resembled the airport at Zurich, in that it has a convex façade on the air side, with a passenger-handling block occupying the centre of the structure, and forming the vertical of the T-plan where it joins the entrance canopy on the land side. As the limited size of the airport does not require two-level circulation, the upper floor is used for a restaurant with a viewing terrace on the air side, overlooking the apron.

Although the structure of the lateral office wings is not remarkable, the central passenger-handling block has many interesting features. Reinforced concrete portal-frames of an unusual design rise from ground level on the air side, and wrap over the headroom of the viewing restaurant, then drop towards the entrance on the land side. Owing to the curvature of the plan, to which the frames are radii, they converge also towards the land side. However, instead of being 'grounded' in the normal way, their ends are attached to a single reinforced concrete beam suspended upon tension members from a parabolic arch, as in the illustration. This obviates obstruction of the entrance wall face which is wholly double glazed in conformity with the rest of the block.

A new jet airport for B.E.A. and British Eagle has been built at a cost of approximately £5,000,000 at Abbotsinch, nine miles outside Glasgow. It was opened on May 2nd, 1966 and the architect is Sir Basil Spence.

SCHIPHOL AIRPORT AMSTERDAM

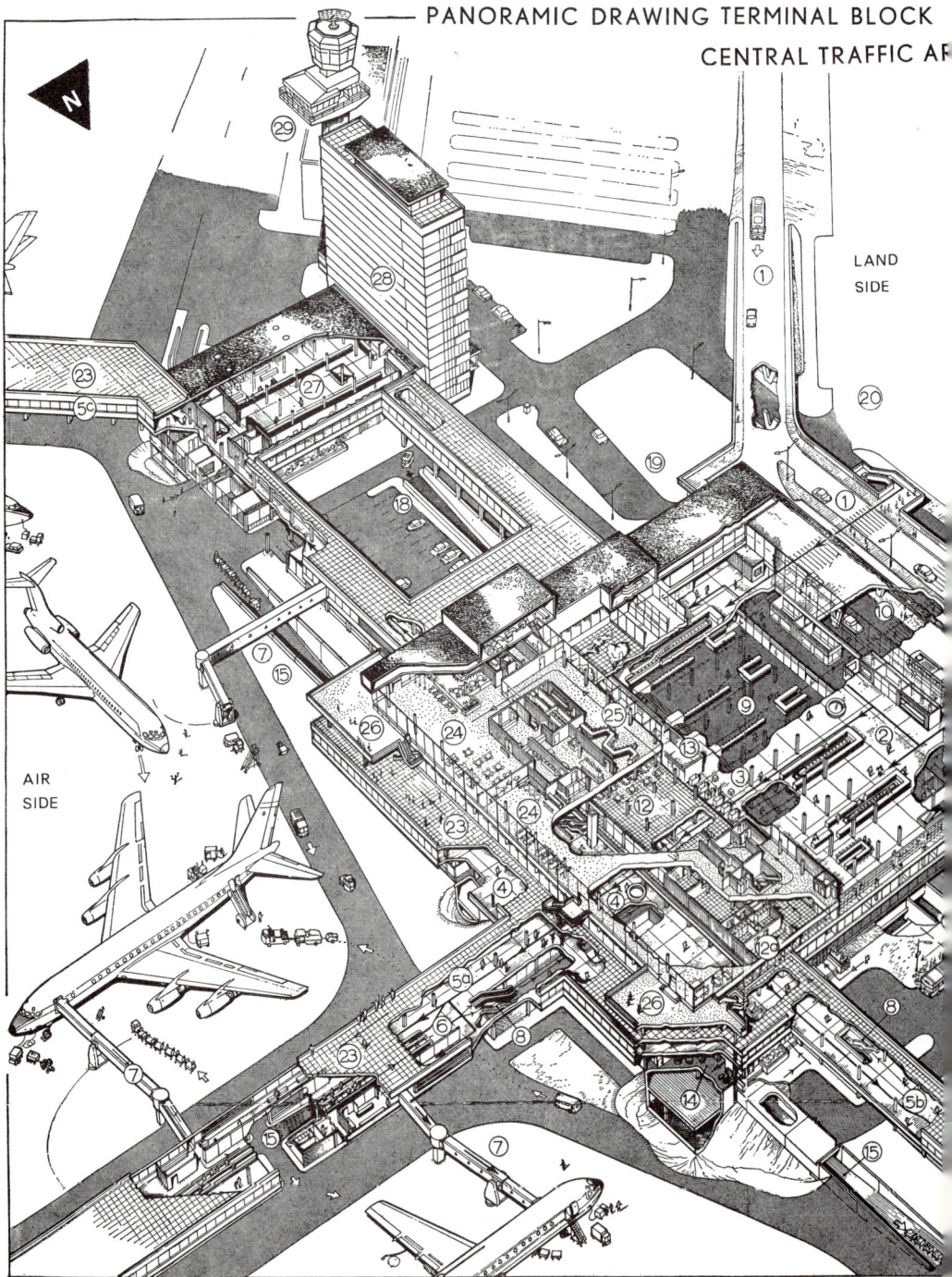

N

LAND SIDE

AIR SIDE

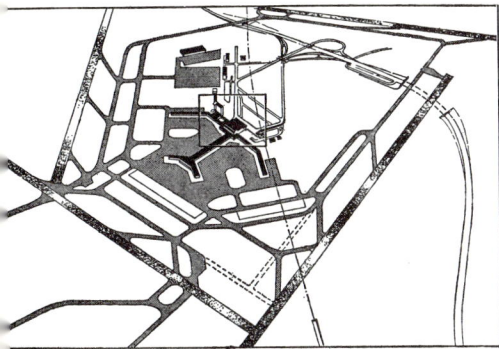

Legend

1. ELEVATED ROAD DEPARTING PASSENGERS	12. TRANSIT RESTAURANT
	12a. KITCHEN TRANSIT RESTAURANT
2. DEPARTURE HALL	13. SHOPS
3. PASSPORT CONTROL	14. VIP., PRESS- AND CONFERENCE ROOMS
4. LOUNGE	15. LUGGAGE ROAD
5a. CENTRAL PIER	16. GARAGE
5b. NORTH PIER	17. EXIT GARAGE
5c. SOUTH PIER	18. SERVICE ROAD
6. MOVING SIDE-WALKS	19. TAXIS
7. AEROBRIDGE	20. CAR PARK
8. STAIRS AND ESCALATOR	21. RAILWAY STATION
9. ARRIVAL HALL	22. VISITORS' ENTRANCE
10. ROAD ARRIVING PASSENGERS	23. PROMENADE
11. BUS TERMINAL	24. VISITORS' RESTAURANT
	24a. KITCHEN VISITORS' RESTAURANT
	25. SNACK BAR
	26. ROOF TERRA
	27. CREW CENTRE
	28. AIRPORT AUTHORITY BUILDING
	29. CONTROL TOWER

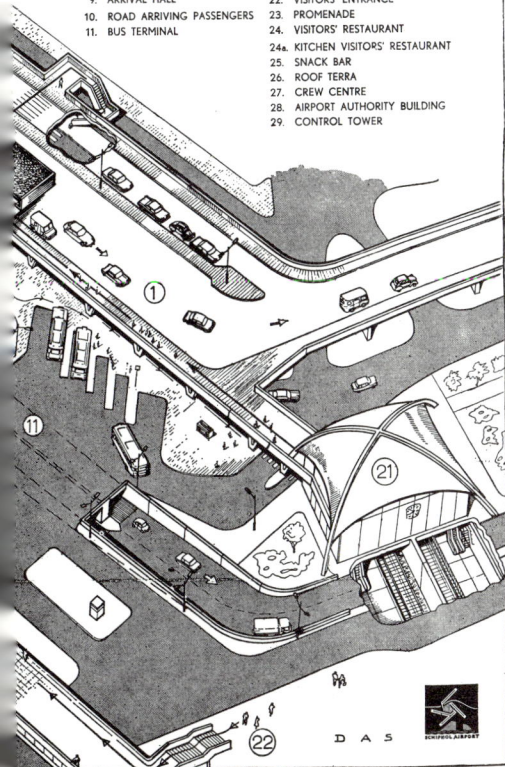

INTRODUCTION—
SCHIPHOL AIRPORT, AMSTERDAM

The development of Schiphol airport embodies several interesting historical facts of special significance to its siting. Large areas of Western Holland formerly comprised a series of vast lakes which, as part of national expediency, were reclaimed; and in the mid-nineteenth century the Haarlam Lake, situated between the cities of Amsterdam, Haarlam and Leyden was similarly reclaimed.

The draining of the lake while resulting in land reclamation for agriculture, was undertaken for the more urgent reasons of protection from the threatening danger caused by turbulent waters, arising from periodic south-west gales in the bay at the north-eastern areas.

The bay was particularly hazardous to coastal shipping and over years many vessels were sunk in an area which for more than five centuries was referred to as 'Schip Holl' meaning, literally the hole or grave of ships. The name was recorded as early as 1447 in documents and in charts dating from 1610.

After the reclamation in 1852 a fortress was built in the north-eastern corner and was given the old name of Schiphol; the recovered area provided adequate space for development at approximately 13 feet below sea-level. In 1917 a military airfield

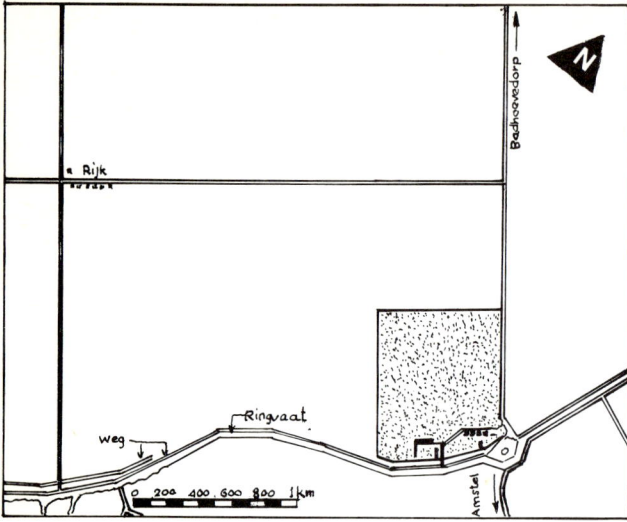

A diagram of Amsterdam Civil Airport in 1920, which originated out of the former military airfield and occupied about 190 acres.

Amsterdam (Schiphol Airport) in 1955. The plan shows the increased area and the primary improved runway layout in triangular form, suggesting the ultimate in the tangential idea.

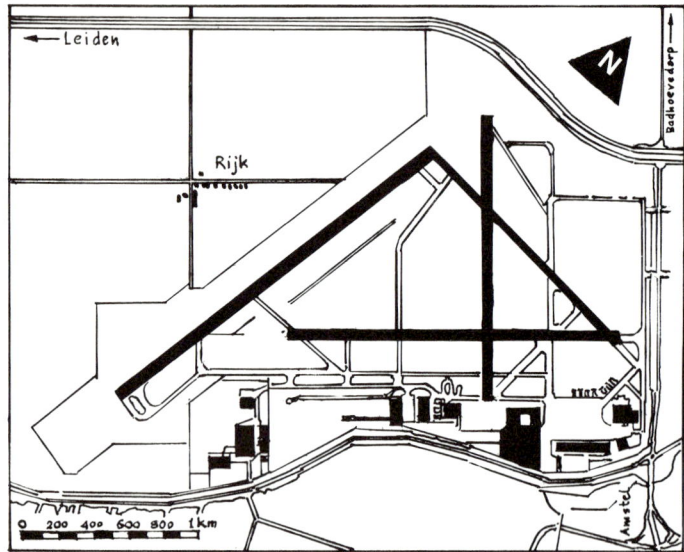

was laid out at the foot of the fortress and it remained operative until civil aviation was introduced in 1920. . . . Six years later the City of Amsterdam took-over the administration and then developed the airfield, from about 190 acres into an airport of about 525 acres. The adjoining diagrams indicate progressive development between the years 1920 and 1967.

THE NEW SCHIPHOL AIRPORT

After the total destruction of the first airport, as a result of World War II, the first aircraft touched down again, on repaired runways in July 1945.

During the years 1945 and 1955, in anticipation of post-war reconstruction, studies and reports were initiated for the preparation of a Master Plan for the new airport. The forecasts estimated an expansion rate in passengers and freight, up to the year 1975 as a basis for determining the initial capacity of buildings to be constructed in the central terminal area, within the space enclosed by the tangential runway system.

In May, 1967, Amsterdam's Schiphol Airport, covering an area of approximately 660 acres in respect of its central area, became operational in its new form. It is an outstanding example of native skill in using reclaimed land.

The adjoining illustration indicates the

A comprehensive plan of Schiphol Airport, showing the tangential runway system surrounding the central terminal buildings. The plan also shows the national highway (A) linking Amsterdam, Rotterdam and the Hague with the airport, and the dotted line (B) represents the Amsterdam-Hague and Rotterdam railway.

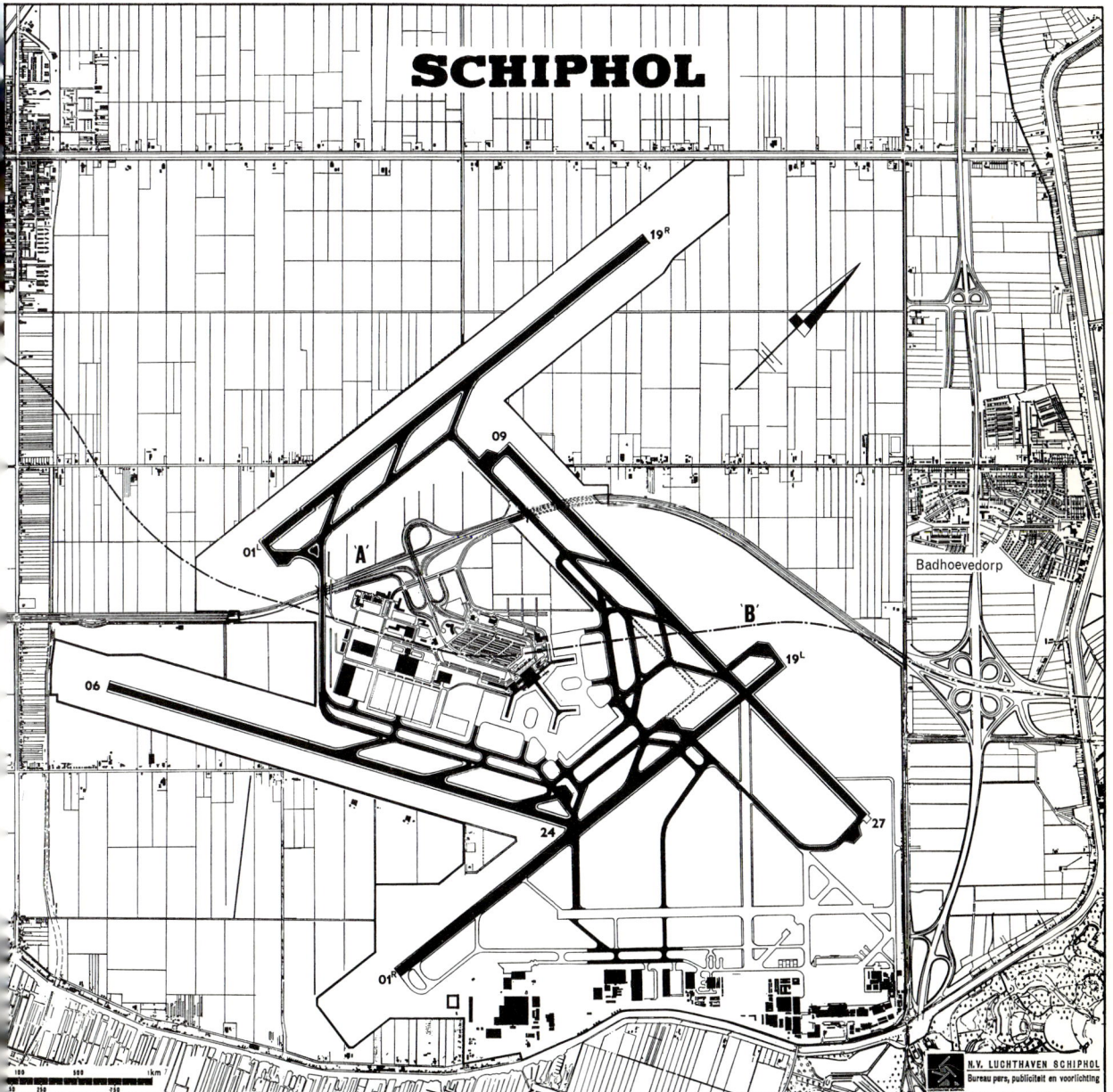

The year 1926 marked the opening of the Amsterdam Air Terminal; a combined bus station and air passenger processing and transit building. It was designed by Joh. H. Groenewegen and H. Mieras; it remained in operation until destroyed during World War II. The illustration at the top indicates a view along the canopied departure building. And below, a general view of the whole building, facing the bus route to the airfield. Now superseded by the new Schiphol complex.

A view of the Airport, with the ramped road on the left of the terminal buildings, and the eighth-floor Airport Authority building, Control Tower and Car-park, centre and right.

new Terminal Building Complex which comprises a rectangular block, forming the focal point. Grouped around the Arrivals Hall are: Passenger Control, Reception Hall and Transit Restaurants, with adjoining kitchens. From the 'land-side', the buildings are reached by means of a ramped road; under this elevated roadway is a drive which receives passengers leaving the airport for interior dispersal.

On the 'air-side' there are 3 pier fingers, which bifurcate at their ends. In the straight stem of the main piers moving footways (Travellators) are installed. Near each aircraft 'gate' position, simple holding rooms, for passengers, are provided, seating 80 passengers, prior to emplaning, via the Aviobridge, also illustrated and described.

The buildings and their layout have many elements similar to those seen at modern Gatwick or Newcastle (Woolsington), and the approach is by way of ramped, elevated roads.

The architects for the new airport

A twilight scene at Schiphol, showing the covered gangways (Aviobridges) which serve as links between aircraft and main pier on the air-side.

The Airport Authority
building and Control Tower.
Arriving and departing
passengers are handled on
different levels; arrivals below,
departures above.

The Main Control Tower, located
between the Airport Authority
building, and the civil aviation
service block. The monumental
symbol (right), gives a feeling of
new design, shape and architecture
for the aviation of tomorrow.

The new Airfreight centre at Schiphol, designed by E. A. Riphagen, consists of a large lightweight single-span roof suspended from tensioned steel cables, and anchored by peripheral concrete buildings. The connected office block, by the same architect is constructed on the 'liftslab' principle, where each 'poured' concrete section is lifted in turn by jacks.

comprised the following groups: Ir.F.C. de Weger b.i. of Rotterdam, and Professor M. Duitjer, architect B.N.A. Amsterdam – in conjunction with 'NACO' (Netherlands Airport Consulting Office), also Bouw-bureau Stationgebou Schiphol (Civil Engineering Contractor, Terminal Building, Schiphol). Additional co-operating architects: L. Jonkers, G. Oostreen, Kho Liang and Ph. M. Simons.

In contrast to current arrangements in most large airports where the buildings provide all handling and Customs services at the airfield, Amsterdam had established a combined bus-terminal, where the processing of air passengers and their baggage began and ended.

THE TERMINAL IN AMSTERDAM

At each end of the building comprising the Amsterdam Terminal (architects: Joh. H. Groenewegen and H. Mieras) there was a counter; one, where the passenger handed over his baggage to the airline at the beginning of the journey, before he boarded the bus which took him to the airport. The other counter was for the collection of his baggage on arrival inwards at the end of his flight. Consequently, the main traffic flow through the building was across the ends, and this was reflected in the design and structural form of the buildings. This is indicated in the illustration, (see p. 178) which shows the ends wholly, or partly, under pent-roofs which, in the case of the departure canopy, are carried on V-strut legs. Between these two ends was an area of less directed circulation, with waiting space, kiosks for magazines, etc., inquiry, ticket, and hotel-booking desks, together with refreshments and a *bureau-de-change*.

All the public part of this area was under a continuous roof, carried on pairs of laminated timber portal-frames, but the purely administrative area of the central block was housed under a lower roof, along the north-west side, leaving clerestory windows above to light the public part. The manager occupied a small raised office at the junction of the arrivals area and the central space; underneath, a cellar accommodated the heating plant.

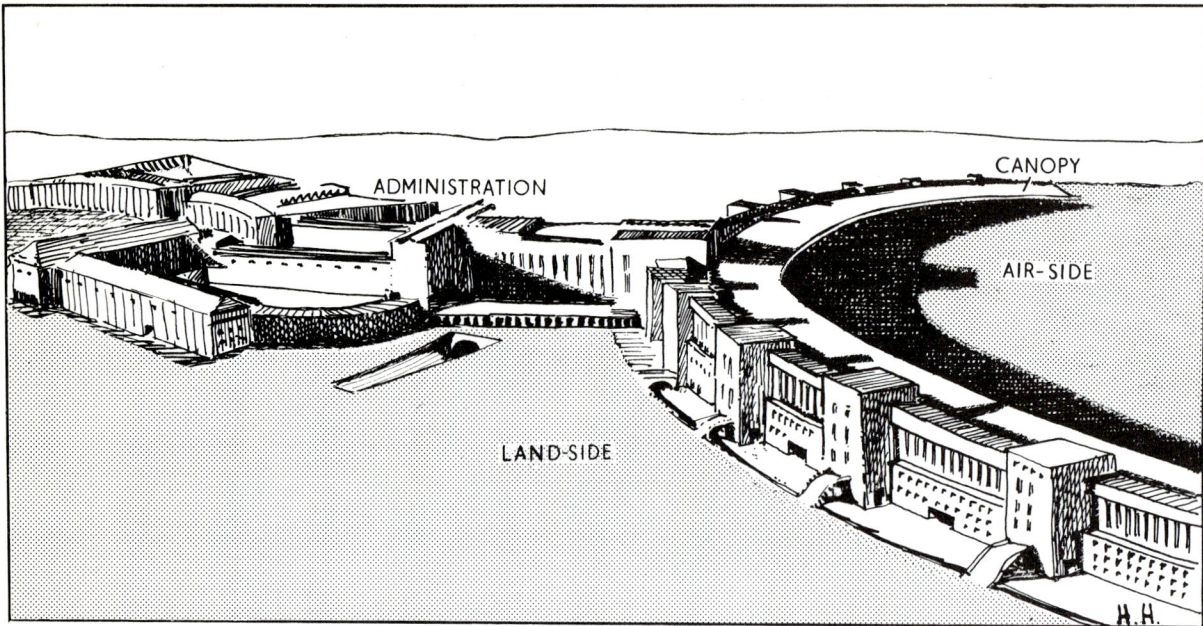

Tempelhof Airport, Berlin, designed by Ernst Sagebiel in 1934. The drawing shows the two-storeyed embarking and landing stage which extends for about 400 yards in the form of a crescent.

BERLIN (TEMPELHOF) AIRPORT

Berlin's Tempelhof Airport (Zentralflughafen), designed by Ernst Sagebiel in 1934, is distinguished by its nearness to the centre of the city and by the two-storeyed embarking and landing stage, which extends for about 400 yards in the form of a crescent. This crescent is significantly apparent in the adjoining drawing of an air view.

The original buildings, heavily damaged during the last war, were rebuilt in their present form, with certain additions. The concourse hall was constructed in 1962 and it has a maximum capacity of 10,000 passengers entering and leaving daily. Offices for the airways companies adjoin the hall on one side and, on the other side are the dispatch halls, also accommodating various booths for trade sales.

A public gallery provides a viewing platform overlooking the airfield, and the airport restaurant, which was opened in 1963, has a glazed balcony extending above the landing stage. This provides weather protection and contains (it is inferred) the germ of an idea, improved upon later, for the development of the designs for the spectacular Pan American airport on New York's Kennedy Airport. This will be discussed in a later chapter.

In addition to the Lufthansa German Airlines, B.E.A. and Pan American planes operate from Tempelhof; approximately 140 aircraft arrive and depart daily.

By way of comparison with Berlin's war-scarred and rebuilt veteran airport, we may follow with the very modern complex of buildings which represent the Bonn-Cologne Airport.

BONN-COLOGNE AIRPORT

Situated at Wahn, this airport serves Bonn, capital of the Federal Republic, and Cologne, a major city of West Germany. The ultimate capacity for which it was planned is approximately 4,000,000 passengers. In 1965 an annual maximum of 300,000 passengers was handled.

The project was designed in three stages by the architect, Prof. Dipl. Ing. Paul Schneider-Esteben. Phase 1 provided for the central building and car-park, and included several 'bridgeheads' or fingers, which penetrated the airfield, the bus and car arrival points being far distant from the aircraft. Phase 2 comprised a compact central building with gangways leading to the bridgeheads; a circular roadway, passing under the gangways, provided shortened approaches for the pedestrians. Phase 3, which is here illustrated, had a central building, shaped like a semi-hexagon; it incorporated a three-storey garage for a large number of cars; the administrative offices, shops, a restaurant, and the services connected therewith.

The building is as near to the bridgeheads as air safety would allow, and an outer ring-road gives access to the bridgeheads, which provide all facilities for arrivals and departures. The distance from the arrival points for motorized vehicles to departure counters is approximately 110 yards. Passengers arrive below ground level and travel up by escalators to departure level; the central building is serviced by a separate ring-road.

Bonn-Cologne Airport, architect Prof. Dip. Paul Schneider-Esteben. The model represents the semi-hexagon central building, with four 'bridgeheads' arranged as satellites, and connected to the central building by short gangways. Note the passenger 'Drive-in' for vehicles direct to the central area.

REFERENCE
A *Charter Companies Waiting & Information*
B *Pan American Airways, S.W.A., K.L.M., Sabena & B.E.A.*
C *Deutsche Lufthansa*
D *Inland Companies Waiting & Information*
P *Parking areas (short term)*

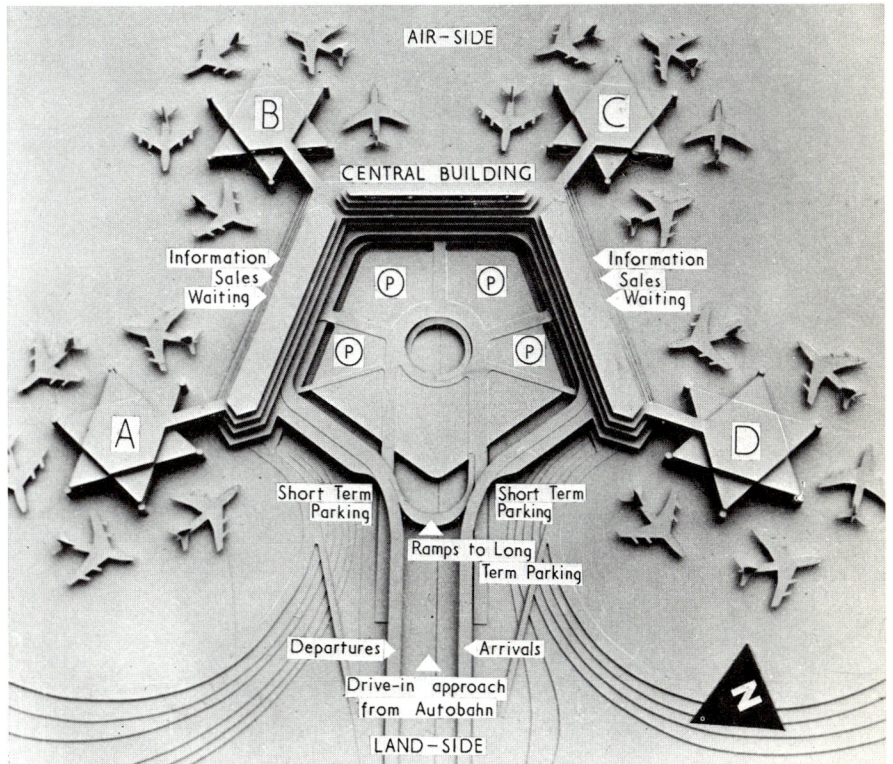

Bonn-Cologne Airport

RIGHT
*The Control Tower dominates
the approach road from the
autobahn to the Terminal
building.*

CENTRE
*The Terminal buildings – from
air-side. Four mobile gangways
resembling the 'Aviobridges'
at Schiphol, are visible.*

BOTTOM
*A detail of Bonn-Cologne Airport
with the 'hinge' of one of the
mobile gangways on the right.*

ROME (LEONARDO DA VINCI) INTERCONTINENTAL AIRPORT

As in the case of the Pan American Airways of Kennedy Airport, New York, the design of Rome's airport (by the architects, A. Luccichento, V. Monaco, R. Morandi, A. Zavitteri, 1963) was the result of long study and research, in this case, over a period of ten years. Work on the construction was accelerated during 1961–5; it was completed in eighteen months, despite the added difficulty of a period of financial stringency.

Fiumicino was selected as an appropriate site for Rome's new airport, as there are no natural obstacles to flight. The airport is located on the Tyrrhenian sea coast near the mouth of the Tiber River, about 20 miles S.W. from Rome and on a 400 acre comparatively level site.

Overland connections comprise three main highways; the Via del Mare, which traverses a corner of the ancient seaport of Ostia, a second road is the old Via Portuense, which serves the south-western part of Rome. The most recent road approach is the high-speed throughway, along the right bank of the Tiber.

An interesting feature of the plan is that it follows the pattern of linear planning – as opposed to the Pan American elliptical form at Kennedy Airport.

Parallel with the finger of considerable length – on the air side, an anti-jet barrier is interposed between the entrances to the gangways and the main finger; this indeed is a novel feature in planning. The runway pattern provides for an aircraft to take off and land every three minutes. About twenty aircraft can, therefore, use a runway in one hour. Assuming a load of 100 passengers for each aircraft, the resultant movement is around 2000 per hour, when working to a tightly organized schedule.

The general layout of the central area of Leonardo da Vinci Airport, Rome. The site is near ancient Rome's port of Ostia on the opposite bank of the Tiber.

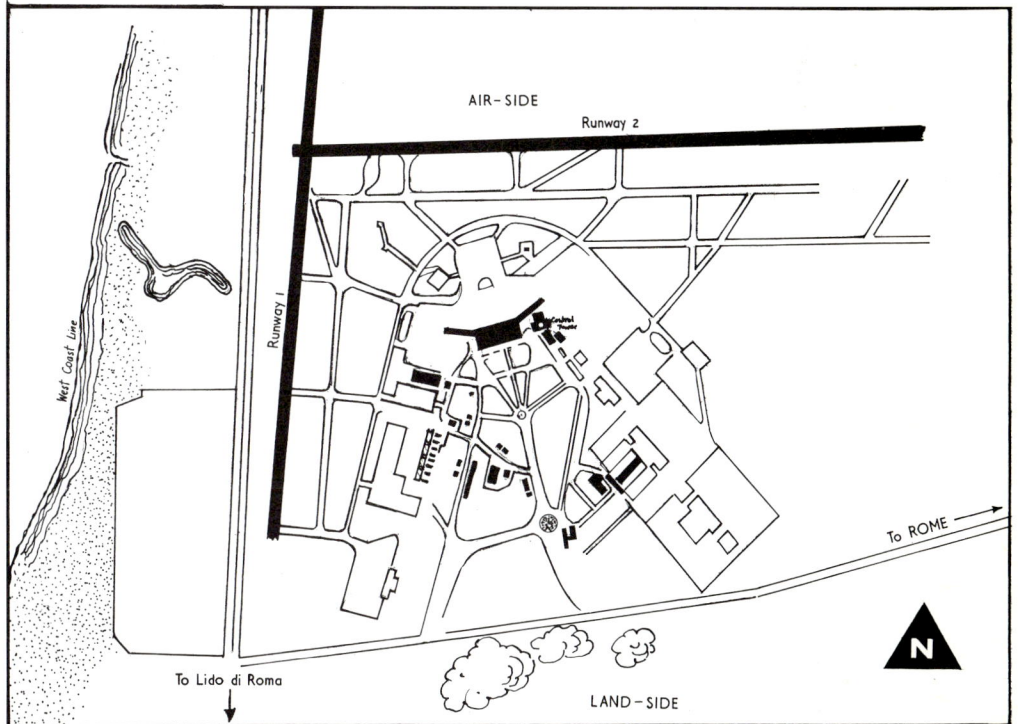

The main Terminal building of Leonardo da Vinci Airport. An interesting feature is the cranked canopy, its fore-edge has angled box-shaped beams which alternate with bands of glass. The free-standing Control Tower is on the right.

In order to deal with motorized vehicles, there are parking aprons adjacent to the passenger fingers for thirteen jet air-liners, and nine propeller-driven aircraft. For aircraft using their power for taxi-ing to and from the terminal, the manœuvring areas required for each jet-liner is approximately 80 yards in diameter and 50 yards for propeller-driven aircraft.

The terminal building operates on three main levels. Passenger movement is concentrated on a *piano nobile*. Luggage is handled and sorted at ground level, and the kitchen services, the ground-staff facilities, and airport storage are also housed here. Restaurants are on the second floor, and passengers have access to them from the concourse below.

The linear plan enables a simplified constructional form, which boldly states a reinforced concrete frame, carrying a light steel roof on lattice single-span beams which

The junction of the main block with the east angled wing, the roof of which forms an extensive viewing deck.

permits a clear floor area, uncluttered by vertical supports. In a building approximately 600 metres (1,970 ft) long, this vista of space along the wings each side of the main block is impressive. The giant-size statue of Leonardo da Vinci, sited axially on the land side approach, will be the centre of a massive rebuilding project, to which we will refer in Section 5; fortunately the airport area was planned to accommodate eventual expansion, which as we have noted, has become a world problem, in air transport.

ZURICH (KLOTEN) AIRPORT

We have referred previously to the importance of land-forms, the term which embraces topography in particular, and here, at Zurich, we have an excellent example of its application to the form of an airport. The architects are A. and H. Oeschger. While many airports are built in areas of relatively level terrain, Zurich (Kloten), as one might anticipate, had to be fitted into an area of low hills with valley bases between them. The latter, of necessity, are utilized for runways, taxi-ways, etc., and the buildings associated with the airport are backed against the hills, which range the site within the 'V' formed by the two minor runways. The taxi-way serving the two runways and the road leading to them, together with the road from the airport, pass around the base of the hill; the building with its apron occupies the area between the road and the taxi-way.

The main façade on the air side has a convex plan with a large central block spreading axially backwards to the entrance canopy on the land side, thus presenting a 'T' outline, which is reminiscent of the aeroplane shape at Elmdon (Birmingham), but upon a larger scale. This central block accommodates all passenger-handling facilities, excepting the restaurant. The fall of the site, from the land side to the air side, is exploited as split-level accommodation for the circulation of passengers and their luggage, thus conforming to present trends in planning.

Travellers enter at either level, their baggage enters at the lower, but they meet in the Customs hall before being conducted to the apron at the lower level. Here they are joined by the 'transit' passengers (i.e., those changing planes) on the air side of the Customs barrier. At Customs hall level is situated the main concourse, which is widened and glazed on the air side to form a great viewing window overlooking the apron.

The restaurant wing serving passengers and visitors is located to the south of the passenger-handling block. It includes long outside terraces on two floor levels, enabling the restaurant users to have extensive views over the apron.

The north wing provides accommodation for administrative and control offices, which serve both the airport operational control and the other lines operating therefrom. The control tower rises four floors clear above the block, in order to ensure both air- and ground-control viewing over their respective operational zones.

The buildings are constructed with mainly reinforced concrete framing, but with 'mushroom'-type supports for the lower levels. Interesting variations for overhead cover have been provided by the use of steel and glass triangular grid techniques which carry the ceiling of the main concourse. A corrugated aluminium vaulting, supported by steel members, forms the *porte-cochère* at the upper level on the land side.

The Pan American Airways Office block, New York. From the flat roof helicopters fly to and from the airport terminal in ten to fifteen minutes.

INTRODUCTION

The progressive successes in orbital adventure from Cape Kennedy compel our admiration and interest in the collateral fields of air services for passenger travel which, since the 1940s, have played a leading part in American airlines' planning.

In order to relate this development to that in Britain and other European countries, it will be appropriate to assess briefly the geographical situation as it affects North American air-routes. The two-ocean concept is a significant fact in trade and transport, also as compared with European landforms the country presents a simpler kind of topography.

Geographically, the sub-division of North

America is comparatively simple; two principal mountain ranges – the Appalachians, on the eastern side – and the western Cordillera. Owing to the fact that the main air-mass movement is influenced by the north-to-south alignment of these mountain ranges, the principal lines of air transport have to cross it, more or less, at right angles, and are thus subjected to a far wider range of weather conditions than are experienced in Europe.

The accompanying diagram map, illustrates the approximate disposition of the principal airports, spread across the North American continent, from New York on the eastern seaboard, to San Francisco on the west, overlooking the North Pacific.

The principal air lanes of the United States run mainly E–W while the barrier mountain ranges and prevailing air currents run counter to them. Inset is an approximate land section which will help explain the problem.

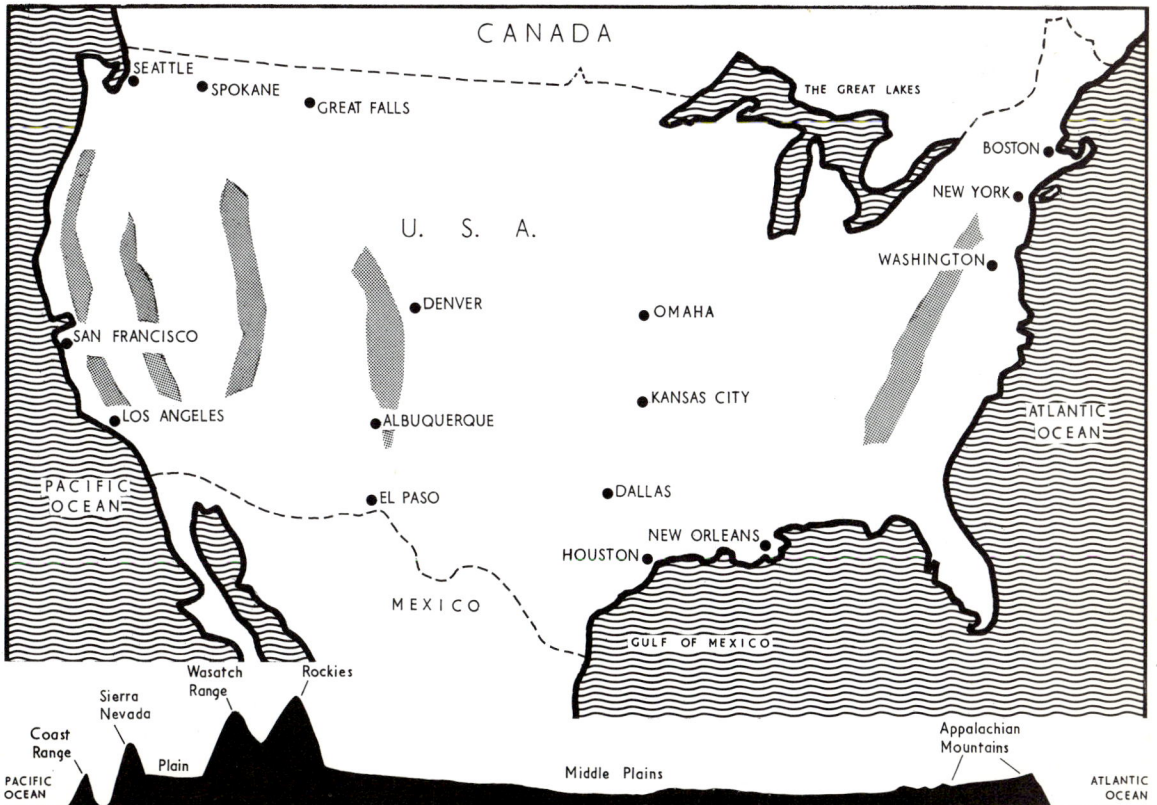

Kennedy Airport, Pan Am Terminal, construction work in progress for the vast extensions necessary to accommodate the Jumbo 747 Jets. The Tower (right) marks the International Arrivals and Foreign building; extreme right background, Eero Saarinen's notable 'flight of fancy' terminal for T.W.A.

From this map we see that the eastward-facing airports on the Atlantic seaboard are those nearest to New York's Kennedy Airport. We may here attempt a comparison between our own major airports, of mainly rectangular elements (except the 'Apex' group at Heathrow) with conventional tiers of circulation, as opposed to the very strikingly unconventional and diverse concepts in design of the termini grouped upon the Kennedy Airport.

From the architectural point of view the approach from the air is of considerable significance as it is the first *coup d'oeil*, the air traveller experiences on his arrival at the end of his journey. That this impression should be satisfactory is certainly of prime importance to the architect as it calls for a disciplined and imaginative concept of his problem in airport design.

KENNEDY AIRPORT, NEW YORK

Our illustration provides a general impression of the main elements of the layout; the ground approach from New York is by the Van Wyck Expressway, which bifurcates as it reaches the perimeter, and loops around the two circular parking areas giving access to the complex of buildings serving this vast airport.

To describe each individual terminal comprising this complex would be a digression – unfavourable to a clear-cut impression of those possessing great understanding of planning and design.

We will, therefore, look at three particular examples, each having an individuality, which raises it to an unfamiliar level of appraisal. For the convenience of comparison, it is appropriate to set a centre of balance between extremes, first by referring

190

to the international arrival terminal and the foreign airline wing-buildings, and secondly to the two adjoining, but dissimilar, terminals of Trans-World Airways and Pan American Airlines, each of which provides an exciting example of the new approach in airport design. On the one hand we have Eero Saarinen's fantastic curvilinear experiment, operationally unsuccessful, while on the other hand, the more recent immaculate 'Pan Am' circular terminal, which 'takes the plane to the passenger'.

The American, Robert Horonjeff, in his interesting and diverse book, *The Planning and Design of Airports*, refers to the differentials which are most apparent in two basic cases: examples being (*a*) the International New York airport, comprising a centralized terminal which combines the activities of all foreign lines (except domestic carriers); and (*b*) in contrast the terminal serving United States-owned internal lines and internationally operating routes.

The Foreign Arrival Wing Airline build-ings, designed by Skidmore, Owings, and Merrill, represents a complex of buildings at Kennedy, where planning and building have stretched over fifteen years at a cost of approximately $235 million for the whole series of termini.

The dominant note of this composition is the control tower block of offices, facing the parking area; beyond this is the vast sweep of the arched roof over the main concourse, the external cladding of which is in stainless steel. Adjacent to the concourse are two long wings which contain the fourteen departure terminals for foreign-owned airlines. The two wings are linked by a central block, from which, on the air side, project two long fingers to the tarmac, similar to those at Gatwick.

A centralized terminal building, as exemplified by the International Airlines Foreign Arrival Wing building, has the advantage of providing a reasonably compact series of operations without the problem of transferring passengers' luggage from one building to another. An important provision

Kennedy Airport, International Arrivals and Foreign building. Interior view of main concourse, showing the plain surfaced sweep of its segmental roof, and the uncluttered floor area.

191

is made for ready expansion as traffic develops.

One of the problems of conveying passengers easily and quickly to the plane has for some years evaded designers, insofar as we note the repetition of the finger principle; but we shall see in a later example how a breakthrough in design has achieved a positive result.

T.W.A. TERMINAL

In striking contrast with its near neighbour, International Airlines (Foreign Arrivals Wing), which we saw was based upon a centralized rectilinear plan, it will be surprisingly refreshing to explore Eero Saarinen's spectacular experiment in fluidity of design.

We have mentioned previously the importance of the approach view from the air, in respect of the grouping of buildings in relation to their surroundings. If the T.W.A. terminal building had been sited upon a green hill, its concept as a bird-like shape might have evoked a sympathetic response. Unfortunately, it so happens that its position at Kennedy at once conflicts with its neighbouring rectilinear and super-functional groups of buildings.

The T.W.A. terminal was commissioned in 1956; its design and construction continued over a period of six years, during which time many models were made before working drawings could be completed, owing to the intricacies of the curvilinear intersections on various planes. To a large extent Saarinen depended upon the engineers, Amman and Whitney, for stabilizing his fantasy into a terrestrial structure. It was inevitable that Eero would display some of the characteristic versatility of his father, Eliel, designer of Helsinki railway terminal, illustrated in an earlier chapter of this book.

One of Eero's contemporaries, speculated that the probable intention was to convey the idea of the 'Drama of Flight'. By discarding a Classical discipline, and relying upon an interwoven series of ramps and curved planes, he achieved a soaring grace.

Some idea of this 'Flight of Fancy' will be evident from the illustration, depicting

Trans-World Airways Terminal at Kennedy Airport. Eero Saarinen designed this revolutionary building in the shape of a bird in flight.

the external view of the building which is the antithesis of regularity; the general appearance is of arrested fluidity of the unrelated curved surfaces leading to nowhere in particular!

Although photography sometimes tends to enlarge the appearance of a building, the facts are that the T.W.A. is rather a small terminal; the total length is around 322 ft, and 222 ft at its broadest extremity. In planning it would seem that the traveller has been given rather less consideration, than has the architect.

A general appraisal would seem to be that, its complexities were part of a broader failure – the architect realized this long before the airport was completed. The final dénouement proceeded from wrong notions of architectural and operational judgement, and arising from a realization that this was so. We may note that it was corrected later in Eero's achievement in the John Foster Dulles Airport at Washington, to be discussed later.

In our introduction to American airports, we referred to the complex of air terminals spread around New York's great airfield. To complete our comparison of the three selected examples in a group, we will now examine the most recent and rational of air terminals.

AIRPORT PASSENGER TERMINAL FOR NEW YORK

This new airport handles all Pan American departures from New York, and the arrivals from Bermuda, Nassau, and Puerto Rico. Passengers arriving on international flights, where they are required to pass health, immigration, and Customs inspection, are handled by the adjoining International Arrival Building, previously described and illustrated.

The relative position will be readily seen in the view from the air over Kennedy (page 190). Its distinctive shape – an ellipse, presents this airport terminal as a complete entity; its plan and design represents the results of a comprehensive study of world airports, combined with over twenty years of airline operation.

Walther Prokosch, partner in the architectural firm of Tippetts, Abbett, McCarthy, and Stratton, was an experienced designer of airports, including those in Puerto Rico and Bolivia; he was able to evolve a solution which satisfied the Pan American criteria for the new terminal at New York International Airport.

The underlying principle of the design and layout was that of conveying the passenger to the plane, easily and with comfort; to eliminate the extensive 'processing' prevalent in many major airports, and where passengers traverse long fingers to reach the plane, finally to mount the gangway under exposed weather conditions.

The designers of this modern airport terminal, by the inversion of current practice, produced the simple expedient of *bringing the plane to the passenger*, or, at least, meeting him more than half-way. The illustration on the next page will indicate how this was achieved.

By expanding the principle of 'bringing the plane to the passenger', the elimination of major inconveniencies of passenger terminals is achieved by a ruse. Primarily it is done by broadening the finger (which is really an extended concourse), so that it surrounds the terminal itself, and then extending the roof in the form of a wide canopy to cover the entrance gangways to the planes. Passengers may then pass directly from comfortable lounges; their luggage, cargo, and mail can also be loaded and unloaded under cover.

A model of the Pan Am Terminal at Kennedy Airport. The overall roof canopy serves the purpose of 'bringing the plane to the passenger'.

The cantilevered roof incorporates ideas from and improves upon the covered appearance at Berlin's Tempelhof Airport, which was built in the 1930s; this is illustrated for comparison.

In the Pan American air terminal the steel and concrete roof-canopy is suspended by 114 ft cables from the top and from the central axis of a three-storey building. The tensioned $2\frac{1}{2}$ in. diameter cables pass over the top of the reinforced concrete piers, which take the main loading. The external edge of the canopy is 50 ft above the apron on the air side, which allows clearance for the tail fins. A photograph of an early model illustrates the manner in which the traveller arrives by car from a ramped roadway on the land side, from which he passes into the building at the level of the concourse.

Thirty-two concrete piers form a peristyle around the glass-enclosed concourse and, radiating from the major axis of the elliptical roof, are a corresponding number of pre-stressed girders which extend to the edge of the canopy; the girders take their fulcrum bearing on the piers and thus support the enormous loads of the mainroof-slab.

While the basic principles of structural design are simple, the resultant achievement is exciting, both from the visual aspect as well as from the underlying calculations of the stresses of velocity wind pressure and turbulence, and of the weight of snow-loads.

The accompanying illustrations show clearly the arrangement of the route by which the traveller arrives at the main entrance at concourse level, either by car or taxi, having come from the Van Wyck Expressway via the eight-laned ramped road system.

The approach to the terminal building is dramatic; the traveller is greeted by a great stilted screen, 200 ft long by 24 ft high, upon which the signs of the Zodiac, in bronze, enrich a series of glass panels which are framed into tapered, vertical ribs. Milton Hebald, a noted American sculptor, was the creator of this imaginative conception.

An interesting feature greets the passenger on arrival at the entrance of the concourse; there are no doors to push open, instead there is a completely unrestricted opening, 94 ft wide and 10 ft high. From overhead slots warmed air circulates through similar slots at floor level, providing an 'air-curtain', between the outer and inner atmosphere and acting as a temperature cushion.

The advantage of this freedom will at once be clear to the passenger, who finds his embarking routine simplified. He arrives directly at the 'check-in' counter, where his baggage is automatically conveyed to the plane, on direct flight, thus enabling him to complete his pre-flight formalities unimpeded.

For the traveller with time to spare may proceed to the adjacent lounge, which is completely glass-enclosed and which provides a view over the airport area.

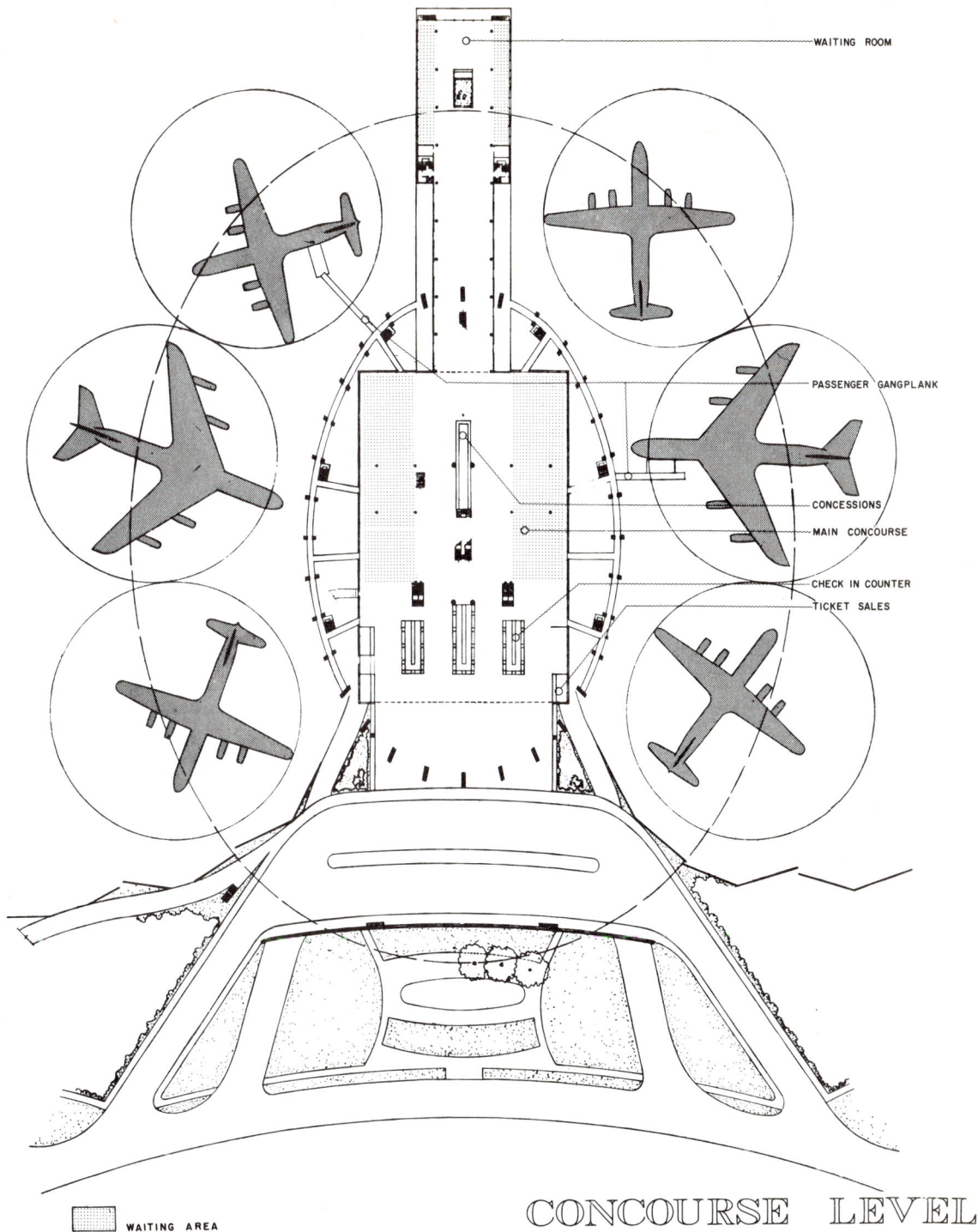

WAITING ROOM

PASSENGER GANGPLANK

CONCESSIONS

MAIN CONCOURSE

CHECK IN COUNTER
TICKET SALES

WAITING AREA

CONCOURSE LEVEL

Plan of the Pan Am Terminal demonstrates how passengers can reach their flights under cover of the oval canopy, indicated by a broken line. At mezzanine level below are restaurants, Clipper Hall and offices.

The plan also shows a mezzanine floor over part of the concourse, providing supplementary lounges and, adjoining the 'Panorama Restaurant', are coffee shops, bars, and an observation deck. Beyond the bar the 'Clipper Hall' is situated; it contains an appropriate innovation – a museum, with models of planes famous in the history of flying, together with trophies and other reminders of the pioneering days, and famous logs of flights of special significance.

These records in the Pan American museum, while they naturally stress American flying achievement, tend also to stimulate interest in the world-wide network of international airlines, which has stemmed from the 'Atlantic Bridge' mentioned in the introduction to this section.

WASHINGTON (FOSTER DULLES) AIRPORT

Sited on the green plains of northern Virginia is the unique airport of Washington designed by the son of Eliel Saarinen, the architect of the famous Helsinki station. Eero has inherited his father's remarkable flair of approach to unusual projects, and it is brought into play in this great undertaking.

The Washington International Airport at Herndon was, from the first, intended for jet planes exclusively; it was designed for future expansion upon a linear plan. The general form of the administrative block is an inverted 'T'-shape, with the short stem forming a link with the rectangular observation tower.

The main building is about 600 ft long and has a range of sixteen columns or ribs on each side, with a maximum height of 65 ft and penetrating the curved roof front to back; each edge is swept back like a wave crest. The illustration emphasizes this most fantastic example of what we might describe as 'frozen flight'.

Operationally, a radically different system of passenger handling was required, and Saarinen found the solution by abandoning the conventional 'finger' corridor, along which passengers proceed to board the aircraft. The system projected at this

Dulles International Airport, Washington. Plan of Eero Saarinen's linear layout, of inverted 'T' form, which provides for lateral extension – a complete contrast to his T.W.A. Terminal.

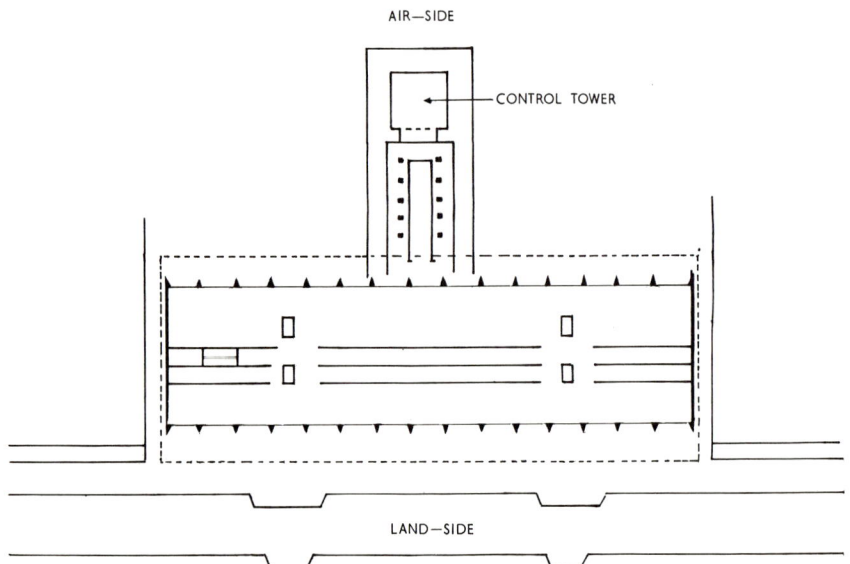

The magnificent sweep of Saarinen's roof construction at Washington is brought out in this night photograph. (RIGHT) *the Control Tower.*

airport is based upon bus transport, as used at some European airports such as at Amsterdam; Saarinen's final solution was an idea of a 'mobile lounge' unit combined with a covered retracting gangway, conceived in discussions with his advisers and associates.

As soon as the mobile lounge was proved feasible, the rest of the programme corresponded with Saarinen's preconceived notion of a 'linear' terminal. This could be extended in each direction at either end, without altering the original thirty-six-gate arrangement, to a total of sixty or ninety gates as need arises.

A major problem for airlines, almost from the beginning, has been to get the passenger to the plane quickly and comfortably across an exposed airfield. Progress in curtailing the finger (or 'sheep-run') has certainly achieved spectacular results, yet much remains to be done to cut down the transit time to and from the airport terminal, immediacy being so important. This brings us back to the interdependence of all forms of transportation.

Philadelphia International Airport, from the air-side, showing Control Tower in middle background.

PHILADELPHIA AIRPORT

The present airport is the result of modifications to an earlier peripheral scheme which had intended to include separate buildings for the several operating companies forming the Philadelphia International Airport.

In the present organized layout (architects: Garrol, Grisdale, and Van Allen) all companies share, in one building, most facilities, except baggage handling. In this case travellers take their baggage up to the first floor, where, after weighing and labelling, it is taken by chutes to the handling area on the floor below. Travellers, meanwhile, remain in the first-floor waiting hall, on the air side overlooking the apron, and when due to emplane pass along one or other of the two projecting covered walkways which extend over the apron. At intervals stairways lead down to the apron, but in the case of international passengers requiring Customs clearance and other formalities, they are dealt with at the western end of the block; the routine is similar for luggage handling, although there is a difference in procedure for Customs clearance.

On the upper floors we have the same types of large deck-restaurants overlooking the apron. Adjoining is a public viewing deck reached by access ramps, which also serve the weather and control offices. The structure is normal reinforced concrete, framework-post and slab, with site-formed portal-frames carrying the roof and windows. The main building is faced with pink brick, aluminium, and blue tiles.

OTTAWA INTERNATIONAL AIR TERMINAL

Work was commenced on this air terminal in 1955 and it was scheduled to be opened for operation in 1959, but the opening was delayed until the following year, owing to damage to the structure as a result of blast from low-flying jet fighter aircraft on exercise.

The general form of building layout of Ottawa terminal (architect: A. W. Ramsey, Department of Transport) is reminiscent of the 'Apex' buildings at London's Heathrow Airport (opened December, 1955). At Ottawa, the apex faces south and comprises two floors, as indicated on the adjoining plan.

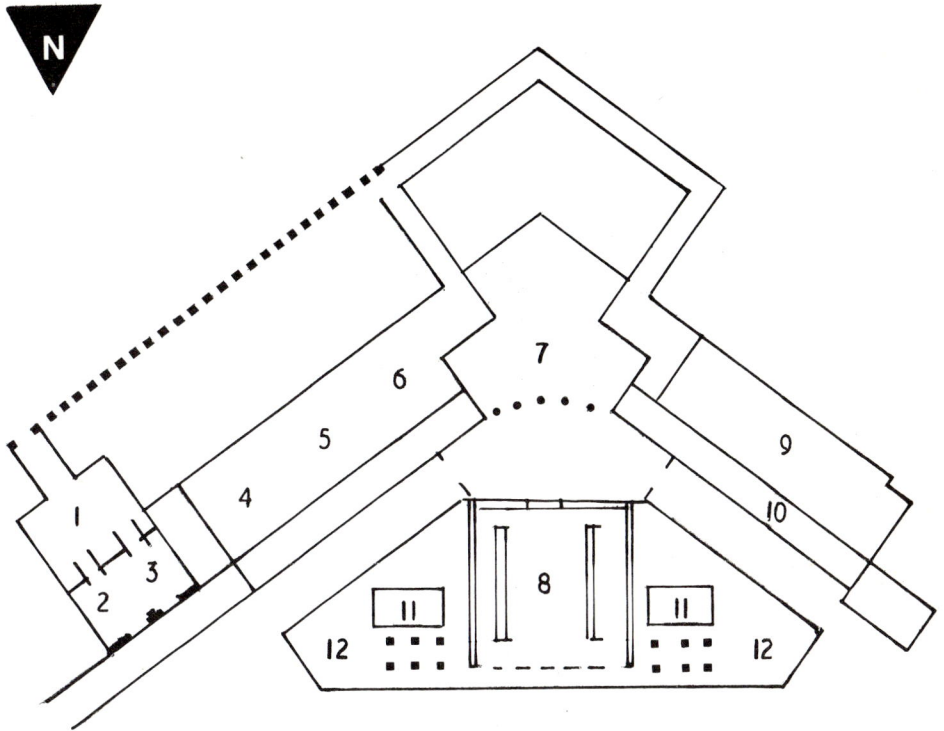

GROUND PLAN

Ottawa International Airport, Canada, built 1955–60, architect: A. W. Ramsey. The plan reflects the influence of London's Heathrow central area 'Apex'.

1 *Incoming Waiting Room* 4 *Customs Inspection* 7 *Main Waiting Area* 10 *Ticket Lobby*
2 *Health Inspection* 5 *Baggage Claim* 8 *D.O.T. Operational Area* 11 *Reflecting Pools*
3 *Immigration* 6 *Coffee Shop* 9 *Airlines Area* 12 *Sunken Gardens*

The main waiting area is centrally placed (7) and on each side the accommodation is arranged for passenger handling; the buildings which form the wings subtend angles roughly corresponding to those at Heathrow. Passengers enter through the incoming waiting room (1), at the eastern end of which are located health inspection (2) and, immigration (3). Passenger movement continues towards the apex by way of Customs inspection (4) and baggage claim (5). To the south of the large circulating area, separated by a corridor, the Director of the Transport Operational Area (8) is sited. Surrounding this area the ground, at a lower level, is laid out in gardens with two rectangular reflecting pools (11). The western wing, connected by the corridor, contains the airlines area (9) and ticket lobby (10).

At first-floor level, following the outline of the wings, the accommodation comprises a centrally placed waiting space from which there is access to a dining room; at the ends of the wings are offices.

As in other airport buildings viewing decks are provided; in the case of Ottawa's air terminal, these are south-east and south-west respectively and are reached by short corridors.

In the three successive chapters of this section, we have considered a variety of

An aerial view of the central area of Ottawa International Air Terminal showing the Control Tower, and the two wings for passenger accommodation and services.

airports in two continents – representative of their development over half a century (certainly including Croydon 1926–8). And, in many instances we find their planning has been lagging behind, in accommodation relating to the phenomenal development of larger and speedier aircraft.

With the introduction of large capacity aircraft, new problems will continue to arise – in respect of the transit of passengers and their baggage, through the airport terminal facilities.

This is for the future, and we shall see in Section 5, examples of the development of new concepts for airport termini – some of which are now actively emerging.

The attractive spaciousness of Ottawa's passenger hall helps to dispel the
tedium of waiting.

'The Shape of Flight'
sculpture outside the main
Terminal building at
Ottawa Airport.

The 'Princess Margaret hovercraft' mounting the ramped apron and hoverpad at Dover Harbour. In the foreground are reception and departure lounges with maintenance area and workshops on the right and the existing car ferry on the left.

CHAPTER **17** SOME PLANS

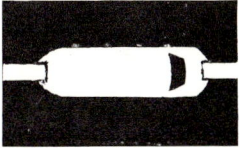

"The man who could predict with certainty the shape of things to come, as regards the railway stations of, say, thirty-five years hence, would be either phenomenally astute – or just curiously clairvoyant."[1] This applied generally to railway termini in any metropolis or large provincial city. One could do little more than explore the tendencies based upon the known facts and examples – which could be examined upon a screen on which are projected the nuclei of future problems. These may embody social, political and industrial trends, relating not only to railways but also to terminal buildings for airports and seaports, and the great variety of road-transport buildings.

In the past two decades, we have considerably extended our horizon in all fields of transport; New Towns, with their industrial areas, have created expanding new problems. The commuter from 'dormitory' towns, the mounting scale of private and commercial motor traffic on the roads, all provided problems which will require from the planners of today an imaginative zeal and technical competence.

In London, as in other great world capitals, there is a growing problem brought about by the lack of space for new and expanding transport routes.

An important point about the London

[1] The above extract is from *Railway Architecture* in 1946 by the author.

plan, for example, is that more than 75 per cent of the new motorways are projected alongside or over existing railway lines; there will be interchanges with the radial motorways, and about twenty-three other interchanges with existing road systems, potentially which will provide not only freedom of movement for travellers but freedom from excessive traffic disturbance in many inner areas.

In an earlier chapter (2), we referred to a system of multi-storey point blocks for parking, situated upon an outer-ring motorway; it would seem that the interchange points with radial roads could fit in with the programme. In the rapid development of motoring over the past two decades, and its effects in cities, the multi-storey garage has tended, in the negative sense, to be regarded as the alternative to the kerbside and a necessary evil. If, however, the trend of current thinking is reversed, the garage is a place where cars naturally come to rest, and the motorist willingly becomes a pedestrian, then the parking garage takes its place as a valid contribution to urban architecture.

As an example of this principle of peripheral multi-storey parking buildings it may be interesting to refer to the large Autorimessa, situated at the landward end of the causeway at Venice, established over thirty years ago; this could be considered, in terms of location, as an almost unsurpassed prototype.

Between the widely separated examples of the Autorimessa in Venice and Chicago's Number 1 City Garage one may find a great variety of types; a notable example in the Hamiel Garage at Dusseldorf, designed by Paul Schneider, Esleben, and Dietricht Hartkopt; a most interesting feature of this building is the external ramps, hanging from roof cantilevers, forming a canopy.

These three examples are simply pointers to various ways of solving particular problems; the answer may lie in the right judgement as between the policy of 'land-use' and the dictates of the town's traffic pattern. This brings us back to London's particular problem; here is an opportunity to produce something really spectacular. London should have, acting as points of emphasis, towering parking structures at the intersections of the great road circuit and the radial motorways.

The design of these 'tower' parking structures could conform to a recognizable form with a symbolic motif which would relate to some organization familiar to the motorist; much in the same way as the Trust Houses have for their own symbol. Where possible, in fortuitous locations, the buildings could serve linked transport and commercial activities.

An example of a multi-purpose parking structure is the interesting American building in Philadelphia's Transportation Center, designed by Vincent J. Kling. The building forms part of the Penn Center, containing, in addition to parking for the large Sheraton Hotel, a Greyhound Bus terminal and restaurant, and an office building; there is also an airline terminal and the building is connected to an underground station, a lower pedestrian concourse, and an underground service street. Here, indeed, is an outstanding achievement in the organization of urban land-use.

Hamiel Garage and Motel at Dusseldorf, Germany. View towards the suspended ramps.

It is conceivable that we may see in the future, in a replanned London, at strategic points along the new 53-mile motorway, parking towers to intercept motor traffic from the principal radial motorways.

Architecturally, in relation to traffic, these buildings could establish an identity, as we have said, in a similar manner to the railway terminal station idea. Motor-parking structures, in this context are, in fact terminals; they would be points of interchange between two forms of progression – the motor car on the one hand, the pedestrian, public transport, escalators, travellators, and the like on the other.

The big cities of America are tackling similar problems in a forthright way. In Chicago, for example, the Number 1 City Garage is connected to the upper and lower levels of the main traffic route at its intersection with one of the approaches to the Loop, the city's central area. It constitutes the kind of peripheral and linked location, which parking buildings must achieve in order to be effective.

This twelve-storey building demonstrates the visual interest created by the open-fronted parking decks in its urban situation. Through the spaces between the safety barriers of tensioned steel cables, the motorist is provided with a new viewpoint, over the motorway and across to the city's distant skyscrapers.

Turning again to transport in Europe, it would be appropriate to examine some of the newer projects on the railways of Britain's near neighbours, more especially now that the Channel Tunnel is likely to increase European co-operation in trade and travel. Perhaps the Netherlands could provide some interesting examples of transport development for the future – at least up to the year 2000.

ROTTERDAM

During May, 1940, the city of Rotterdam received overwhelming bombing from the air which obliterated almost two square miles of the central area of the city. Railway stations on the north side of the river Maas: Delftsche, Hopplein, and Maal, were all badly damaged. By 1942 the invaders had prepared plans for rebuilding the city, visualizing the retention of the then existing layout of railway lines on viaducts.

Those proposals disregarded the plans of the Dutch city engineer previously prepared, which provided for the removal of the line from the centre of the city, the construction of a central station to the west of the city, with an eastern, wider loop linking the Amsterdam and Antwerp lines respectively. Van der Gaast was appointed as architect to the Town Development Department, to assist in this comprehensive plan, incorporating all forms of transportation and, its flexibility assumed an optimum population of the order of one million by the year 2000.

The scope of the Rotterdam project for embracing all forms of transportation becomes clear from its environmental facts. The city's emergence as a great maritime port began when an artificial channel to the Hook of Holland was opened to permit the largest ships to enter and leave Rotterdam docks at any state of the tide. The most important docks are on the southern sector of the city, while near the river Maas on the north side lies the city centre.

Here is a complex situation arising from traffic movement between the two halves of the city. The inadequacy of the river crossings to meet the increasing volume of passenger traffic on the central cross-over routes, predicated an organized traffic flow. A review of alternative systems produced the conclusion that a conventional railway – partly underground – would provide the required capacity and cause less disturbance to existing houses and other facilities.

Owing to the unstable foundations, due to the fact that most of the city of Rotterdam is built upon piles driven down into the sand sub-soil, the level of which is only a few feet above sea-level, normal tunnelling methods would be inadmissible. The tunnel was therefore formed with prefabricated units which were constructed within two temporary 'docks'; the docks were linked together by a wide and deep trench, or small canal, which was flooded to enable the units to be towed into position and joined up.

Regarding the new Metro line, commenced in 1960, this runs north to south from the Netherlands Railways Central station to the residential and dock areas; four stations are situated on the north side, and are underground.

A second Metro, planned to cross the first, and to run east to west, is due for completion around 1975. In the latter system all stations are elevated, with a concourse beneath, while on the northern line the concourse is between the station and the street, with escalator approaches.

Having examined the development plan for Rotterdam, it will be appropriate to refer to the station at Utrecht in order to bring into relief the alert and progressive actions of the municipal governments of both cities and the co-operation of the Netherlands Railways managements.

UTRECHT

Utrecht occupies a strategic position in the Rhine delta; it is the central exchange point for all lines to north, south, east, and west, passing through Holland. These radiating railway routes serve the iron and steel areas in Holland, Belgium, France, Germany, and Luxembourg.

During the twenty-four years between 1938 and 1962, the volume of passenger traffic through Utrecht was doubled and the Netherlands Railways planned an additional two-berth platform at the station. At that juncture, a private development company N.V. Empeo, part of the Bredero undertaking, offered its services and co-operation to the municipality of Utrecht for a large development project which included re-building the railway station. The offer was accepted as part of a staged development,

Track and platform layout of the re-built Utrecht Central Station.

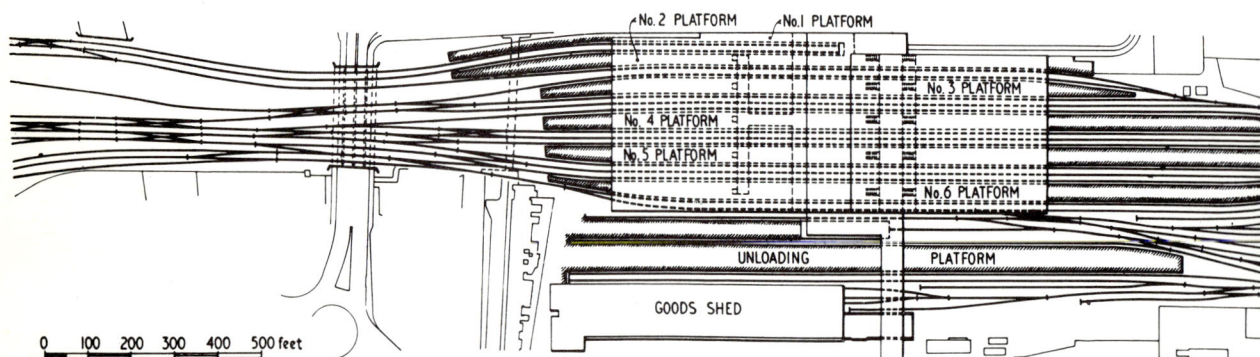

up to the year 2000; this development envisages a drastic rebuilding over a large area.

One of the effects of the N.V. Empeo proposals was that the railway administration widened the scope of its original scheme, in order to achieve the benefits accruing from a consortium of commercial planners, and so take its place in the redevelopment plan for the city of Utrecht.

Isometric view of Utrecht Central Station complex in relation to the city development.

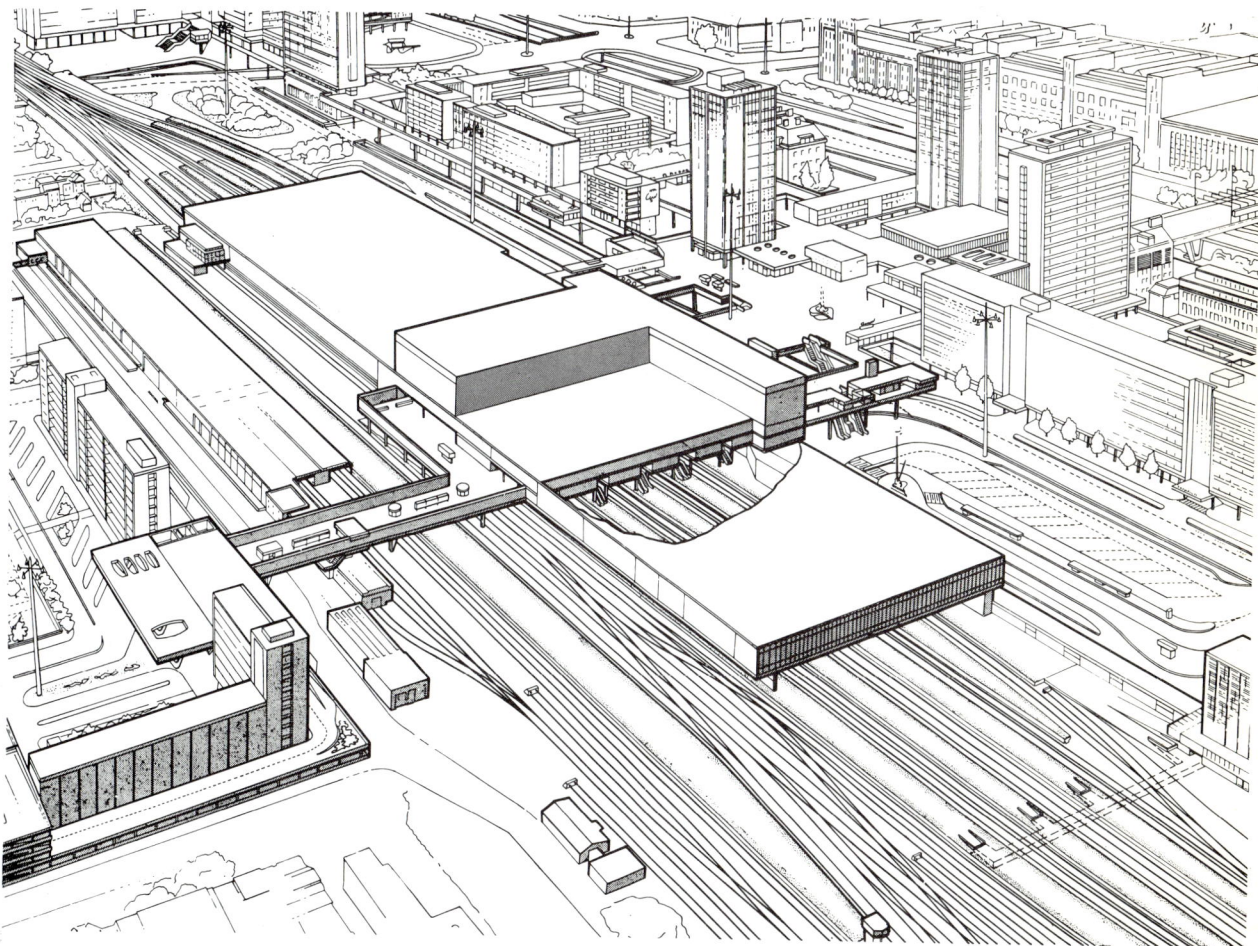

Japanese National Railways

Japan's contribution to modern travel is the spectacular development of high-speed railway trains here epitomized by one passing Mount Fuji. Architectural design is mainly concentrated on the twelve stations on the new Tokaido line where the equipment, such as ticket windows, barriers, escalators and vending machines conform to a uniform design. The line takes its name from the ancient highway linking Tokyo and the former capital, Kyoto.

At one end of the Tokaido line is the fine modern Shinjuka station in Tokyo, completed in 1964 and handling more than 100,000 passengers daily. Quite apart from the space occupied by the Japanese National Railway its eleven floors accommodate shops, restaurants, reception halls, and even a school.

Associated with Shinjuka station is this striking commercial complex on three levels. On the ground floor is the terminal for 68 bus routes; and open space, shopping area, and passenger access occupy the upper basement, while at the lowest level is parking for 420 cars.

Situated at the western end of the line is the Shin-Osaka Terminal which handles about 60 trains a day. As in the other stations on the line there is easy interchange with the older Tokaido system.

SAN FRANCISCO BAY AREA —RAPID TRANSIT

We have previously described two projects in the Netherlands: the great port of Rotterdam and the N.V. Empeo complex which embraced the rebuilding of Utrecht station.

In the case of Rotterdam part of the interest lies in the unique problem of tunnelling for rail-tracks under water. Prefabricated concrete units were floated out to their required positions and then sunk.

In California, at the port of San Francisco, development has currently been proceeding since its inception in June 1951. The scope of the Bay Area Rapid Transit (known as BART) suburban commuter railway includes, as the first stage of construction, the linking up of San Francisco with the junction at Oakland, and thence to Richmond (N), Concord (E), and Fremont (S). Building operations started in 1964.

The route is planned at various levels to meet the conditions imposed by the topography. In the Bay area of the suburbs, adjoining San Francisco and Oakland, the tracks will be at ground level, then for 31 miles through the inner suburbs upon 20 foot high viaducts. Finally through the actual centres of the two cities the tracks will run underground.

Under San Francisco Bay there is a four-mile earthquake-proof tube of prefabricated concrete and steel; the sections here were also floated into a pre-dredged trench, a hundred feet below water level.

For the architecturally inclined traveller, whose technical interest extends towards the forward trends of transportation, there are other aspects of this rapid transit system which he should note. Initially two types of monorail were investigated for this area of varied terrain, but they were discarded in favour of the more adaptable twin-rail, bottom-supported metal, standard track.

A 5 ft 6 in. gauge was adopted, which provided an increased carrying capacity with comfort, quietness, and flexibility, while at the same time satisfying the requirements for stability at a projected speed of 80 m.p.h. power being provided by electric traction with conductor rail supply.

A high degree of automation over the system operates between stations; a separate 'take-over' passenger control operates when approaching the station to stop the train at a precise point along the platform.

HOVERCRAFT AND PORT EXPANSION —DOVER

In Section 4 we followed the development of aircraft and airports and the modification to the latter necessitated by the introduction of jet propulsion into the former. Vertical take off (VTO) by its greater manœuvrability produced problems and opportunities of even more complex nature.

These include the provision for handling revolutionary craft, such as helicopters and hydrofoils. As far back as 1958 it was necessary to make adaptations for the newly introduced hovercraft by providing flat areas, known as pads, and ramped apron connexions with the water surface.

It therefore followed that such a hoverport should form an integral part of a modern harbour, and this was what was done at Dover, already described in Chapter 12. The International Hoverport was installed alongside the car ferry to form a car ferry terminal complex, as can be seen

Provision was made to accommodate the projected hovercraft service between Dover and Boulogne in the development plan for Dover harbour in 1967. We see here the hoverport in mid-distance between the existing car ferry and the entrance.

in the accompanying photographs. Provision was planned for the increasing size of these craft, which originally were 30 ft long and weighing $3\frac{1}{2}$ tons, but now as large as 130 ft and 165 tons, and carrying cars as well as passengers.

The great advance in this type of travel and the fast 'turn-round' requirements made it clear that the then existing facilities at Dover were not adequate and predicated the present expansion programme.

In passing, we should refer also to the other recent cross-channel service operating hovercraft transit, between Pegwell Bay, Ramsgate, and Calais, where a hoverport has been constructed; initiated by Swedish shipping interests. Ramsgate was chosen because of its ready access both to London and to the east and north of England, through the Dartford Tunnel.

The new Dover layout was designed as the first phase of a wide extension; it embodies the reclaiming of about $6\frac{1}{2}$ acres of land from Dover Harbour and using excavated chalk (from the widened A2 road) to form additional ramps.

From the layout plan, apart from the eastward extension, the whole of the area to the westward has been replanned and reorganized to increase the Customs 'sufferance areas' and to utilize all available shore space; the whole project is now in operation.

The site is bounded to the north by 150 ft sheer cliffs and to the south by the waters of the harbour. At the west end are sited the passengers' Booking Hall and Nos. 1 and 2 Control Buildings, providing maximum 'in bond' parking space.

The largest structure, No. 1 Control Building, covers an area of about 225 ft × 275 ft; the Car Ticket Check Point and Booking Hall building, 126 ft × 450 ft.

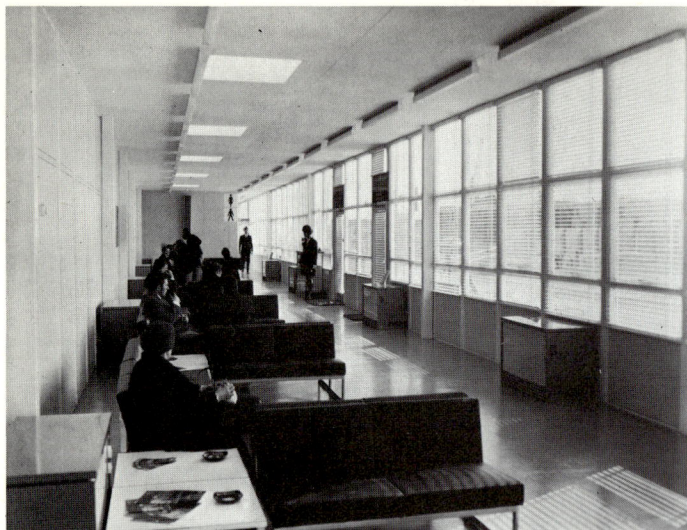

A view of the light and airy Departure Lounge provided for hovercraft passengers at Dover.

The maximum use of ground level for traffic flow necessitates a first floor level for the Booking Hall Car Park, alongside which are the Multistorey Car Park and the main office accommodation. Site and vehicular traffic movement dictated a framed construction, with wide spans and embodying steel structure, with concrete plank floors.

External materials in the seaside environment required minimum maintenance; the Booking Hall and No. 1 Control Building have a 5 ft deep band of pre-cast concrete panels at first-floor level, below which glass panels provide for maximum natural light.

No. 2 Control Building is basically a single storey through-way; long elevations consist of folding doors, shutter type, punctuated with glazing. Roof lighting is provided by a monitor roof, providing maximum headroom to traffic lanes and standard room height to offices.

The ancillary buildings are constructed and finished – employing the traditional building techniques – in a modern idiom. Load-bearing brickwork perforated with standard window and door panels supports a flat roof.

The development was planned by the Board's Engineering Research Staff, in conjunction with the Architects to the Board, Dudley Marsh, Son and Partner.

The computerised check points for passengers and vehicles in the new Dover Eastern Docks Terminal. In mid-distance is a multi-storeyed car park and the Booking Hall building and in the far background is the old harbour and port.

London's Proposed Third Airport at Foulness

One of the schemes for the building of a third London airport at Foulness, off the east coast. The model demonstrates how runways, taxiing areas, car parks and full airport facilities are built out over the sea, and moored to the 18 ft sea-bed. There are jagged reinforced concrete barriers at the end of the runways which are designed to break up large waves, and the causeway on the left is for rapid road and rail connexion with the metropolis.

NEW CONCEPTS IN
AIRPORT PLANNING

In chapter 14, we referred to Bonn-Cologne airport which is one of the more recent of the German Federal Republic's air terminals. The form of the plan is an indication of advanced study in respect of the whole trend of future needs in air transport.

As a continuation of the process of investigation, the Ground Operations Department, Frankfurt/Main (Deutsche Lufthansa A.G.), produced a new 'Concept' for airports in the future – reviewing the whole field of ground operations, in the service of passengers and commercial air transportation. In discussion with airport planners and airline authorities in other fields, during a period of years, a basic concept emerged; its application, however, had to be sufficiently flexible to enable development by architects and planning engineers to meet varying local conditions.

In previous chapters we referred to the need for providing easy and rapid means of transfer, between aircraft and land vehicle at the airport – and thence to his nearest city or provincial town. In too many instances the static central building – in relation to the activities on the 'air side', and the 'land side', as traffic increases in volume and outward spread – a position

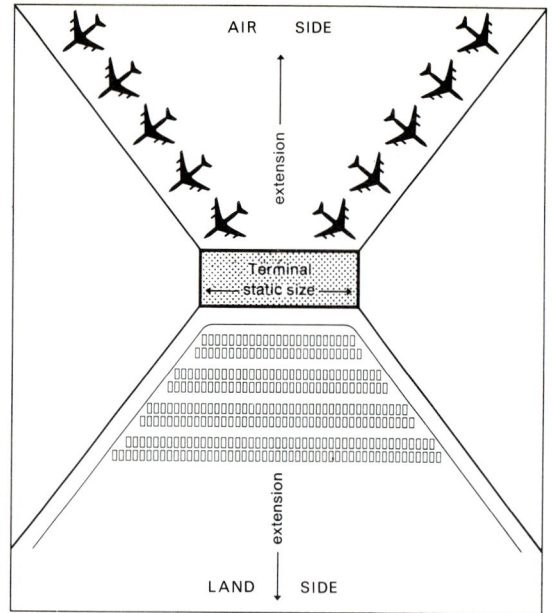

Conventional airport layout with central terminal. Hour glass system.

arises where a bottle-neck is created. This may be apparent from the adjacent diagram.

By the process of ratiocination, a break-away from this impasse appears feasible by applying a modular and linear principle of development, which, combined with parallel road and rail through access – having connections at intervals with check-in and general services buildings, permits lateral expansion each way. Alternative plan types here illustrate basic layout units.

In addition to horizontal circulation we have also to consider the vertical lines of communication, equally important in time-

Module system with linear extension. At Foster Dulles Airport, Washington.

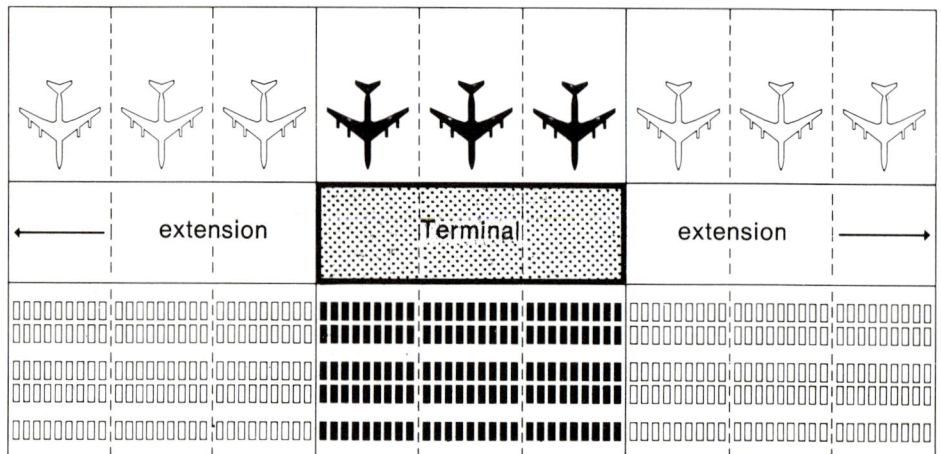

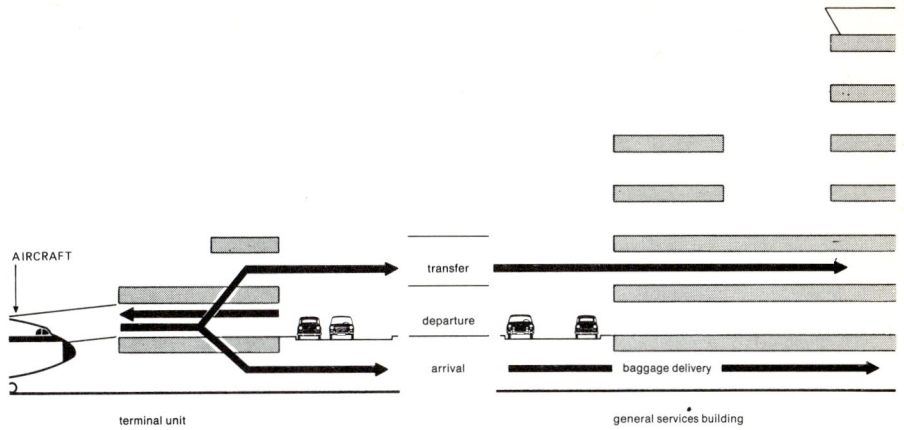

Cross section of module and linear planning, Lufthansa Dutch Airlines.

saving – and still more so, in energy conservation for the traveller.

The adjoining cross-section indicates a convenient formula for the adjustment between arrival, departure and transfer – in relation to the aircraft.

To sum up the desirable principles to be observed in formulating an ideal system of planning for efficient and comfortable airport operation, the following elements have been given priority:

(a) Decentralization of processing functions, as near as possible to the aircraft.

(b) Provision of terminal elements giving a balanced capacity between: one aircraft position, waiting lounge, check-in, lobby space, curb side, and car parking area (see diagram).

(c) Grouping the several elements into one unit in a manner that the road

system will provide direct access to each element (see diagram).

(d) Connexion of two units to a General Services Building to house restaurants, bars, concessions, banks and other amenities.

(e) Planning the available terminal area for a phased linear expansion programme.

The grouping of elements system, compare with Bonn-Cologne airport.

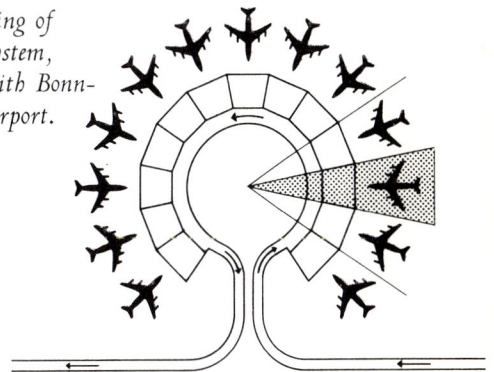

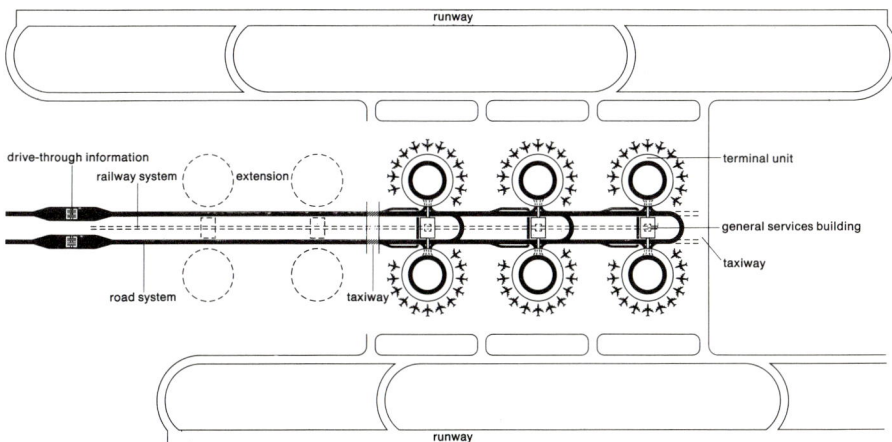

Unit concept with 'drive-in and gate check-in' facilities.

215

OPPOSITE PAGE
*A cut-away and section view of
the new Pan American World
Airways Passenger Terminal.*

*A model of the new Pan American
World Airways terminal complex
at Kennedy International Airport.
The two-level roadway system
penetrates the heart of the building.*

AIRPORT EXPANSION
IN THE U.S.A.

With the emergence of the Boeing 747 Jumbo Jets, to which we have referred before, as it affected London's Heathrow Airport, it will be interesting to project our view further afield and examine how some of the premier airlines of the Western hemisphere have dealt with the problems.

There is an indication that by 1971 approximately 186 of the 747 aircraft may be operating from 45 airports throughout the world, including 21 in the United States of America.

At New York's Kennedy Airport, both Pan American Airways and Trans-World Airways are involved in massive reconstruction and expansion of their original terminal buildings and ground areas.

Having described both these terminals in an earlier chapter (16), it should now be possible to assess the extent of their present problems and the manner in which they are being resolved.

At the Pan American terminal the existing accommodation will ultimately expand to six and a half times its original compass. This new project has been designed by Tippetts-Abbett-McCarthy-Stratton, the architect-engineering partnership, which also designed the original oval terminal.

The photograph of the model provides a vivid impression of the wedge-shaped extension of the accommodation and its link with the existing buildings, also the new two-level roadway system which penetrates to the heart of the terminal in the foreground.

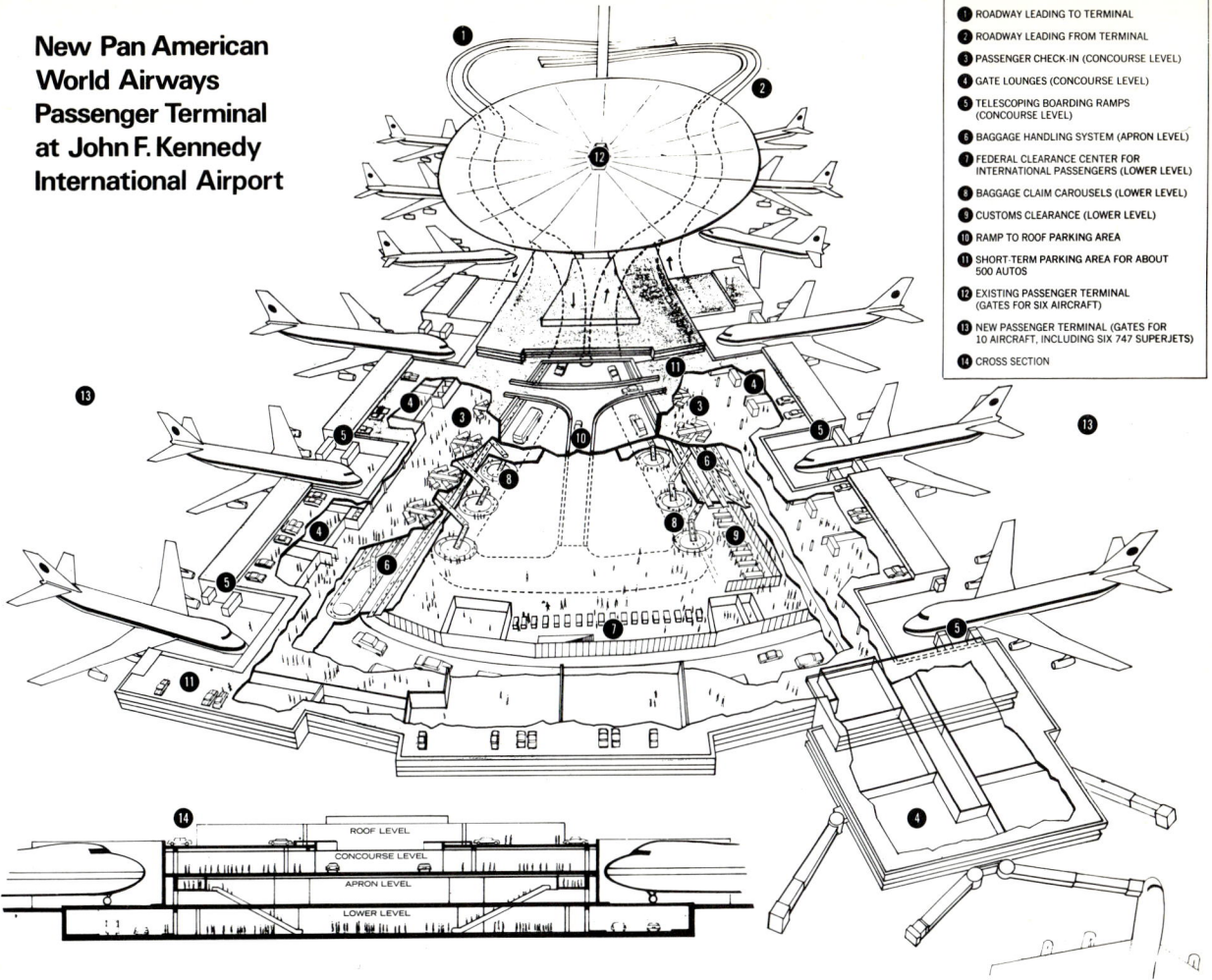

New Pan American World Airways Passenger Terminal at John F. Kennedy International Airport

① ROADWAY LEADING TO TERMINAL
② ROADWAY LEADING FROM TERMINAL
③ PASSENGER CHECK-IN (CONCOURSE LEVEL)
④ GATE LOUNGES (CONCOURSE LEVEL)
⑤ TELESCOPING BOARDING RAMPS (CONCOURSE LEVEL)
⑥ BAGGAGE HANDLING SYSTEM (APRON LEVEL)
⑦ FEDERAL CLEARANCE CENTER FOR INTERNATIONAL PASSENGERS (LOWER LEVEL)
⑧ BAGGAGE CLAIM CAROUSELS (LOWER LEVEL)
⑨ CUSTOMS CLEARANCE (LOWER LEVEL)
⑩ RAMP TO ROOF PARKING AREA
⑪ SHORT-TERM PARKING AREA FOR ABOUT 500 AUTOS
⑫ EXISTING PASSENGER TERMINAL (GATES FOR SIX AIRCRAFT)
⑬ NEW PASSENGER TERMINAL (GATES FOR 10 AIRCRAFT, INCLUDING SIX 747 SUPERJETS)
⑭ CROSS SECTION

ROOF LEVEL
CONCOURSE LEVEL
APRON LEVEL
LOWER LEVEL

In order to provide the maximum amount of space within the terminal, a four-level building was planned, the lower level of which is at 16 ft below apron level. This basement storey, which has Customs Clearance, Baggage Claims and Federal Clearance Center for international passengers – is of special significance, because this Center will enable travellers arriving under the same roof from foreign countries, the convenience of clearance instead of having to pass through the existing International Arrivals Building; it also eliminates the shuttling of aircraft on taxiways between terminals.

The accommodation on the floors at apron level and above, include Baggage Handling systems – linked with Basement Claims. Passenger check-in, gate lounges and boarding ramps are at main Concourse level, while the roof accommodation allows 'short-term' parking areas for about 500 cars.

The adjoining cut-away and section provide a comprehensive and integrated view of the accommodation and the lines of communication throughout the building. It is anticipated that the new terminal will become operative for the full services in 1971.

An aerial view of the new extensions from T.W.A.'s main terminal building at Kennedy airport, showing the 221 ft tubular bridge to the new Flight Wing One building, beyond which can be seen Flight Wing Two, similarly connected.

TRANSWORLD AIRWAYS TERMINAL, KENNEDY AIRPORT

With the same object in view, the Pan American terminal's near neighbour T.W.A., has been extending from its original curvilinear building to provide ten additional aircraft gates and passenger amenities to cope with the influx from 747 Jumbo Jets. The new Flight Wing One is being carried out by the former Saarinen office, by Kelvin Roche, John Dinkelo, and Associates, and will double the accommodation.

The accompanying air view of the new Flight Wing One building, which was described on page 190, is connected with the main terminal on the right by a tubular bridge 221 ft long; beyond can be seen Flight Wing Two (1962), similarly connected, and the wide expanse of the runways dotted with aircraft. It will be observed that the new building has been provided with a roof-top heliport – a distinct advantage. Another facility, duplicated at the Pan American terminal, is the provision of Federal and Customs clearance within the complex, as well as level access from aircraft to passenger concourse.

CANADIAN AIRPORTS

In Chapter 16 we described the international airport at Ottawa, built between 1955–59; it was one of a number constructed under the Department of Transport's $100,000,000 programme for airport construction in the 1950s; included was the $32,000,000 new Vancouver Airport, opened in the autumn of 1968.

Within the current new expansion programme, Ottawa Airport will be remodelled to accommodate heavier passenger loads in the seventies; this project includes improvement to the health, immigration, Customs and baggage-handling facilities.

Among the major projects, planning has been scheduled for Calgary, Toronto, and Montreal international airports to provide additional terminal buildings for the accommodation of the new era of 400–500 capacity passenger-carrying jet aircraft. Also included are Halifax and Winnipeg.

We may here briefly refer to two examples involving major expansion projects initially phased to the year 1974, allowing for interim buildings, satellite and feeder-line airports.

At the existing circular terminal airport building, No. 1, in Toronto, some interim improvements have currently (1970) been carried out in the trans-border processing area, in respect of Customs and Immigration authorities. A new waiting room has also been provided above a section of the outdoor observation deck.

In the case of the new Terminal 2, the phased construction has commenced, with foundation and steelwork for the stage to enable it to face the large-capacity jets, early in 1971. The estimated cost is around $63,000,000.

Regarding Montreal international airport, mentioned above, at Dorval, there are two related projects. The first relates to re-designing the present air terminal and 'aeroquay' to provide additions to both buildings for handling the 747 Jumbo Jets during the interim period before the new international airport becomes operative. The selected site for this is situated at Saint Scholastique, about 26 miles north of the centre of Montreal.

The project at Montreal (Dorval) Airport includes the extension of the aircraft apron area and car-parking accommodation for a total of 4,500 cars, a 95 per cent increase (approximately).

In the main terminal building the trans-border 'finger' will have two additional gates, two storeys high for serving the Boeing 747 jet aircraft. In the main ground-floor area the entire layout is being re-designed to improve Customs, Health and Immigration services, and the related accommodation for air travellers. Also initiated is an extension of the ground-floor area to provide additional and improved baggage-handling.

The layout of first-floor areas includes reorganization of the offices of Air Canada and the international airlines. This $10,000,000 Montreal project is due for completion early in 1971.

In connexion with the new international airport No. 2 (St Scholastique) it may be interesting to record an outline of the intensive review of the airport requirements in the selected area, resulting from studies made between 1966 and 1968.

Twenty possible sites were reviewed; the technical criteria included geographical location and communications, landforms and urban areas, atmospheric conditions, fog and freezing rain hazards. Following the assessment of the technical cost and development factors, revealed by these studies, the location of the new airport was confirmed. In January 1970 a management contract for all the physical aspects of the airport's development was awarded to a consortium of surveyors, engineers, and architects. Land clearance commenced in May 1970, and the completion of the airport is due in 1974.

The new terminal is associated with the following transport routes: motorways include the Laurentian Motorway and Route II (Montreal–St Jerome), Route 8 (Lachute–St Eustache), and Route 41 (Lachute–St Jerome). For the railways, Canadian Pacific and Canadian National serve the immediate area south-west of the new airport.

Obviously at this planning stage no comprehensive picture of the terminal buildings can yet emerge. It would be interesting to speculate whether it will follow a radial pattern (as Pan American) or the modular-linear system as exemplified by Washington (Foster Dulles), and in more detail, the examples referred to on a previous page under the heading of 'New Concepts in Airport Planning'.

An artist's impression of a city-centre airport for vertical take-off passenger aircraft.

BIBLIOGRAPHY

Travel by Road

THE ENGLAND OF NIMROD & SURTEES, 1815–1854, E. W. Bovill, *O.U.P., 1959.* CHAUCER'S WORLD, Edith Rickert, *O.U.P., London. Columbian Univ., New York, 1962.* THE ROLLING ROAD, L. A. G. Strong, *Hutchinson, 1956.* BRITISH ROADS, Geoffrey Boumphrey, *Thomas Nelson & Sons Ltd.* TRAVEL, Lt.-Col. F. S. Brereton, *B. T. Batsford Ltd, 1931.* THE COACHING AGE, S. Harris, *R. Bentley & Sons, 1885.* STAGE COACH TO JOHN O'GROATS, Leslie Gardiner, *Hollis & Carter, 1961.* THE ENGLISH INN, Thomas Burke, *Herbert Jenkins, 1947.* A SCRAPBOOK OF INNS, Rowland Watson, *T. Werner Laurie, 1949.* THE ENGLISH INN, Denzil Batchelor, *B. T. Batsford Ltd, 1963.* THE OLD INNS OF ENGLAND, A. E. Richardson, *B. T. Batsford Ltd, 1935.* THE DEVELOPMENT OF TRANSPORTATION IN MODERN ENGLAND, W. T. Jackman, *H.M.S.O.* THE TOWN: A VISUAL HISTORY OF BRITAIN, Geoffrey Martin, *Vista Books, 1961.* TRAFFIC IN TOWNS, Buchanan Report, *Min. of Transport, 1963.* MOTOPIA, G. A. Jellicoe, *Studio Books, 1961.*

Travel by Rail

THE EVOLUTION OF RAILWAYS, Charles E. Lee, *Tothill Press (2nd edn. 1943).* THE RAILWAY STATION, Carroll L. V. Meeks, *Yale Univ. Press, 1957.* THE RAILWAYS OF BRITAIN, Prof. Jack Simmons, *Routledge & Kegan Paul.* A REGIONAL HISTORY OF THE RAILWAYS OF GREAT BRITAIN, H. P. White, *Phoenix House.* THE RAILWAY LOVER'S COMPANION, Edited by Bryan Morgan, *Eyre & Spottiswoode, 1963.* RAILWAYS FOR BRITAIN, Patrick Thornhill, *Methuen, 1954.* THE METROPOLITAN DISTRICT RAILWAY, Charles E. Lee, *Oakwood Press, 1956.* MORE UNUSUAL RAILWAYS, J. R. Day, *Frederick Müller Ltd, 1960.* NEXT STATION, Christian Barman, *G. Allen & Unwin, 1947.* EARLY VICTORIAN ARCHITECTURE IN BRITAIN (Vol. 2), Henry Russell Hitchcock; Editor: George Kebler, *Yale Historical Publishers; New Haven Press: Architectural Press, London, 1954.* AN INTRODUCTION TO RAILWAY ARCHITECTURE, Christian Barman, *Art & Technics Ltd, 1950.* THE MAKING OF MODERN BRITAIN, T. K. Derry & T. L. Jarman, *John Murray, 1962.* THE GEOGRAPHY OF COMMUNICATIONS IN BRITAIN, J. H. Appleton, *Univ. of Hull Publications, 1962.* A VISUAL HISTORY OF MODERN BRITAIN, Prof. Jack Simmons, *Vista Books Ltd.* U.S.A. ARCHITECTURE, Ian McCullum, *Architectural Press.* TRANSPORT, R. A. S. Hennesey, *B. T. Batsford Ltd.* GUIDE TO MODERN ARCHITECTURE, Reyner Banham, *Architectural Press, 1962.*

Travel by Sea

BOAT TRAINS & CHANNEL PACKETS, Rixon Bucknall, *Vincent Stuart, 1957.* BRITISH PORTS & SHIPPING, Henry Rees, *George G. Harrap & Co. Ltd, 1958.* THE GATEWAY OF ENGLAND, Rivers Scott, *Dover Harbour Board, 1956.*

Travel by Air

THE PLANNING & DESIGN OF AIRPORTS (U.S.A.), Robert Horonjeff, *Yale Univ. Press (U.S.A.).* EERO SAARINEN, Allan Temko, *Prentice Hall International Press.* ATLANTIC BRIDGE, Official account of R.A.F. Transport Command, *H.M.S.O., 1945.* GATEWAY TO THE WORLD, *Pan American Airways, New York.* GEOGRAPHY OF AIR TRANSPORT, Kenneth R. Sealy, *Hutchinson Univ. Library, 1957.*

Periodicals

ARCHITECTURAL REVIEW
ARCHITECTS JOURNAL
PROGRESSIVE ARCHITECTURE (U.S.A.)
ARCHITECTURAL RECORD (U.S.A.)
ARCHITECTURAL FORUM (U.S.A.)
L'ARCHITECTURE D'AUJOURD'HUI
REVISTA TECNICA ITALIANE
R.I.B.A. JOURNAL
RAILWAY GAZETTE
MODERN RAILWAYS

INDEX

References to illustrations are shown in italics.